MW01532139

HARDPRESS.NET

ISBN: 9781313535045

Published by:
HardPress Publishing
8345 NW 66TH ST #2561
MIAMI FL 33166-2626

Email: info@hardpress.net
Web: http://www.hardpress.net

BS
2560
S17P2r

INTER·FOLIA·FRUCTUS

ANDREW DICKSON WHITE

Cornell University Library

BS2560.S17 P2
+

Parallel gospels : exhibiting at one vie

olin   3 1924 029 339 433

Overs

OLIN

DATE DUE

GAYLORD			PRINTED IN U.S.A.

THE PARALLEL GOSPELS.

THE
PARALLEL GOSPELS:

EXHIBITING AT ONE VIEW, IN

FOUR COLLATERAL COLUMNS,

EVERY CONCURRENT, CONFLICTING, AND ADDITIONAL PASSAGE OF EACH EVANGELIST;

FORMING ALSO, OF THE FOUR,

ONE CONTINUOUS GOSPEL.

INTENDED FOR THE USE OF

RELIGIOUS STUDENTS OF ALL DENOMINATIONS.

COLLATED BY

EDWARD SALMON,

LATE BARRISTER-AT-LAW.

London:

LONGMANS, GREEN & CO., PATERNOSTER ROW,

1876.

D

CORNELL UNIVERSITY.
The
President White
Library
RECEIVED 1891.

PRELIMINARY REMARKS.

IN THIS COLLATION the Gospel of St. Matthew has been accepted as the STANDARD to which the other three Evangelists are adjusted ; not only as being reputed to be the Primitive Gospel, and to have been written by the hand of that Apostle ; but, because, in a Work which is not intended merely as a Concordance, but as the UNITED TEXT to assist a Student in forming his own tenets in consistency with the supreme authority of the Gospels, it was necessary to preserve one Evangelist in the original order, with which every passage in the other three might be compared. The texts of St. Mark, of St. Luke, and of St. John are disarranged only so far as necessary to exhibit the extent of their parallelism with St. Matthew ; And reference is given to the *Page* at which every displaced passage may be read in the order of its own Gospel. Such corresponding, or additional, or dissimilar portions as could not be so brought into juxta-position, are referred to by notes in the margin, or in the blank spaces of the text.

An Index to the chapters and verses of each Evangelist precedes the Gospels. A Compendium of the leading Texts of each of them, and a Synopsis of Miracles, are subjoined.

The Collation has been made from that Edition of the New Testament printed at the Clarendon Press, Oxford, by Collingwood and Co., A.D. 1821.

ABREVIATIONS EMPLOYED.

M. *for St. Matthew.*

Mk. *for St. Mark.*

L. *for St. Luke.*

J. *for St. John.*

For a Summary of what is known of the early history of the Gospels, the Inquirer may refer to
Paley's Evidences of Christianity,
Chap. X. P. 104 to 187.

The four Gospels are reputed to have

been written about

		A.D.
St. Matthew	...	41
St. Mark ...	...	44
St. Luke ...	...	53
St. John ...	...	96

Lond.: Encycl.: 1829.

" *Matthew, Mark, Luke, John.*"

THE PARALLEL GOSPELS.

GENERAL INDEX to the CHAPTERS and VERSES.

INDEX, Continued.

INDEX, Continued.

INDEX, Continued.

ST. JOHN.

CHRONOLOGY OF EARLY FATHERS.

HERMAS.	"Cotemporary with St. Paul."	Paley's Evid., P. 113.
IGNATIUS.	"Bishop of Antioch about 37 years after the Ascension."	Idem 114.
POLYCARP.	"Cotemporary with Ignatius."	Idem 115.
PAPIAS.	"A hearer of John and Companion of Polycarp."	Idem 117.
IRENÆUS.	"A.D. 178." (Martyred A.D. 202.)	Idem 113.
CLEMENT.	"Followed Irenæus at distance of 16 years."	Idem 126.
TERTULLIAN.	"Joins on with Clement."	Idem 127.
ORIGEN.	"A.D. 230."	Idem 113.
JUSTIN.	{ "(Martyr). 20 years after Origen." Idem 118. "Converted about A.D. 132."	Lond. Encyc., "Justin."
EUSEBIUS.	"Bishop of Cæsarea, A.D. 315."	Paley's Evid., P. 133.
JEROME.	"Son of Eusebius. Born about A.D. 340."	Lond. Encyc., "Jerome."

HISTORICAL NOTES.

Papias* *(a hearer of St. John and companion of Polycarp, as Irenæus†
attests, and of that age as all agree) in a passage quoted by Eusebius,‡ from
a work now lost, expressly ascribes their respective Gospels to Matthew and
Mark.*

C. X., S. 6, P. 107, *Paley's Evidences,* 1818

" *Irenæus saith, that Matthew among the Jews writ a Gospel in their
own language, while Peter and Paul were preaching the Gospel at Rome and
founding a church there.   After their exit, Mark the disciple and interpreter
of Peter, delivered to us in writing the things that had been preached by Peter:
and Luke, the companion of St. Paul, put down in a book the Gospel preached
by him.   Afterwards, John, the disciple of the Lord, published a Gospel
while he dwelt at Ephesus.*

" *Also, that only four Gospels were at that time publicly read and
acknowledged.   He mentions how Matthew begins his Gospel; how Mark
begins and ends his; enumerates the several passages in Luke which are not
found in the other Evangelists; states the design with which John composed
his Gospel; and accounts for the doctrinal declaration which precedes his
narrative.*"

Paley's Evidences, C. X., S. 10. P. 123, 124.

Papias, Irenæus, Origen, Jerome, assert that Matthew composed a
Hebrew Gospel.   The Greek translation only is extant.

Gibbon's Decl. and Fall, C. XLVII., Note E.

" *All the books of the New Testament were written in Greek, except the
Gospel of St. Matthew, who, according to St. Jerome (A.D. 392), first wrote
in Judea in the Hebrew language.*"

Lond. Encylop. " *Bible.*" 1829.

---

* *Papias martyred A.D. 167.*
† *Irenæus martyred A.D 202*
‡ *Eusebius born A.D. 333.*

THE GOSPEL OF ST. JOHN.

CHAP. I.

N.B. All words written within square brackets [ ] are the variations of Dean Alford's version.

1. *In the beginning* was the Word, and the Word was with God, and the Word was God.

2. The same was in the beginning with God.

3. All things were made by him ; and without him was not any thing made that was made.

4. In him was life ; and the life was the light of men.

5. And the light shineth in darkness ; and the darkness comprehended it not.

M. III. 1.

6. ¶ There was a man sent from God, whose name *was* John.

7. The same came for a witness, to bear witness of the Light, that all *men* through him might believe.

8. He was not that Light, but *was sent* to bear witness of that Light.

9. *That* was the true Light, which lighteth every man that cometh into the world.

10. He was in the world, and the world was made by him, and the world knew him not.

11. He came unto his own, and his own received him not.

12. But as many as received him, to them gave he power to become the sons of God, *even* to them that believe on his name :

13. Which were born, not of blood, nor of the will of the flesh, nor of the will of man, but of God.

14. And the Word was made flesh, and dwelt among us, (and we beheld his glory, the glory as of the only begotten of the Father,) full of grace and truth.

15. ¶ John bare witness of him, and cried, saying, This was he of whom I spake, He that cometh after me is preferred before me : for he was before me.

16. And of his fulness have all we received, and grace for grace.

17. For the law was given by Moses, *but* grace and truth came by Jesus Christ

18. No man hath seen God at any time ; the only begotten Son, which is in the bosom of the Father, he hath declared *him.*

THE GOSPEL OF ST. LUKE.

Continued P. 15.

CHAP. I.

1. FORASMUCH as many have taken in hand to set forth in order a declaration of those things which are most surely believed among us,

2. Even as they delivered them unto us, which from the beginning were eyewitnesses and ministers of the word ;

3. It seemed good to me also, having had perfect understanding of all things from the very first, to write unto thee in order, most excellent Theophilus,

4. That thou mightest know the certainty of those things wherein thou hast been instructed.

5. ¶ There was in the days of Herod, the king of Judea, a certain priest named Zacharias, of the course of Abia : and his wife *was* of the daughters of Aaron, and her name *was* Elisabeth.

6. And they were both righteous before God, walking in all the commandments and ordinances of the Lord blameless.

7. And they had] no child, because that Elisabeth was barren, and they both were *now* well stricken in years.

8. And it came to pass, that while he executed the priest's office before God in the order of his course,

9. According to the custom of the priest's office, his lot was to burn incense when he went into the temple of the Lord.

10. And the whole multitude of the people were praying without at the time of incense.

11. And there appeared unto him an angel of the Lord standing on the right side of the altar of incense.

12. And when Zacharias saw *him,* he was troubled, and fear fell upon him.

13. But the angel said unto him, Fear not, Zacharias : for thy prayer is heard ; and thy wife Elisabeth shall bear thee a son, and thou shalt call his name John.

14. And thou shalt have joy and gladness ; and many shall rejoice at his birth.

15. For he shall be great in the sight of the Lord, and shall drink neither wine nor strong drink ; and he shall be filled with the Holy Ghost, even from his mother's womb.

16. And many of the children of Israel shall he turn to the Lord their God.

17. And he shall go before him in the spirit and power of Elias, to turn the hearts of the fathers to the children, and the disobedient to the wisdom of the just ; to make-ready a people prepared for the Lord.

18. And Zacharias said unto the angel, Whereby shall I know this? for I am an old man, and my wife well stricken in years.

19. And the angel answering said unto him, I am Gabriel, that stand in the presence of God ; and am sent to speak unto thee, and to shew thee these glad tidings.

20. And, behold, thou shalt be dumb, and not able to speak, until the day that these things shall be performed, because thou believest not my words, which shall be fulfilled in their season.

21. And the people waited for Zacharias, and marvelled that he tarried so long in the temple.

22. And when he came out he could not speak unto them : and they perceived that he had seen a vision in the temple : for he beckoned unto them, and remained speechless.

23. And it came to pass, that, as soon as the days of his ministration were accomplished, he departed to his own house.

24. And after those days his wife Elisabeth conceived, and hid herself.

THE GOSPEL OF ST. MATTHEW.

CHAP. I.

1. THE BOOK of the generation of JESUS CHRIST, the son of David, the son of Abraham.

2. Abraham begat Isaac; and Isaac begat Jacob; and Jacob begat Judas and his brethren;

3. And Judas begat Phares and Zara of Thamar; and Phares begat Esrom; and Esrom begat Aram;

4. And Aram begat Aminadab; and Aminadab begat Naasson; and Naasson begat Salmon;

5. And Salmon begat Booz of Rachab; and Booz begat Obed of Ruth; and Obed begat Jesse;

6. And Jesse* begat David the king; and David the king begat Solomon of her *that had been the wife* of Urias;

7. And Solomon begat Roboam; and Roboam begat Abia; and Abia begat Asa;

8. And Asa begat Josaphat; and Josaphat begat Joram; and Joram begat Ozias;

9. And Ozias begat Joatham; and Joatham begat Achaz; and Achaz begat Ezekias;

10. And Ezekias begat Manasses; and Manasses begat Amon; and Amon begat Josias;

11. And Josias begat Jechonias and his brethren, about the time they were carried away to Babylon:

12. And after they were brought to Babylon, Jechonias begat Salathiel; and Salathiel begat Zorobabel;

13. And Zorobabel begat Abiud; and Abiud begat Eliakim; and Eliakim begat Azor;

14. And Azor begat Sadoc; and Sadoc begat Achim; and Achim begat Eliud;

15. And Eliud begat Eleazar; and Eleazar begat Matthan; and Matthan begat Jacob;

five months, saying,

25. Thus hath the Lord dealt with me in the days wherein he looked on *me*, to take away my reproach among men.

Continued P. 5.

L. III. 34 to 51. P. 17. ¹

*L. III. 31. P. 16, 17.

Note.—For the genealogy by St. Luke see P. 16, 17.

The two genealogies cannot be placed together here; one being in the ascending, the other in the descending line. But a comparative table will be found at the end of the Gospels.

Contra. L. III. 31 to 20. P. 16.

ST. MATTHEW, I.　　ST. MARK.　　ST. LUKE, I.　　ST. JOHN, I.

16. And Jacob begat Joseph the husband of Mary; of whom was born Jesus, who is called Christ.

17. So all the generations from Abraham to David *are* fourteen generations; and from David until the carrying away into Babylon *are* fourteen generations; and from the carrying away into Babylon unto Christ *are* fourteen generations.

26. And in the sixth month the angel Gabriel was sent from God unto a city of Galilee, named Nazareth,

18. Now the birth of Jesus Christ was on this wise:

when as his mother Mary was espoused to Joseph,

before they came together she* was found with child of the Holy Ghost.

27. To a virgin espoused to a man whose name was Joseph, of the house of David; and the virgin's name *was* Mary.

`L. I. 35.　P. 6.`

28. And the angel came in unto her, and said, Hail, *thou that art* highly favoured, the Lord *is* with thee: blessed *art* thou among women.

29. And when she saw *him,* she was troubled at his saying, and cast in her mind what manner of salutation this should be.

30. And the angel said unto her, Fear not, Mary: for thou hast found favour with God.

19. Then Joseph her husband, being a just *man,* and not willing to make her a public example, was minded to put her away privily.

20. But while he thought on these'things, behold, the angel of the Lord appeared unto him in a dream, saying, Joseph, thou son of David, fear not to take unto thee Mary thy wife: for that which is conceived in her is of the Holy Ghost.

21. And she shall bring forth a son, and thou shalt call his name JESUS: for he shall save his people from their sins.

31. And, behold, thou shalt conceive in thy womb, and bring forth a son, and shalt call his name JESUS.

32. He shall he great, and shall he called the Son of the Highest: and the Lord God shall give unto him the throne of his father David:

33. And he shall reign over the house of Jacob for ever; and of his kingdom there shall be no end.

34. Then said Mary unto the angel, How shall this be, seeing I know not a man?

35. And the angel answered and said unto her, The Holy [Ghost] shall come upon thee, *[Spirit.—A.]* and the power of the Highest shall overshadow thee: there- M. I. 18. fore also that holy thing which shall be born of thee shall be called the Son of God. L. I. 22

22. Now all this was done, that it might be fulfilled which was spoken of the Lord by the prophet, saying,

23. Behold, a virgin shall be with child, and shall bring forth a son, and they shall call his name Emmanuel, which being interpreted is, God with us.

24. Then Joseph, being raised from sleep, did as the angel of the Lord had bidden him, and took unto him his wife:

25. And knew her not till she had brought forth her first-born son: and he called his name JESUS.

36. And, behold, thy cousin Elisabeth, she hath also conceived a son in her old age: and this is the sixth month with her, who was called barren.

37. For with God nothing shall be impossible.

38. And Mary said, Behold the handmaid of the Lord; be it unto me according to thy word. And the angel departed from her.

39. And Mary arose in those days, and went into the hill country with haste, into a city of Juda;

40. And entered into the house of Zacharias, and saluted Elisabeth.

41. And it came to pass that when Elisabeth heard the salutation of Mary, the babe leaped in her womb; and Elisabeth was filled with the Holy Ghost:

42. And she spake out with a loud voice, and said, Blessed *art* thou among women; and blessed is the fruit of thy womb.

43. And whence *is* this to me, that the mother of my Lord should come to me?

44. For, lo, as soon as the voice of thy salutation sounded in mine ears, the babe leaped in my womb for joy.

45. And blessed *is* she that believed: for there shall be a performance of those things

which were told her from the Lord.

46. And Mary said, My soul doth magnify the Lord,

47. And my spirit hath rejoiced in God my Saviour.

48. For he hath regarded the low estate of his handmaiden: for, behold, from henceforth all generations shall call me blessed.

49. For he that is mighty hath done to me great things; and holy *is* his name.

50. And his mercy *is* on them that fear him from generation to generation.

51. He hath shewed strength with his arm; he hath scattered the proud in the imagination of their hearts.

52. He hath put down the mighty from *their* seats, and exalted them of low degree.

53. He hath filled the hungry with good things; and the rich he hath sent empty away.

54. He hath holpen his servant Israel, in remembrance of *his* mercy;

55. As he spake to our fathers, to Abraham, and to his seed for ever.

56. And Mary abode with her about three months, and returned to her own house.

57. Now Elisabeth's full time came that she should be delivered; and she brought forth a son.

58. And her neighbours and her cousins heard how the Lord had showed great mercy upon her; and they rejoiced with her.

59. And it came to pass, that on the eighth day they came to circumcise the child; and they called him Zacharias, after the name of his father.

60. And his mother answered and said, Not *so*; but he shall be called John.

61. And they said unto her, There is none of thy kindred that is called by this name.

62. And they made signs to his father, how he would have him called.

63. And he asked for a writing table, and wrote, saying, His name is John. And they marvelled all.

64. And his mouth was opened immediately, and his tongue *loosed*, and he spake and praised God.

65. And fear came on all that dwelt round about them : and all these sayings were noised abroad throughout all the hill country of Judea.

66. And all they that heard *them* laid *them* up in their hearts, saying, What manner of child shall this be ? And the hand of the Lord was with him.

67. And his father Zacharias was filled with the Holy Ghost, and prophesied, saying,

68. Blessed *be* the Lord God of Israel ; for he hath visited and redeemed his people,

69. And hath raised up an horn of salvation for us in the house of his servant David ;

70. As he spake by the mouth of his holy prophets, which have been since the world began :

71. That we should be saved from our enemies, and from the hand of all that hate us ;

72. To perform the mercy *promised* to our fathers, and to remember his holy covenant ;

73. The oath which he sware to our father Abraham,

74. That he would grant unto us, that we being delivered out of the hand of our enemies might serve him without fear,

75. In holiness and righteousness before him all the days of our life.

76. And thou, child, shalt be called the prophet of the Highest : for thou shalt go before the face of the Lord to prepare his ways ;

77. To give knowledge of salvation unto his people by the remission of their sins,

78. Through the tender mercy of our God ; whereby the dayspring from on high hath visited us,

79. To give light to them that sit in darkness and *in* the shadow of death, to guide our feet into the way of peace.

80. And the child grew, and waxed strong in spirit, and was in the deserts till the day of his showing unto Israel.

CHAP. II.

1. And it came to pass in those days, that there went out a decree from Cæsar Augustus, that all the world should be taxed.
2. (And this taxing was first made when Cyrenius was governor of Syria.)
3. And all went to be taxed, every one into his own city.
4. And Joseph also went up from Galilee, out of the city of Nazareth, into Judea, unto the city of David, which is called Bethlehem ;

(because he was of the house and lineage of David :)
5. To be taxed with Mary his espoused wife, being great with child.
6. And so it was, that, while they were there, the days were accomplished that she should be delivered.
7. And she brought forth her firstborn son, and wrapped him in swaddling clothes, and laid him in a manger ; because there was no room for them in the inn.
8. And there were in the same country shepherds abiding in the field, keeping watch over their flock by night.
9. And, lo, the angel of the Lord came upon them, and the glory of the Lord shone round about them : and they were sore afraid.
10. And the angel said unto them, Fear not : for behold I bring you good tidings of great joy, which shall be to all people.
11. For unto you is born this day in the city of David a Saviour, which is Christ the Lord.
12. And this shall be a sign unto you ; Ye shall find the babe wrapped in swaddling clothes, lying in a manger.
13. And suddenly there was with the angel a multitude of the heavenly host praising God, and saying,
14. Glory to God in the highest, and on earth peace, good will toward men.
15. And it came to pass, as the angels were gone away from them into heaven, the shep-

CHAP. II.

1. Now when Jesus was born in Bethlehem of Judea in the days of Herod the king, *   L. II. 4, 6, 7.   * 1st. Herod

behold, there came wise men from the east to Jerusalem,
2. Saying, Where is he that is born King of the Jews ? for we have seen his star in the east, and are come to worship him.
3. When Herod the king had heard these things, he was troubled, and all Jerusalem with him.
4. And when he had gathered all the chief priests and scribes of the people together, he demanded of them where Christ should be born.
5. And they said unto him, In Bethlehem of Judea : for thus it is written by the prophet,
6. And thou Bethlehem, in the land of Juda, art not the least among the princes of Juda : for out of thee shall come a Governor, that shall rule my people Israel.
7. Then Herod, when he had privily called the wise men, inquired of them diligently what time the star appeared.

3

8. And he sent them to Bethlehem, and said, Go and search diligently for the young child; and when ye have found *him*, bring me word again, that I may come and worship him also.

9. When they had heard the king, they departed; and, lo, the star, which they saw in the east, went before them, till it came and stood over where the young child was.   L. II. 12.

10. When they saw the star, they rejoiced with exceeding great joy.

11. ¶ And when they were come into the house, they saw the young child with Mary his mother, and fell down, and worshipped him: and when they had opened their treasures, they presented unto him gifts; gold, and frankincense, and myrrh.   L. II. 16.

12. And being warned of God in a dream that they should not return to Herod, they departed into their own country another way.

13. And when they were departed, behold the angel of the Lord appeareth to Joseph in a dream, saying, Arise, and take the young child and his mother, and flee into Egypt, and be thou there until I bring thee word: for Herod will seek the young child to destroy him.

14. When he arose, he took the young child and his mother by night, and departed into Egypt: L. II. 22.

herds said one to another, Let us now go even unto Bethlehem, and see this thing which is come to pass, which the Lord hath made known unto us.

16. And they came with haste, and found Mary, and Joseph, and the babe lying in a manger.

17. And when they had seen *it*, they made known abroad the saying which was told them concerning this child.

18. And all they that heard *it* wondered at those things which were told them by the shepherds.

19. But Mary kept all these things, and pondered *them* in her heart.

20. And the shepherds returned, glorifying and praising God for all the things that they had heard and seen, as it was told unto them.

21. And when eight days were accomplished for the circumcising of the child, his name was called JESUS, which was so named of the angel before he was conceived in the womb.

22. And when the days of her purification according to the law of Moses were accomplished, they brought him to Jerusalem, to present *him* to the Lord;   M. II. 14.

23. (As it is written in the law of the Lord, Every male that openeth the womb shall be called holy to the Lord;)

24. And to offer a sacrifice according to that which is said in the law of the Lord, A pair of turtledoves, or two young pigeons.

25. And, behold, there was a man in Jerusalem, whose name *was* Simeon; and the same man *was* just and devout, waiting for the consolation of Israel: and the Holy Ghost was upon him.

26. And it was revealed unto him by the Holy Ghost, that he should not see death, before he had seen the Lord's Christ.

27. And he came by the

Spirit into the temple ; and when the parents brought in the child Jesus, to do for him after the custom of the law,

28. Then took he him up in his arms, and blessed God, and said,

29. Lord, now lettest thou thy servant depart in peace, according to thy word :

30. For mine eyes have seen thy salvation,

31. Which thou hast prepared before the face of all people ;

32. A light to lighten the Gentiles, and the glory of thy people Israel.

33. And Joseph and his mother marvelled at those things which were spoken of him.

34. And Simeon blessed them, and said unto Mary his mother, Behold this *child* is set for the fall and rising again of many in Israel ; and for a sign which shall be spoken against ;

35. (Yea, a sword shall pierce through thy own soul also,) that the thoughts of many hearts may be revealed.

36. And there was one Anna, a prophetess, the daughter of Phanuel, of the tribe of Aser : she was of a great age, and had lived with an husband seven years from her virginity ;

37. And she *was* a widow of about fourscore and four years, which departed not from the temple, but served *God* with fastings and prayers night and day.

38. And she coming in that instant gave thanks likewise unto the Lord, and spake of him to all them that looked for redemption in Jerusalem.

15. And was there until the death of Herod :* that it might be fulfilled which was spoken of the Lord by the prophet, saying, Out of Egypt have I called my son.

* *A.D. 3. Encycl London : 1829. (Or rather A.D. 1. Smith's Classical Dicty., " Herod.')*

39. And when they had performed all things according to the law of the Lord, they returned into Galilee, to their own city Nazareth.

See V. 22.

M. II. 14.

40. And the child grew, and waxed strong in spirit, filled with wisdom : and the grace of God was upon him.

16. ¶ Then Herod, when he saw that he was mocked of the wise men, was exceeding wroth, and sent forth, and slew all the children that were in Bethlehem, and in all the coasts

thereof, from two years old and
under, according to the time
which he had diligently enquired of the wise men.

17. Then was fulfilled that
which was spoken by Jeremy
the prophet, saying,

18. In Rama was there a
voice heard, lamentation, and
weeping, and great mourning,
Rachel weeping *for* her children, and would not be comforted, because they are not.

19. ¶ But when Herod was
dead,* behold, an angel of the
Lord appeareth in a dream to
Joseph in Egypt,

20. Saying, Arise, and take
the young child and his mother,
and go into the land of Israel:
for they are dead which sought
the young child's life.

21. And he arose, and took
the young child and his mother,
and came into the land of Israel.

22. But when he heard that
Archelaus did reign in Judea
in the room of his father Herod,
he was afraid to go thither:
notwithstanding, being warned
of God in a dream, he turned
aside into the parts of Galilee:

A.D. 1.

41. Now his parents went to
Jerusalem every year at the
feast of the passover.

42. And when he was twelve
years old, they went up to Jerusalem after the custom of the
feast.

43. And when they had fulfilled the days, as they returned,
the child Jesus tarried behind
in Jerusalem; and Joseph and
his mother knew not *of it.*

44. But they, supposing him
to have been in the company,
went a day's journey; and they
sought him among *their* kinsfolk and acquaintance.

45. And when they found
him not, they turned back
again to Jerusalem, seeking
him.

46. And it came to pass, that
after three days they found him
in the temple, sitting in the
midst of the doctors, both hearing them, and asking them
questions.

47. And all that heard him
were astonished at his understanding and answers.

48. And when they saw him,
they were amazed: and his
mother said unto him, Son,
why hast thou thus dealt with
us? behold, thy father and I
have sought thee sorrowing.

49. And he said unto them,
How is it that ye sought me?
wist ye not that I must be
about my Father's business?

50. And they understood not
the saying which he spake unto
them.

| St. MATTHEW, III. | St. MARK, I. | St. LUKE, III. | St. JOHN, 1. |

ST. MATTHEW, III.

23. And he came and dwelt in a city called Nazareth :

that it might be fulfilled which was spoken by the prophets, He shall be called a Nazarene.

The 2 first chapters of Matt. did not exist in the Ebionite copies.
Epiphan : Hœres. XXX. 13, & see L, II. 39 to 51.

ST. LUKE, III.

51. And he went down with them, and came to Nazareth, and was subject unto them :

but his mother kept all these sayings in her heart.
52. And Jesus increased in wisdom and stature, and in favour with God and man.

THE GOSPEL OF ST. MARK.

| CHAP. III. | CHAP. I. | CHAP. III. |

ST. LUKE, III.

1. Now in the fifteenth year of the reign of Tiberius Cæsar, Pontius Pilate being governor of Judea, and Herod being tetrarch of Galilee, and his brother Philip tetrarch of Iturea and of the region of Trachonitis, and Lysanias the tetrarch of Abilene,
2. Annas and Caiaphas * being the high priests,

* M. XXVI. 3. 57. J. XI. 49. P. 114. J. XVIII. 13. P. 164.

ST. MARK, I.

1. The beginning of the gospel of Jesus Christ, the Son of God ;
2. As it is written in the prophets, Behold, I send my messenger before thy face, which shall prepare thy way before thee.
3. The voice of one crying in the wilderness, Prepare ye the way of the Lord, make his paths straight. (1)

ST. MATTHEW, III.

1. In those days came John the Baptist preaching in the wilderness of Judea, (1)
2. And saying, Repent ye : for the kingdom of heaven is at hand. (2)

ST. MARK, I.

4. John did baptize in the wilderness, and preach the baptism of repentance for the remission of sins.
5. And there went out unto him all the land of Judea, and they of Jerusalem, and were all baptized of him in the river of Jordan, confessing their sins. (2)

ST. LUKE, III.

the word of God came unto John the son of Zacharias in the wilderness.
3. And he came into all the country about Jordan, preaching the baptism of repentance for the remission of sins ;

(1) J. I. 6. P. 1.
(2) M. IV. 17. XXIV. 3, 6, 14, 29, 30. 42. M. XXV. 13. XXVIII. 20.

(1) M. III. 3.
(2) M. I. 2, 5, 6.

ST. MATTHEW, III.　　ST. MARK, I.　　ST. LUKE, III.　　ST. JOHN, I.

3. For this is he that was spoken of by the prophet Esaias, saying, The voice of one crying in the wilderness, Prepare ye the way of the Lord, make his paths straight.

4. As it is written in the book of the words of Esaias the prophet, saying, The voice of one crying in the wilderness, Prepare ye the way of the Lord, make his paths straight.
J. I. 23.　P. 15.

5. Every valley shall be filled, and every mountain and hill shall be brought low ; and the crooked shall be made straight, and the rough ways *shall be* made smooth ;

6. And all flesh shall see the salvation of God.

4. And the same John had his raiment of camel's hair, and a leathern girdle about his loins ; and his meat was locusts and wild honey.

6 And John was clothed with camel's hair, and with a girdle of a skin about his loins ; and he did eat locusts and wild honey ;

5. Then went out to him Jerusalem, and all Judea, and all the region round about Jordan,

6. And were baptized of him in Jordan, confessing their sins.

7. ¶ But when he saw many of the Pharisees and Sadducees come to his baptism, he said unto them, O generation of vipers, who hath warned you to flee from the wrath to come ?

7. Then said he to the multitude that came forth to be baptized of him, O generation of vipers, who hath warned you to flee from the wrath to come ?

8. Bring forth therefore fruits meet for repentance :

8. Bring forth therefore fruits worthy of repentance, and begin not to say within yourselves, We have Abraham to *our* father : for I say unto you, That God is able of these stones to raise up children unto Abraham.

9. And think not to say within yourselves, We have Abraham to *our* father : for I say unto you, that God is able of these stones to raise up children unto Abraham.

10. And now also the axe is laid unto the root of the trees : therefore every tree which bringeth not forth good fruit is hewn down and cast into the fire.

9. And now also the axe is laid unto the root of the trees : every tree therefore which bringeth not forth good fruit is hewn down, and cast into the fire.

10. And the people asked him, saying, What shall we do then ?

11. He answereth and saith unto them, He that hath two coats, let him impart to him that hath none ; and he that hath meat, let him do likewise.

12. Then came also publicans to be baptized, and said unto him, Master, what shall we do ?

13. And he said unto them, Exact no more than that which is appointed you.

14. And the soldiers likewise demanded of him, saying, And what shall we do ? And he said unto them, Do violence

to no man, neither accuse *any* falsely ; and be content with your wages.

15. And as the people were in expectation, and all men mused in their hearts of John, whether he were the Christ, or not ;

Continued from P. 2.

19. ¶ And this is the record of John, when the Jews sent priests and Levites from Jerusalem to ask him, Who art thou ?

20. And he confessed, and denied not ; but confessed, I am not the Christ.

21. And they asked him, What then ? Art thou Elias ? And he saith, I am not. (1) Art thou that prophet ? And he answered, No.

22. Then said they unto him, Who art thou ? that we may give an answer to them that sent us. What sayest thou of thyself ?

23. He said, I *am* the voice of one crying in the wilderness, Make straight the way of the Lord, as said the prophet Esaias. (2)

24. And they which were sent were of the Pharisees.

25. And they asked him, and said unto him, Why baptizest thou then, if thou be not that Christ, nor Elias, neither that prophet ?

11. I indeed baptize you with water unto repentance : but he that cometh after me is mightier than I, whose shoes I am not worthy to bear :

he shall baptize you with the Holy [Ghost,]* and *with* fire.

12. Whose fan *is* in his hand, and he will throughly purge his floor, and gather his wheat into the garner ; but he will burn up the chaff with unquenchable fire.

7. And preached, saying, There cometh one mightier than I after me, the latchet of whose shoes I am not worthy to stoop down and unloose.

8. I indeed have baptized you with water : but he shall baptize you with the Holy Ghost.

16. John answered, saying unto *them* all, I indeed baptize you with water : but one mightier than I cometh, the latchet of whose shoes I am not worthy to unloose :

he shall baptize you with the Holy Ghost and with fire :

17. Whose fan *is* in his hand, and he will throughly purge his floor, and will gather the wheat into his garner ; but the chaff he will burn with fire unquenchable.

18. And many other things in his exhortation preached he unto the people.

26. John answered them, saying, I baptize with water : but there standeth one among you, whom ye know not ;

27. He it is, who coming after me is preferred before me, whose shoe's latchet I am not worthy to unloose.

13. ¶ Then cometh Jesus from Galilee to Jordan unto John, to be baptized of him.

14. But John forbad him, saying, I have need to be baptized of thee, and comest thou to me ?

15. And Jesus answering said unto him, Suffer *it to be so* now : for thus it becometh us to fulfil all righteousness.

9. And it came to pass in those days, that Jesus came from Nazareth of Galilee,

19. *Continued P. 73.*
20.
21. Now when all the people were baptized, it came to pass, that Jesus also

28. These things were done in Bethabara * beyond Jordan, where John was baptizing.

29. ¶ The next day † John seeth Jesus coming unto him, and saith, Behold the Lamb of God, which taketh away the sin of the world.

30. This is he of whom I said, After me cometh a man which is preferred before me :

* [*Spirit.—A.*]

(1) M. XI. 14.
(2) M. III. 3.
* "*Bethany.*" So all the oldest MSS.—*Alford.*
† J. I. 35—43. II. 1.

Then he suffered him.

16. And Jesus, when he was baptized, went up straightway out of the water: and, lo, the heavens were opened unto him, and he saw the Spirit of God descending like a dove, and [lighting] upon him: [coming. —A.]

17. And lo a voice from heaven, saying, This is my beloved Son, in whom I am well pleased. (1)

and was baptized of John in Jordan.

10. And straightway coming up out of the water, he saw the heavens opened, and the Spirit, like a dove descending upon him;

11. And there came a voice from heaven, saying, Thou art my beloved Son, in whom I am well pleased.

being baptized, and praying,

the heaven was opened.

22. And the Holy Ghost descended in a bodily shape like a dove upon him,

and a voice came from heaven, which said, Thou art my beloved Son; in thee I am well pleased.

31. And I knew him not: but that he should be made manifest to Israel, therefore am I come baptizing with water:

32. And John bare record, saying, I saw the Spirit descending from heaven like a dove, and it abode upon him.

33. And I knew him not: but he that sent me to baptize with water, the same said unto me, Upon whom thou shalt see the Spirit descending, and remaining on him, the same is he which baptizeth with the Holy Ghost.

34. And I saw, and bare record that this is the Son of God. (1)

Continued at P. 17.

[* Was about thirty years of age when he began.—Alford.]

For the Genealogy according to St. Matthew, see M. I., P. 3, and the note at P. 4.—See also the comparative table at P. 185.

23. And Jesus himself [began to be about thirty years of age,]* being (as was supposed) the son of Joseph, which was *the son* of Heli,

24. Which was *the son* of Matthat, which was *the son* of Levi, which was *the son* of Melchi, which was *the son* of Janna, which was *the son* of Joseph,

25. Which was *the son* of Mattathias, which was *the son* of Amos, which was *the son* of Naum, which was *the son* of Esli, which was *the son* of Nagge,

26. Which was *the son* of Maath, which was *the son* of Mattathias, which was *the son* of Semei, which was *the son* of Joseph, which was *the son* of Juda,

27. Which was *the son* of Joana, which was *the son* of Rhesa, which was *the son* of Zorobabel, which was *the son* of Salathiel, which was *the son* of Neri,

28. Which was *the son* of Melchi, which was *the son* of Addi, which was *the son* of Cosam, which was *the son* of Elmodam, which was *the son* of Er,

29. Which was *the son* of Jose, which was *the son* of Eliezer, which was *the son* of Jorim, which was *the son* of Matthat, which was *the son* of Levi,

30. Which was *the son* of Simeon, which was *the son* of

Juda, which was *the son* of Joseph, which was *the son* of Jonan, which was *the son* of Eliakim,

31. Which was *the son* of Melea, which was *the son* of Menan, which was *the son* of Mattatha, which was *the son* of Nathan,* which was *the son* of David,

32. Which was *the son* of Jesse, which was *the son* of Obed, which was *the son* of Booz, which was *the son* of Salmon, which was *the son* of Naasson,

33. Which was *the son* of Aminadab, which was *the son* of Aram, which was *the son* of Esrom, which was *the son* of Phares, which was *the son* of Juda,

34. Which was *the son* of Jacob, which was *the son* of Isaac, which was *the son* of Abraham, which was *the son* of Thara, which was *the son* of Nachor,

35. Which was *the son* of Saruch, which was *the son* of Ragau, which was *the son* of Phalec, which was *the son* of Heber, which was *the son* of Sala,

36. Which was *the son* of Cainan, which was *the son* of Arphaxad, which was *the son* of Sem, which was *the son* of Noe, which was *the son* of Lamech,

37. Which was *the son* of Mathusala, which was *the son* of Enoch, which was *the son* of Jared, which was *the son* of Maleleel, which was *the son* of Cainan,

38. Which was *the son* of Enos, which was *the son* of Seth, which was *the son* of Adam, which was *the son* of God.

Continued from P. 16.

35. ¶ Again the next day after* John stood, and two of his disciples ;

36. And looking upon Jesus as he walked, he saith, Behold the Lamb of God !

Continued at P. 19.

Contra J. I. 29, 35, 43.   II. 1.

CHAP. IV.

1. Then was Jesus led up of the spirit into the wilderness to be tempted of the devil.

2. And when he had fasted forty days and forty nights, he was afterward an hungred.

3. And when the tempter came to him, he said, If thou be the Son of God, command that these stones be made bread.

4. But he answered and said, It is written, Man shall not live by bread alone, but by every word that proceedeth out of the mouth of God.

5. Then the devil taketh him up into the holy city, and setteth him on a pinnacle of the temple,

6. And saith unto him, If thou be the Son of God, cast

12. And immediately* the spirit driveth him into the wilderness.

13. And he was there* in the wilderness forty days, tempted of Satan ; and was with the wild beasts ;

CHAP. IV.

1. And Jesus being full of the Holy Ghost returned from Jordan, and was led by the Spirit into the Wilderness,

2. Being forty days tempted of the devil. And in those days he did eat nothing : and when they were ended, he afterward hungered.

3. And the devil said unto him, If thou be the Son of God, command this stone that it be made bread.

4. And Jesus answered him, saying, It is written, That man shall not live by bread alone, but by every word of God.

Continued P. 18.

9. And he brought him to Jerusalem, and set him on a pinnacle of the temple, and said unto him, If thou be the Son of God, cast thyself down from hence :

St. MATTHEW, IV.

`hyself down : for it is written, He shall give his angels charge concerning thee : and in *their* hands they shall bear thee up, lest at any time thou dash thy foot against a stone.

7. Jesus said unto him, It is written again, Thou shalt not tempt the Lord thy God.

8. Again, the devil taketh him up into an exceeding high mountain, and sheweth him all the kingdoms of the world, and the glory of them ;

9. And saith unto him, All these things will I give thee, if thou wilt fall down and worship me.

10. Then saith Jesus unto him, Get thee hence, Satan : for it is written, Thou shalt worship the Lord thy God, and him only shalt thou serve.

11. Then the devil leaveth him,

and, behold, angels came and ministered unto him.

12. ¶ Now when Jesus had heard that John was cast into prison, he departed into Galilee ; (1)

13. And leaving Nazareth, he came and dwelt in Capernaum, which is upon the sea coast, in the borders of Zabulon and Nephthalim :

14. That it might be fulfilled which was spoken by Esaias the prophet, saying,

15. The land of Zabulon, and the land of Nephthalim, *by the* way of the sea, beyond Jordan, Galilee of the Gentiles ;

16. The people which sat in

(1) J. III. 24. P. 24.

St. MARK, I.

and the angels ministered unto him.

14. Now after that John was put in prison, Jesus came into Galilee, preaching the gospel of the kingdom of God,

15. And saying, The time is fulfilled, and the kingdom of God is at hand : repent ye, and believe the gospel. (1)

V. 16 to 20 continued P. 19 & 20.
From P. 20.
21. And they went into Capernaum ;

(-) M. IV. 17.

St. LUKE, IV.

10. For it is written, He shall give his angels charge over thee, to keep thee :

11. And in *their* hands they shall bear thee up, lest at any time thou dash thy foot against a stone.

12. And Jesus answering said unto him, It is said, Thou shalt not tempt the Lord thy God.

Continued below.

From P. 17.

5. And the devil, taking him up into an high mountain, shewed unto him all the kingdoms of the world in a moment of time.

6. And the devil said unto him, All this power will I give thee, and the glory of them : for that is delivered unto me ; and to whomsoever I will I give it.

7. If thou therefore wilt worship me, all shall be thine.

8. And Jesus answered and said unto him, [Get thee behind me, Satan :] for it is written, Thou shalt worship the Lord thy God, and him only shalt thou serve.

Not in Alford's version.

Continued P. 17.

13. And when the devil had ended all the temptation, he departed from him for a season.

14. ¶ And Jesus returned in the power of the Spirit into Galilee : and there went out a fame of him through all the region round about.

15. And he taught in their synagogues, being glorified of all.

Continued P. 71.

From P. 72.
31. And came down to Capernaum, a city of Galilee,

St. JOHN, I.

ST. MATTHEW, IV.   ST. MARK, I.   ST. LUKE, IV. V.   ST. JOHN, I.

darkness saw great light ; and to them which sat in the region and shadow of death light is sprung up.

17. ¶ From that time Jesus began to preach, and to say, Repent : for the kingdom of heaven is at hand. (1)

and straightway on the sabbath day he entered into the synagogue, and taught.

22. And they were astonished at his doctrine ; for he taught them as one that had authority, and not as the scribes. (1)

23. And there was in their synagogue a man with an unclean spirit ; and he cried out,

24. Saying, Let *us* alone; what have we to do with thee, thou Jesus of Nazareth ? art thou come to destroy us ? I know thee who thou art, the Holy One of God.

25. And Jesus rebuked him, saying, Hold thy peace, and come out of him.

26. And when the unclean spirit had torn him, and cried with a loud voice, he came out of him.

27. And they were all amazed, insomuch that they questioned among themselves saying, What thing is this ? what new doctrine *is* this ? for with authority commandeth he even the unclean spirits, and they do obey him.

28. And immediately his fame spread abroad throughout all the region round about Galilee.

29 *to* 34 *continued P.* 44.

35. And in the morning, rising up a great while before day, he went out, and departed into a solitary place, and there prayed.

36. And Simon and they that were with him followed after him.

37. And when they had found him, they said unto him, All *men* seek for thee.

38. And he said unto them, Let us go into the next towns, that I may preach there also : for therefore came I forth.

39. And he preached in their synagogues throughout all Galilee,

and cast out devils.

Continued P. 42.
From P. 18.

16. Now as he walked by the sea of Galilee,

he saw Simon and Andrew his brother

and taught them on the sabbath days.

32. And they were astonished at his doctrine : for his word was with power.

33. ¶ And in the synagogue there was a man, which had a spirit of an unclean devil, and cried out with a loud voice,

34. Saying, Let *us* alone; what have we to do with thee, *thou* Jesus of Nazareth ? art thou come to destroy us ? I know thee who thou art ; the Holy One of God.

35. And Jesus rebuked him, saying Hold thy peace, and come out of him. And when the devil had thrown him in the midst, he came out of him,

and hurt him not.

36. And they were all amazed and spake among themselves, saying, What a word *is* this !

for with authority and power he commandeth the unclean spirits, and they come out.

37. And the fame of him went out into every place of the country round about.

38 *to* 41 *continued P.* 44.

42. And when it was day, he departed and went out into a desert place :

and the people sought him, and came unto him, and stayed him, that he should not depart from them.

43. And he said unto them, I must preach the kingdom of God to other cities also : for therefore am I sent.

44. And he preached in the synagogues of Galilee.

CHAP. V.

1. And it came to pass, that, as the people pressed upon him to hear the word of God, he stood by the lake of Gennesaret,

2. And saw two ships standing by the lake : but the fishermen were

Continued from P. 17.

37. And the two disciples heard him speak, * and they followed Jesus.

38. Then Jesus turned, and saw them following, and saith unto them, What seek ye ? They said

18. ¶ And Jesus, walking by the sea of Galilee,

saw two brethren, Simon called Peter, and Andrew his brother*

(1) M. III. 2. Mk. I. 15. M. XXIV. 3, 5, 14, 29, 30.
(*) J. I. 40. P. 20.

(1) M. VII. 28, 29.

* M. IV. 12. Mk. I. 14. P. 18.

St. MATTHEW, IV.   St. MARK, I.   St. LUKE, V.   St. JOHN, I.

casting a net into the sea : for they were fishers.

casting a net into the sea : for they were fishers.

gone out of them, and were washing *their* nets.

unto him, Rabbi, (which is to say, being interpreted, Master,) where dwellest thou ?

3. And he entered into one of the ships, which was Simon's, and prayed him that he would thrust out a little from the land. And he sat down, and taught the people out of the ship.

4. Now when he had left speaking, he said unto Simon, Launch out into the deep, and let down your nets for a draught.

5. And Simon answering said unto him, Master, we have toiled all the night, and have taken nothing : nevertheless at thy word I will let down the net. (1)

6. And when they had this done, they inclosed a great multitude of fishes : and their net brake. (2)

7. And they beckoned unto *their* partners, which were in the other ship, that they should come and help them.* And they came, and filled both the ships, so that they began to sink.

8. When Simon Peter saw *it*, he fell down at Jesus' knees, saying, Depart from me; for I am a sinful man, O Lord.

9. For he was astonished, and all that were with him, at the draught of the fishes which they had taken :

10. And so *was* also James, and John, the sons of Zebedee, which were partners with Simon. And Jesus said unto Simon, Fear not ; from henceforth thou shalt catch men.

39. He saith unto them, Come and see. They came and saw where he dwelt, and abode with him that day : for it was about the tenth hour.

40. One of the two which heard John *speak*, and followed him, was Andrew, Simon Peter's brother.

41. He first findeth his own brother Simon, and saith unto him, We have found the Messias, which is, being interpreted, the Christ.

42. And he brought him to Jesus. And when Jesus beheld him, he said,

19. And he saith unto them, Follow me, and I will make you fishers of men.

17. And Jesus said unto them, Come ye after me, and I will make you to become fishers of men.

11. And when they had brought their ships to land, they forsook all, and followed him,

Thou art Simon the son of Jona: thou shalt be called Cephas, which is by interpretation, A stone.

20. And they straightway left *their* nets, and followed him.

18. And straightway they forsook their nets, and followed him.

Continued P. 42.

21. And going on from thence he saw other two brethren, James *the son* of Zebedee, and John his brother, in a ship with Zebedee their father, mending their nets ; and he called them.

19. And when he had gone a little farther thence, he saw James the son of Zebedee, and John his brother, who also were in the ship mending their nets.

22. And they immediately left the ship and their father, and followed him.

Continued P. 60.

20. And straightway he called them : and they left their father Zebedee in the ship with the hired servants, and went after him.

Continued P. 18.

43. ¶ The day following * Jesus would go forth into Galilee, and findeth Philip, and saith unto him, Follow me.

44. Now Philip was of Bethsaida, the city of Andrew and Peter.

45. Philip findeth Nathanael, and saith unto him, We have found him, of whom Moses in the law,

(1) J. XXI. 3—4—6. P. 183.
(2) J. XXI. 11.
* J. XXI. 8.

* J. I. 29. P. 15. II. 1. P. 21. Mk. I. 13. P. 17. L. IV. 1. P. 17. M. IV. 1, 2.

21

ST. MATTHEW, IV.   ST. MARK, I.   ST. LUKE, V.   ST. JOHN, II.

and the prophets, did write'
Jesus of Nazareth, the son o
Joseph.

46. And Nathanael said unto
him, Can there any good thing
come out of Nazareth? Philip
saith unto him, Come and see.

47. Jesus saw Nathanael
coming to him, and saith of
him, Behold an Israelite indeed,
in whom is no guile!

48. Nathanael said unto him,
Whence knowest thou me?
Jesus answered and said unto
him, Before that Philip called
thee, when thou wast under the
fig tree, I saw thee.

49. Nathanael answered and
saith unto him, Rabbi, thou
art the Son of God; thou art
the King of Israel.

50. Jesus answered and said
unto him, Because I said unto
thee, I saw thee under the fig
tree, believest thou? thou shalt
see greater things than these.

51. And he saith unto him,
Verily, verily, I say unto you,
Hereafter ye shall see heaven
open, and the angels of God
ascending and descending upon
the Son of man.

CHAP. II.

* J. I. 29, 35, 43.   Ps. 15. 17, 20.
II. 1. P. 21. Mk. I. 13. P. 17.
L. IV. 1. P. 17. M. IV. 1, 2.

1. And the third day* there
was a marriage in Cana of Galilee; and the mother of Jesus
was there:

2. And both Jesus was called,
and his disciples, to the marriage.

3. And when they wanted
wine, the mother of Jesus saith
unto him, They have no wine.

4. Jesus saith unto her,
Woman, what have I to do
with thee? mine hour is not
yet come.

5. His mother saith unto the
servants, Whatsoever he saith
unto you, do it.

6. And there were set there
six waterpots of stone, after
the manner of the purifying of
the Jews, containing two or
three firkins apiece.

7. Jesus saith unto them, Fill
the waterpots with water. And
they filled them up to the brim.

8. And he saith unto them,
Draw out now, and bear unto
the governor of the feast. And

they bare it.

9. When the ruler of the feast had tasted the water that was made wine, and knew not whence it was: (but the servants which drew the water knew;) the governor of the feast called the bridegroom,

10. And saith unto him, Every man at the beginning doth set forth good wine; and when men have well drunk, then that which is worse: but thou hast kept the good wine until now.

* Mk. I. 20. P. 19.

11. This beginning* of miracles did Jesus in Cana of Galilee, and manifested forth his glory; and his disciples believed on him.

M. IV. 13.

12. ¶ After this he went down to Capernaum, he, and his mother, and his brethren, and his disciples: and they continued there not many days.

J. III. 22. P. 24.

13. ¶ And the Jews' passover was at hand, and Jesus went up to Jerusalem,

14. And found in the temple those that sold oxen and sheep and doves, and the changers of money sitting:

15. And when he had made a scourge of small cords, he drove them all out of the temple, and the sheep, and the oxen; and poured out the changers' money, and overthrew the tables;

M. XXI. 12, 13. Mk. XI. 15, 16.
L. XIX. 45. P. 125.

16. And said unto them that sold doves, Take these things hence; make not my Father's house an house of merchandise.

17. And his disciples remembered that it was written, The zeal of thine house hath eaten me up.

18. ¶ Then answered the Jews and said unto him, What sign shewest thou unto us, seeing that thou doest these things?

19. Jesus answered and said unto them, Destroy this temple, and in three days I will raise it up

20. Then said the Jews, Forty and six years was this temple in building, and wilt thou rear it up in three days?

21. But he spake of the temple of his body.

22. When therefore he was risen from the dead, his disciples remembered that he had said this unto them; and they believed the scripture, and the word which Jesus had said.

23. ¶ Now when he was in Jerusalem at the passover, in the feast day, many believed in his name, when they saw the miracles which he did.

24. But Jesus did not commit himself unto them, because he knew all *men*,

25. And needed not that any should testify of man : for he knew what was in man.

CHAP. III.

1. There was a man of the Pharisees, named Nicodemus, a ruler of the Jews :

2. The same came to Jesus by night, and said unto him, Rabbi, we know that thou art a teacher come from God : for no man can do these miracles that thou doest, except God be with him.

3. Jesus answered and said unto him, Verily, verily, I say unto thee, Except a man be born again, he cannot see the kingdom of God.

4. Nicodemus saith unto him, How can a man be born when he is old? can he enter the second time into his mother's womb, and be born?

5. Jesus answered, Verily, verily, I say unto thee, Except a man be born of water and *of* the Spirit, he cannot enter into the kingdom of God.

6. That which is born of the flesh is flesh ; and that which is born of the Spirit is spirit.

7. Marvel not that I said unto thee, Ye must be born again.

8. The wind bloweth where it listeth, and thou hearest the sound thereof, but canst not tell whence it cometh, and whither it goeth : so is every one that is born of the Spirit.

9. Nicodemus answered and said unto him, How can these things be?

10. Jesus answered and said unto him, Art thou a master of Israel, and knowest not these things?

11. Verily, verily, I say unto thee, We speak that we do know, and testify that we have seen ; and ye receive not our witness.

12. If I have told you earthly things, and ye believe not, how shall ye believe, if I tell you *of* heavenly things?

13. And no man hath ascended up to heaven, but he that came down from heaven,

even the Son of man which is in heaven.

14. ¶ And as Moses lifted up the serpent in the wilderness, even so must the Son of man be lifted up:

15. That whosoever believeth in him should not perish, but have eternal life.

16. ¶ For God so loved the world, that he gave his only begotten Son, that whosoever believeth in him should not perish, but have everlasting life.

17. For God sent not his Son into the world to condemn the world; but that the world through him might be saved.

18. ¶ He that believeth on him is not condemned: but he that believeth not is condemned already, because he hath not believed in the name of the only begotten Son of God.

19. And this is the condemnation, that light is come into the world, and men loved darkness rather than light, because their deeds were evil.

20. For every one that doeth evil hateth the light, neither cometh to the light, lest his deeds should be reproved.

21. But he that doeth truth cometh to the light, that his deeds may be made manifest, that they are wrought in God.

22. ¶ After these things came Jesus and his disciples into the land of Judea; and there he tarried with them, and baptized.* 　J. IV. 2. P. 25.

23. And John also was baptizing in Ænon near to Salim, because there was much water there: and they came and were baptized.

24. For John was not yet cast into prison. 　M. IV. 12. XI. 2.

25. ¶ Then there arose a question between *some* of John's disciples and the Jews about purifying.

26. And they came unto John, and said unto him, Rabbi, he that was with thee beyond Jordan, to whom thou barest witness, behold, the same baptizeth, and all *men* come to him.

27. John answered and said, A man can receive nothing, except it be given him from heaven.

28. Ye yourselves bear me witness, that I said, I am not the Christ, but that I am sent before him.

29. He that hath the bride is the bridegroom; but the friend of the bridegroom, which standeth and heareth him, rejoiceth greatly because of the bridegroom's voice: this my joy therefore is fulfilled.

30. He must increase, but I *must* decrease.

31. He that cometh from above is above all : he that is of the earth is earthly, and speaketh of the earth : he that cometh from heaven is above all.

32. And what he hath seen and heard, that he testifieth ; and no man receiveth his testimony.

33. He that hath received his testimony hath set to his seal that God is true.

34. For he whom God hath sent speaketh the words of God : for God giveth not the Spirit by measure *unto him.*

35. The Father loveth the Son, and hath given all things into his hand.

36. He that believeth on the Son hath everlasting life : and he that believeth not the Son shall not see life ; but the wrath of God abideth on him.

CHAP. IV.

1. When therefore the Lord knew how the Pharisees had heard that Jesus made and baptized more disciples than John,

2. (Though Jesus himself baptized not, but his disciples,)

J. III. 22. P. 24.

3. He left Judea, and departed again into Galilee.

4. And he must needs go through Samaria.

5. Then cometh he to a city of Samaria, which is called Sychar, near to the parcel of ground that Jacob gave to his son Joseph.

6. Now Jacob's well was there. Jesus therefore, being wearied with *his* journey, sat thus on the well : *and* it was about the sixth hour.

7. There cometh a woman of Samaria to draw water : Jesus saith unto her, Give me to drink.

8. (For his disciples were gone away unto the city to buy meat.)

9. Then saith the woman of Samaria unto him, How is it that thou, being a Jew, askest drink of me, which am a woman of Samaria ? for the Jews have no dealings with the Samaritans.

10. Jesus answered and said unto her, If thou knewest the gift of God, and who it is that saith to thee, Give me to drink ; thou wouldest have asked of

him, and he would have given thee living water.

11. The woman saith unto him, Sir, thou hast nothing to draw with, and the well is deep: from whence then hast thou that living water?

12. Art thou greater than our father Jacob, which gave us the well, and drank thereof himself, and his children, and his cattle?

13. Jesus answered and said unto her, Whosoever drinketh of this water shall thirst again:

14. But whosoever drinketh of the water that I shall give him shall never thirst; but the water that I shall give him shall be in him a well of water springing up into everlasting life.

15. The woman saith unto him, Sir, give me this water, that I thirst not, neither come hither to draw.

16. Jesus saith unto her, Go, call thy husband, and come hither.

17. The woman answered and said, I have no husband. Jesus said unto her, Thou hast well said, I have no husband:

18. For thou hast had five husbands; and he whom thou now hast is not thy husband: in that saidst thou truly.

19. The woman saith unto him, Sir, I perceive that thou art a prophet.

20. Our fathers worshipped in this mountain; and ye say, that in Jerusalem is the place where men ought to worship.

21. Jesus saith unto her, Woman, believe me, the hour cometh, when ye shall neither in this mountain, nor yet at Jerusalem, worship the Father.

22. Ye worship ye know not what: we know what we worship: for salvation is of the Jews.

23. But the hour cometh, and now is, when the true worshippers shall worship the Father in spirit and in truth: for the Father seeketh such to worship him.

24. God *is* a Spirit: and they that worship him must worship *him* in spirit and in truth.

25. The woman saith unto him, I know that Messias cometh, which is called Christ: when he is come, he will tell us all things.

26. Jesus saith unto her, I

that speak unto thee am *he.*

27. ¶ And upon this came his disciples, and marvelled that he talked with the woman : yet no man said, What seekest thou ? or, Why talkest thou with her ?

28. The woman then left her waterpot, and went her way into the city, and saith to the men,

29. Come, see a man, which told me all things that ever I did : is not this the Christ ?

30. Then they went out of the city, and came unto him.

31. ¶ In the mean while his disciples prayed him, saying, Master, eat.

32. But he said unto them, I have meat to eat that ye know not of.

33. Therefore said the disciples one to another, Hath any man brought him *aught* to eat ?

34. Jesus saith unto them, My meat is to do the will of him that sent me, and to finish his work.

35. Say not ye, There are yet four months, and *then* cometh harvest ? behold, I say unto you, Lift up your eyes, and look on the fields ; for they are white already to harvest.

36. And he that reapeth receiveth wages, and gathereth fruit unto eternal life : that both he that soweth and he that reapeth may rejoice together.

37. And herein is that saying true, One soweth, and another reapeth.

38. I sent you to reap that whereon ye bestowed no labour: other men laboured, and ye are entered into their labours.

39. ¶ And many of the Samaritans of that city believed on him for the saying of the woman, which testified, He told me all that ever I did.

40. So when the Samaritans were come unto him, they besought him that he would tarry with them : and he abode there two days.

41. And many more believed because of his own word ;

42. And said unto the woman, Now we believe, not because of thy saying : for we have heard *him* ourselves, and know that this is indeed the Christ, the Saviour of the world.

43. ¶ Now after two days he departed thence, and went into Galilee.

M. XIII. 57.   44. For Jesus himself testified, that a prophet hath no honour in his own country.

45. Then when he was come into Galilee, the Galileans received him, having seen all the things that he did at Jerusalem at the feast : for they also went unto the feast.

46. So Jesus came again into Cana of Galilee, where he made the water wine. And there was a certain nobleman, whose son was sick at Capernaum.

M. VIII. 5—13.

47. When he heard that Jesus was come out of Judea into Galilee, he went unto him, and besought him that he would come down, and heal his son : for he was at the point of death.

48. Then said Jesus unto him, Except ye see signs and wonders, ye will not believe.

49. The nobleman saith unto him, Sir, come down ere my child die.

50. Jesus saith unto him, Go thy way; thy son liveth. And the man believed the word that Jesus had spoken unto him, and he went his way.

51. And as he was now going down, his servants met him and told *him*, saying, Thy son liveth.

52. Then enquired he of them the hour when he began to amend. And they said unto him, Yesterday at the seventh hour the fever left him.

53. So the father knew that *it was* at the same hour, in the which Jesus said unto him, Thy son liveth : and himself believed, and his whole house.

J. II. 11. P. 22, Mk. I. 25. P. 19.   54. This *is* again the second miracle *that* Jesus did, when he was come out of Judea into Galilee.

CHAP. V.

J. VI. 1, P. 74. VII. 1. 9, P. 89.   1. After this there was a feast of the Jews ; and Jesus went up to Jerusalem.*

* Second visit.

2. Now there is at Jerusalem by the sheep *market* a pool, which is called in the Hebrew

29

ST. MATTHEW, IV.   ST. MARK, 1.   ST. LUKE, V.   ST. JOHN. V.

tongue Bethesda, having five porches.

3. In these lay a great multitude of impotent folk, of blind, halt, withered, waiting for the moving of the water.

4. For an angel went down at a certain season into the pool, and troubled the water: whosoever then first after the troubling of the water stepped in was made whole of whatsoever disease he had.

[These words are not in the majority of ancient MSS.—A.]

5. And a certain man was there, which had an infirmity thirty and eight years.

6 When Jesus saw him lie and knew that he had been now a long time *in that case*, he saith unto him, Wilt thou be made whole?

7. The impotent man answered him, Sir, I have no man when the water is troubled, to put me into the pool: but while I am coming, another steppeth down before me.

8. Jesus saith unto him, Rise, take up thy bed and walk.

9. And immediately the man was made whole, and took up his bed and walked: and on the same day was the sabbath.

10 ¶ The Jews therefore said unto him that was cured, It is the sabbath day: it is not lawful for thee to carry *thy* bed.

11. He answered them, He that made me whole, the same said unto me, Take up thy bed, and walk.

12. Then asked they him, What man is that which said unto thee, Take up thy bed, and walk?

13. And he that was healed wist not who it was: for Jesus had conveyed himself away, a multitude being in *that* place.

14. Afterward Jesus findeth him in the temple, and said unto him, Behold, thou art made whole: sin no more, lest a worse thing come unto thee.

15. The man departed, and told the Jews that it was Jesus, which had made him whole.

16. And therefore did the Jews persecute Jesus, and sought to slay him, because he had done these things on the Sabbath day.

" And sought to slay him." [Not in the oldest MSS.—A.]

17. ¶ But Jesus answered them, My Father worketh hitherto, and I work.

18. Therefore the Jews sought the more to kill him, because he not only had broken the sabbath, but said also that God was his Father, making himself equal with God.

19. Then answered Jesus and said unto them, Verily, verily, I say unto you, The Son can do nothing of himself, but what he seeth the Father do˙: for what things soever he doeth, these also doeth the Son likewise.

20. For the Father loveth the Son, and sheweth him all things that himself doeth : and he will shew him greater works than these, that ye may marvel.

21. For as the Father raiseth up the dead,¹ and quickeneth *them ;* even so the Son quickeneth whom he will.

22. For the Father judgeth no man, but hath committed all judgment unto the Son :

23. That all *men* should honour the Son, even as they honour the Father. He that honoureth not the Son honoureth not the Father which hath sent him.

24. Verily, verily, I say unto you, He that heareth my word, and believeth on him that sent me, hath everlasting life, and shall not come into condemnation ; but is passed from death unto life.

25. Verily, verily, I say unto you, The hour is coming, and now is, when the dead shall hear the voice of the Son of God: and they that hear shall live.

26. For as the Father hath life in himself ; so hath he given to the Son to have life in himself.

27. And hath given him authority to execute judgment also because he is the Son of man.

28. Marvel not at this : for the hour is coming, in the which all that are in the graves shall hear his voice,

29. And shall come forth ; they that have done good, unto the resurrection of life; and they that have done evil, unto the resurrection of damnation.

30. I can of mine own self do nothing : as I hear, I judge : and my judgment is just ; because I seek not mine own will, but the will of the Father which hath sent me.

St. MATTHEW, IV.   St. MARK, I.   St. LUKE, V.   St. JOHN, V.

31. If I bear witness of myself, my witness is not true.

32. ¶ There is another that beareth witness of me ; and I know that the witness which he witnesseth of me is true.

33. Ye sent unto John, and he bare witness unto the truth.

34. But I receive not testimony from man : but these things I say, that ye might be saved.

35. He was a burning and a shining light : and ye were willing for a season to rejoice in his light.

36. ¶ But I have greater witness than *that* of John : for the works which the Father hath given me to finish, the same works that I do, bear witness of me, that the Father hath sent me.

37. And the Father himself, which hath sent me, hath borne witness of me. Ye have neither heard his voice at any time, nor seen his shape.

38. And ye have not his word abiding in you : for whom he hath sent, him ye believe not.

39. ¶ Search the scriptures ; for in them ye think ye have eternal life : and they are they which testify of me.

40. And ye will not come to me, that ye might have life.

41. I receive not honour from men.

42. But I know you, that ye have not the love of God in you.

43. I am come in my Father's name, and ye receive me not : if another shall come in his own name, him ye will receive.

44. How can ye believe, which receive honour one of another, and seek not the honour that *cometh* from God only ?

45. Do not think that I will accuse you to the Father: There is *one* that accuseth you, *even* Moses, in whom ye trust.

46. For had ye believed Moses, ye would have believed me : for he wrote of me.

47. But if ye believe not his writings, how shall ye believe my words?

From P. 20.

23. ¶ And Jesus went about all Galilee, teaching in their synagogues, and preaching the gospel of the kingdom, and healing all manner of sickness and all manner of disease among the people.

CHAP. VI.

See P. 74.

ST. MATTHEW, V.   ST. MARK, 1.   ST. LUKE, VI.   ST. JOHN, VI.

24. And his fame went throughout all Syria : and they brought unto him all sick people that were taken with divers diseases and torments, and those which were possessed with devils, and those which were lunatick, and those which had the palsy ; and he healed them.

25. And there followed him great multitudes of people from Galilee, and *from* Decapolis, and *from* Jerusalem, and *from* Judea, and *from* beyond Jordan.

CHAP. V.

1. And seeing the multitudes, he went up into a mountain : and when he was set, his disciples came unto him :

2. And he opened his mouth, and taught them, saying,

3. Blessed *are* the poor in spirit : for their's is the kingdom of heaven.

4. Blessed *are* they that mourn : for they shall be comforted.

5. Blessed *are* the meek : for they shall inherit the earth.

6. Blessed *are* they which do hunger and thirst after righteousness : for they shall be filled.

7. Blessed *are* the merciful : for they shall obtain mercy.

8. Blessed *are* the pure in heart : for they shall see God.

9. Blessed *are* the peacemakers : for they shall be called the children of God.

10. Blessed *are* they which are persecuted for righteousness' sake : for their's is the kingdom of heaven.

11. Blessed are ye when *men* shall revile you, and persecute *you*, and shall say all manner of evil against you falsely, for my sake.

12. Rejoice, and be exceeding glad : for great *is* your reward in heaven : for so persecuted they the prophets which were before you.

CHAP. VI.

1 to 11 (see P. 61).

12 to 16 (see P. 52).

17 to 19 (see P. 63)

Continued from P. 63.
20. ¶ And he lifted up his eyes on his disciples, and said, Blessed *be ye* poor : for your's is the kingdom of God.

21. Blessed *are ye* that hunger now :   for ye shall be filled.

M. V. 4.   Blessed *are ye* that weep now : for ye shall laugh.

L. VI. 36. P. 33

22. Blessed are ye, when men shall hate you, and when they shall separate you *from their company*, and shall reproach *you*, and cast out your name as evil, for the Son of man's sake.

23. Rejoice ye in that day : and leap for joy : for, behold, your reward *is* great in heaven ; for in the like manner did their fathers unto the prophets.

24. But woe unto you that are rich ! for ye have received your consolation.

St. MATTHEW, V.   St. MARK, I., IV.   St. LUKE, VI., XIV., VIII.   St. JOHN, VI.

25. Woe unto you that are full! for ye shall hunger. Woe unto you that laugh now! for ye shall mourn and weep.

26. Woe unto you, when all men shall speak well of you! for so did their fathers to the false prophets.

Continued at P. 35.

---

13. ¶ Ye are the salt of the earth : but if the salt have lost his savour, wherewith shall it be salted ?
it is thenceforth good for nothing, but to be cast out, and to be trodden under foot of men.

IX. 50.—P. 91.

Chap. XIV. from P. 56.
34. ¶ Salt *is* good : but if the salt have lost his savour, wherewith shall it be seasoned ?

35. It is neither fit for the land, nor yet for the dunghill ; *but* men cast it out.
He that ears to hear, let him hear.

For Chap. XV. see P. 91.

14. Ye are the light of the world. A city that is set on an hill cannot be hid.

15. Neither do men light a candle, and put it under a bushel, but on a candlestick ; and it giveth light unto all that are in the house.

Chap. IV.—from P. 68.
21. ¶ And he said unto them, Is a candle brought to be put under a bushel, or under a bed ? and not to be set on a candlestick ?

Continued at P. 55.

Chap. VIII. from P. 68.
16. ¶ No man, when he hath lighted a candle, covereth it with a vessel, or putteth *it* under a bed ; but setteth *it* on a candlestick, that they which enter in may see the light.

17. For nothing is secret, that shall not be made manifest ; neither *any thing* hid, that shall not be known and come abroad.

Continued at P. 67.

16. Let your light so shine before men, that they may see your good works, and glorify your Father which is in heaven.

17. ¶ Think not that I am come to destroy the law, or the prophets : I am not come to destroy, but to fulfil.

18. For verily I say unto you, Till heaven and earth pass, one jot or one tittle shall in no wise pass from the law, till all be fulfilled.

L. XVI. 16, 17, P. 94.

19. Whosoever therefore shall break one of these least commandments, and shall teach men so, he shall be called the least in the kingdom of heaven : but whosoever shall do and teach *them*, the same shall be called great in the kingdom of heaven.

20. For I say unto you, That except your righteousness shall exceed *the righteousness* of the scribes and Pharisees, ye shall in no case enter into the kingdom of heaven.

21. ¶ Ye have heard that it

was said by them of old time, Thou shalt not kill: and whosoever shall kill shall be in danger of the judgment:

22. But I say unto you, That whosoever is angry with his brother without a cause shall be in danger of the judgment: and whosoever shall say to his brother, Raca, shall be in danger of the council: but whosoever shall say, Thou fool, shall be in danger of hell fire.

23. Therefore if thou bring thy gift to the altar, and there rememberest that thy brother hath ought against thee;

24. Leave there thy gift before the altar, and go thy way; first be reconciled to thy brother, and then come and offer thy gift.

25. Agree with thine adversary quickly, whiles thou art in the way with him; lest at any time the adversary deliver thee to the judge, and the judge deliver thee to the officer, and thou be cast into prison.

26. Verily I say unto thee, Thou shalt by no means come out thence, till thou hast paid the uttermost farthing.

27. ¶ Ye have heard that it was said by them of old time, Thou shalt not commit adultery:

28. But I say unto you, That whosoever looketh on a woman to lust after her hath committed adultery with her already in his heart.

29. And if thy right eye offend thee, pluck it out, and cast *it* from thee: for it is profitable for thee that one of thy members should perish, and not *that* thy whole body should be cast into hell.

30. And if thy right hand offend thee, cut it off, and cast *it* from thee: for it is profitable for thee that one of thy members should perish, and not *that* thy whole body should be cast into hell. (1)

31. It hath been said, Whosoever shall put away his wife, let him give her a writing of divorcement:

32. But I say unto you, That whosoever shall put away his wife, saving for the cause of fornication, causeth her to commit adultery: and whosoever shall marry her that is divorced

(1) See M. XVIII., 8, 9; Mk. IX., 47, 43; P. 91.

Chap. XII. from P. 83.

58. ¶ When thou goest with thine adversary to the magistrate, *as thou art* in the way, give diligence that thou mayest be delivered from him; lest he hale thee to the judge, and the judge deliver thee to the officer, and the officer cast thee into prison.

59. I tell thee, thou shalt not depart thence, till thou hast paid the very last mite.

For Chap. XIII. see P. 60.

See Mk. IX., 47, P. 91

and IX., 43, P. 90.

M. XIX., 9.

committeth adultery.

33. ¶ Again, ye have heard that it hath been said by them of old time, Thou shalt not forswear thyself, but shalt perform unto the Lord thine oaths :

34. But I say unto you, Swear not] at all; neither] by heaven ; for it is God's throne :

35. Nor by the earth ; for, it is his footstool : neither by Jerusalem ; for it is the city of the great King.

36. Neither shalt thou swear by thy head, because thou canst not make one hair white or black.

37. But let your communication be, Yea, yea ; Nay, nay : for whatsoever is more than these cometh of evil.

38. ¶ Ye have heard that it hath been said, An eye for an eye, and a tooth for a tooth :

39. But I say unto you, That ye resist not evil : but whosoever shall smite thee on thy right cheek, turn to him the other also.

VI.

29. And unto him that smiteth thee on the *one* cheek offer also the other ;

40. And if any man will sue thee at the law, and take away thy coat, let him have *thy* cloke also.

and him that taketh away thy cloke forbid not *to take thy* coat also.

41. And whosoever shall compel thee to go a mile, go with him twain.

42. Give to him that asketh thee, and from him that would borrow of thee turn not thou away.

30. Give to every man that asketh of thee ; and of him that taketh away thy goods ask *them* not again.

31. And as ye would that men should do to you, do ye also to them likewise.

See M. VII., 12.

Continued below.

M. VII, 12.

43. ¶ Ye have heard that it hath been said, Thou shalt love thy neighbour, and hate thine enemy.

44. But I say unto you, Love your enemies, bless them that curse you, do good to them that hate you, and pray for them which despitefully use you, and persecute you ;

L. VI. 35, P. 36.

" Love your enemies, and pray for them which persecute you."--Alford.

Chap. VI. from P. 33.

27. ¶ But I say unto you which hear, Love your enemies, do good to them which hate you.

28. Bless them that curse you, and pray for them which despitefully use you.

Continued above.

45. That ye may be the children of your Father which is in heaven : for he maketh his sun to rise on the evil and on the good, and sendeth rain on the just and on the unjust.

46. For if ye love them which love you, what reward have ye? do not even the publicans the same?

32. For if ye love them which love you, what thank have ye? for sinners also love those that love them.

33. And if ye do good to them which do good to you, what thank have ye? for sinners also do even the same.

34. And if ye lend *to them* of whom ye hope to receive, what thank have ye? for sinners also lend to sinners, to receive as much again.

47. And if ye salute your brethren only, what do ye more *than others?* do not even the publicans so?

35. But love ye your enemies, and do good, and lend, hoping for nothing again; and your reward shall be great, and ye shall be the children of the Highest: for he is kind unto the unthankful and *to* the evil.   M. V. 44, 45.

36. Be ye therefore merciful, as your Father also is merciful. *Continued P. 39.*

48. Be ye therefore perfect, even as your Father which is in heaven is perfect.

CHAP. VI.

1. Take heed that ye do not your alms before men, to be seen of them: otherwise ye have no reward of your Father which is in heaven.

2. Therefore when thou doest *thine* alms, do not sound a trumpet before thee, as the hypocrites do in the synagogues and in the streets, that they may have glory of men. Verily I say unto you, They have their reward.

3. But when thou doest alms, let not thy left hand know what thy right hand doeth:

4. That thine alms may be in secret: and thy Father which seeth in secret, himself shall reward thee openly.

5. ¶ And when thou prayest, thou shalt not be as the hypocrites *are;* for they love to pray standing in the synagogues and in the corners of the streets, that they may be seen of men. Verily I say unto you, They have their reward.

6. But thou, when thou prayest, enter into thy closet, and when thou hast shut thy door, pray to thy Father which is in secret; and thy Father which seeth in secret shall reward thee openly.

7. But when ye pray, use not vain repetitions, as the heathen *do:* for they think that they shall be heard for their much speaking.

8. Be not ye therefore like unto them: for your Father knoweth what things ye have need of, before ye ask him.

Chap. XI.

From P. 125.

1. And it came to pass, that, as he was praying in a certain place, when he ceased, one of his disciples said unto him, Lord, teach us to pray, as John also taught his disciples.

2. And he said unto them, When ye pray say,

9. After this manner therefore pray ye: Our Father which art in heaven, Hallowed be thy name.

10. Thy kingdom come. Thy will be done in earth, as *it is in* heaven.

11. Give us this day our daily bread.

12. And forgive us our debts, as we forgive our debtors.

13. And lead us not into temptation, but deliver us from evil:
*For thine is the kingdom, and the power, and the glory, for ever. Amen.

14. For if ye forgive men their trespasses, your heavenly Father will also forgive you:

15. But if ye forgive not men their trespasses, neither will your Father forgive your trespasses.

Our Father which art in heaven, Hallowed be thy name. Thy kingdom come. Thy will be done, as in heaven, so in earth.

3. Give us day by day our daily bread.

4. And forgive us our sins; for we also forgive every one that is indebted to us. And lead us not into temptation'; but deliver us from evil.

Continued P. 39.

[" *As in heaven so also in earth.*"
" *Our necessary bread.*"—*Alford.*]

Chap. XI. from P. 126.

25. And when ye stand praying, forgive, if ye have ought against any: that your Father also which is in heaven may forgive you your trespasses.

26. But if ye do not forgive, neither will your Father which is in heaven forgive your trespasses.

Continued P. 126.

" *Our*"—" *which art in heaven,*"

" *thy will be done, as in heaven so in earth.*"

" *but deliver us from evil.*"

Not in Alford's version.

(*v. 26.* " *Not in the oldest MSS. and some others.*"—*Alford.*)

16. ¶ Moreover when ye fast, be not, as the hypocrites, of a sad countenance: for they disfigure their faces, that they may appear unto men to fast. Verily I say unto you, They have their reward.

17. But thou, when thou fastest, anoint thine head, and wash thy face;

18. That thou appear not unto men to fast, but unto thy Father which is in secret: and thy Father, which seeth in secret, shall reward thee openly.

19. ¶ Lay not up for yourselves treasures upon earth, where moth and rust doth corrupt, and where thieves break through and steal:

20. But lay up for yourselves treasures in heaven, where neither moth nor rust doth corrupt, and where thieves do not break through nor steal:

21. For where your treasure is, there will your heart also.

L. XII. 33, 34. P. 143.

Chap. XI. from P. 65.

33. No man, when he hath   M. V, 15; L. VIII., 16; P. 33.

* Not in Alford's version.

lighted a candle, putteth *it* in a secret place, neither under a bushel, but on a candlestick, that they which come in may see the light.

34. The light of the body is the eye : therefore when thine eye *is* single, thy whole body also is full of light ; but when *thine eye* is evil, thy body also *is* full of darkness.

35. Take heed therefore that the light which is in thee be not darkness.

36. If thy whole body therefore *be* full of light, having no part dark, the whole shall be full of light, as when the bright shining of a candle doth give thee light.
Continued P. 136.

22. The light of the body is the eye :
if therefore thine eye be single, thy whole body shall be full of light.

23. But if thine eye be evil, thy whole body shall be full of darkness.
If therefore the light that is in thee be darkness, how great *is* that darkness !

Chap. XVI. from P. 94.
13. ¶ No servant can serve two masters : for either he will hate the one, and love the other ; or else he will hold to the one, and despise the other. Ye cannot serve God and mammon.
Continued P. 94.

24. ¶ No man can serve two masters :
for either he will hate the one, and love the other ; or else he will hold to the one and despise the other.
Ye cannot serve God and mammon.

Chap. XII. from P. 54.
22. ¶ And he said unto his disciples, Therefore I say unto you, Take no thought for your life, what ye shall eat ; neither for the body, what ye shall put on.

23. The life is more than meat, and the body *is more* than raiment.

24. Consider the ravens : for they neither sow nor reap ; which neither have storehouse nor barn ; and God feedeth them : how much more are ye better than the fowls ?

25. And which of you with taking thought can add to this stature one cubit ?

26. If ye then be not able to do that thing which is least, why take ye thought for the rest ?

27. Consider the lilies how they grow : they toil not, they spin not ; and yet I say unto you, that Solomon in all his glory was not arrayed like one of these.

28. If then God so clothe the grass, which is to day in the field, and to morrow is cast into the oven ; how much more *will he clothe* you, O ye of little faith ?

25. Therefore I say unto you, Take no thought for your life, what ye shall eat, or what ye shall drink : nor yet for your body, what ye shall put on.
Is not the life more than meat, and the body than raiment ?

26. Behold the fowls of the air : for they sow not, neither do they reap, nor gather into barns ; yet your heavenly Father feedeth them. Are ye not much better than they ?

27. Which of you by taking thought can add one cubit unto his stature ?

28. And why take ye thought for raiment ?
Consider the lilies of the field, how they grow ; they toil not, neither do they spin :

29. And yet I say unto you, That even Solomon in all his glory was not arrayed like one of these.

30. Wherefore if God so clothe the grass of the field, which to day is, and to morrow is cast into the oven, *shall he* not much more *clothe* you, O ye of little faith ?

ST. MATTHEW, VII.   ST. MARK, I.   ST. LUKE, XII. VI. XI.   ST. JOHN, VI.

31. Therefore take no thought, saying, What shall we eat? or, What shall we drink? or Wherewithal shall we be clothed?

32. (For after all these things do the Gentiles seek :) for your heavenly Father knoweth that ye have need of all these things.

33. But seek ye first the kingdom of God, and his righteousness ; and all these things shall be added unto you.

34. Take therefore no thought for the morrow : for the morrow shall take thought for the things of itself. Sufficient unto the day is the evil thereof.

29. And seek not ye what ye shall eat, or what ye shall drink, neither be ye of doubtful mind.

30. For all these things do the nations of the world seek after : and your Father knoweth that ye have need of these things.

31. ¶ But rather seek ye the kingdom of God ; and all these things shall be added unto you.

Continued P. 143.

CHAP. VII.

1. Judge not, that ye be not judged.

2. For with what judgment ye judge, ye shall be judged :

Chap. VI. from P. 36.

37. Judge not, and ye shall not be judged : condemn not, and ye shall not be condemned : forgive, and ye shall be forgiven :

38. Give, and it shall be given unto you ; good measure, pressed down, and shaken together, and running over, shall men give into your bosom.

and with what measure ye mete, it shall be measured to you again.

For with the same measure that ye mete withal it shall be measured to you again.

39.—Continued P. 80.
40.—Continued P. 54.

From P. 54.

3. And why beholdest thou the mote that is in thy brother's eye, but considerest not the beam that is in thine own eye ?

4. Or how wilt thou say to thy brother, Let me pull out the mote out of thine eye ; and behold a beam is in thine own eye ?

5. Thou hypocrite, first cast out the beam out of thine own eye ; and then shalt thou see clearly to cast out the mote out of thy brother's eye.

41. And why beholdest thou the mote that is in thy brother's eye, but perceivest not the beam that is in thine own eye?

42. Either how canst thou say to thy brother, Brother, let me pull out the mote that is in thine eye, when thou thyself beholdest not the beam that is in thine own eye? Thou hypocrite, cast out first the beam out of thine own eye, and then shalt thou see clearly to pull out the mote that is in thy brother's eye.

43.—Continued P. 41.

6. ¶ Give not that which is holy unto the dogs, neither cast ye your pearls before swine, lest they trample them under their feet, and turn again and rend you.

Chap. XI. from P. 37.

5. And he said unto them, Which of you shall have a

friend, and shall go unto him at midnight, and say unto him, Friend, lend me three loaves ;

6. For a friend of mine in his journey is come to me, and I have nothing to set before him?

7. And he from within shall answer and say, Trouble me not : the door is now shut, and my children are with me in bed ; I cannot rise and give thee.

8. I say unto you, Though he will not rise and give him, because he is his friend, yet because of his importunity he will rise and give him as many as he needeth.

9. And I say unto you, Ask, and it shall be given you ; seek, and ye shall find ; knock, and it shall be opened unto you.

7. ¶ Ask, and it shall be given you ; seek, and ye shall find ;
knock, and it shall be opened unto you :

8. For everyone that asketh receiveth ; and he that seeketh findeth ; and to him that knocketh it shall be opened.

9. Or what man is there of you, whom if his son ask bread, will he give him a stone

10. Or if he ask a fish, will he give him a serpent ?

10. For every one that asketh receiveth ; and he that seeketh findeth ; and to him that knocketh it shall be opened.

11. If a son shall ask bread of any of you that is a father, will he give him a stone?
or if *he ask* a fish, will he for a fish give him a serpent ?

12. Or, if he shall ask an egg, will he offer him a scorpion ?

13. If ye then, being evil, know how to give good gifts unto your children : how much more shall *your* heavenly Father give the Holy Spirit to them that ask him ?

11. If ye then, being evil, know how to give good gifts unto your children, how much more shall your Father which is in heaven give good things to them that ask him ?

12. Therefore all things whatsoever ye would that men should do to you, do ye even so to them : for this is the law and the prophets.

L. VI. 31. P. 35

M. XXII. 39. 4C.

Continued P. 63.

See VI. 31. P. 35.

Chap. XIII. from P. 69.

22. And he went through the cities and villages, teaching, and journeying towards Jerusalem.

23. Then said one unto him, Lord, are there few that be saved? And he said unto them,

24. ¶ Strive to enter in at the strait gate ; for many, I say unto you, will seek to enter in, and shall not be able.

13. ¶ Enter ye in at the strait gate : for wide *is* the gate, and broad *is* the way, that leadeth to destruction, and many there be which go in thereat :

14. Because strait *is* the gate : and narrow *is* the way, which leadeth unto life, and few there be that find it.

15 ¶ Beware of false pro-

Continued P. 41.

ST. MATTHEW, VII.   ST. MARK, I.   ST. LUKE, VI., XIII.   ST. JOHN, VI.

phets, which come to you in sheep's clothing, but inwardly they are ravening wolves.

16. Ye shall know them by their fruits. Do men gather grapes of thorns, or figs of thistles?

17. Even so every good tree bringeth forth good fruit; but a corrupt tree bringeth forth evil fruit.

18. A good tree cannot bring forth evil fruit, neither can a corrupt tree bring forth good fruit.

M. III. 10.

19. Every tree that bringeth not forth good fruit is hewn down and cast into the fire.

20. Wherefore by their fruits ye shall know them.

Chap. VI. from P. 39.

43. For a good tree bringeth not forth corrupt fruit; neither doth a corrupt tree bring forth good fruit.

44. For every tree is known by his own fruit. For of thorns men do not gather figs, nor of a bramble bush gather they grapes.

45. A good man out of the good treasure of his heart bringeth forth that which is good; and an evil man out of the evil treasure of his heart bringeth forth that which is evil: for of the abundance of the heart his mouth speaketh.

46. ¶ And why call ye me, Lord, Lord, and do not the things which I say?

Continued P. 42.

21. ¶ Not every one that saith unto me, Lord, Lord, shall enter into the kingdom of heaven; but he that doeth the will of my Father which is in heaven.

Chap. XIII. from P. 40.

25. When once the master of the house is risen up, and hath shut to the door, and ye begin to stand without, and to knock at the door, saying, Lord, Lord, open unto us; and he shall answer and say unto you, I know you not whence ye are:

26. Then shall ye begin to say, We have eaten and drunk in thy presence, and thou hast taught in our streets.

27. But he shall say, I tell you, I know you not whence ye are; depart from me, all *ye* workers of iniquity.

22. Many will say to me in that day, Lord, Lord, have we not prophesied in thy name? and in thy name have cast out devils; and in thy name done many wonderful works?

23. And then will I profess unto them, I never knew you: depart from me ye that work iniquity.

(See M. VIII. 11. 12.)

M. VIII. 11. 12.

28. There shall be weeping and gnashing of teeth, when ye shall see Abraham, and Isaac, and Jacob, and all the prophets, in the kingdom of God, and you *yourselves* thrust out.

29. And they shall come from the east, and *from* the west, and from the north, and *from* the south, and shall sit down in the kingdom of God.

30. And, behold, there are last which shall be first, and there are first which shall be last.

Continued P. 137.
Chap. VI. from P. 41.
47. Whosoever cometh to me, and heareth my sayings, and doeth them, I will shew you to whom he is like :
48. He is like a man which built an house, and digged deep, and laid the foundation on a rock : and when the flood arose, the stream beat vehemently upon that house, and could not shake it : for it was founded upon a rock.
49. But he that heareth, and doeth not, is like a man that without a foundation built an house upon the earth ; against which the stream did beat vehemently, and immediately it fell ; and the ruin of `that house was great.

For Chap. VII. see P. 43.

24. ¶ Therefore whosoever heareth these sayings of mine, and doeth them, I will liken him unto a wise man, which

built his house upon a rock :
25. And the rain descended, and the floods came, and the winds blew, and beat upon that house ; and it fell not : for it was founded upon a rock.
26. And every one that heareth these sayings of mine, and doeth them not, shall be likened unto a foolish man, which built his house upon the sand ;
27. And the rain descended, and the floods came, and the winds blew, and beat upon that house ; and it fell : and great was the fall of it.
28. And it came to pass, when Jesus had ended these sayings, the people were astonished at his doctrine :
29. For he taught them as *one* having authority, and not as the scribes.

CHAP. VIII.

1. When he was come down from the mountain, great multitudes followed him.
2. And, behold, there came a leper and worshipped him, saying, Lord, if thou wilt, thou canst make me clean.
3. And Jesus put forth *his* hand, and touched him, saying, I will ; be thou clean.

　　And immediately his leprosy was cleansed.

4. And Jesus saith unto him, See thou tell no man ; but go thy way, shew thyself to the priest, and offer the gift that Moses commanded, for a testimony unto them.

From P. 19.
40. And there came a leper to him, beseeching him, and kneeling down to him, and saying unto him, if thou wilt, thou canst make me clean.
41. And Jesus, moved with compassion, put forth *his* hand, and touched him, and saith unto him, I will ; be thou clean.
42. And as soon as he had spoken, immediately the leprosy departed from him, and he was cleansed.
43. And he straitly charged him, and forthwith sent him away ;
44. And saith unto him, See thou say nothing to any man : but go thy way, shew thyself to the priest, and offer for thy cleansing those things which Moses commanded, for a testimony unto them.

Chap. V. from P. 20.
12. ¶ And it came to pass, when he was in a certain city, behold a man full of leprosy : who seeing Jesus fell on *his* face, and besought him, saying, Lord, if thou wilt, thou canst make me clean.
13. And he put forth *his* hand, and touched him, saying, I will : be thou clean. And immediately the leprosy departed from him.
14. And he charged him to tell no man :
but go, and shew thyself to the priest, and offer for thy cleansing, according as Moses commanded, for a testimony unto them.

ST. MATTHEW, VIII.   ST. MARK, I.   ST. LUKE, V., VII.   ST. JOHN, VI.

45. But he went out, and began to publish it much, and to blaze abroad the matter, insomuch that Jesus could no more openly enter into the city, but was without in desert places : and they came to him from every quarter.

For Chap. II., see P. 47.

15. But so much the more went there a fame abroad of him : and great multitudes came together to hear, and to be healed by him of their infirmities.

16. ¶ And he withdrew himself into the wilderness, and prayed.

Continued P. 47.

CHAP. VII.

From P. 42.

1. Now when he had ended all his sayings in the audience of the people, he entered into Capernaum.

2. And a certain centurion's servant, who was dear unto him,
was sick, and ready to die.

3. And when he heard of Jesus, he sent unto him the elders of the Jews, beseeching him that he would come and heal his servant.

4. And when they came to Jesus, they besought him instantly, saying, That he was worthy for whom he should do this :

5. For he loveth our nation, and he hath built us a synagogue.

6. Then Jesus went with them ; And when he was now not far from the house,
the centurion sent friends to him, saying unto him, Lord, trouble not thyself : for I am not worthy that thou shouldest enter under my roof :

7. Wherefore neither thought I myself worthy to come unto thee :
but say in a word, and my servant shall be healed.

8. For I also am a man set under authority, having under me soldiers, and I say unto one, Go, and he goeth ; and to another, Come, and he cometh ; and to my servant, Do this, and he doeth it.

9. When Jesus heard these things, he marvelled at him, and turned him about, and said unto the people that followed him, I say unto you, I have not found so great faith, no, not in Israel.

J. IV. 46 to 53, P. 28.
(Quere, same miracle?)

5. ¶ And when Jesus was entered into Capernaum, there came unto him a centurion, beseeching him,

6. And saying, Lord, my servant lieth at home sick of the palsy, grievously tormented.

7. And Jesus saith unto him, I will come and heal him.

8. The centurion answered and said,
Lord, I am not worthy that thou shouldest come under my roof :

but speak the word only, and my servant shall be healed.

9. For I am a man under authority, having soldiers under me : and I say to this man, Go, and he goeth ; and to another, Come, and he cometh ; and to my servant, Do this, and he doeth it.

10. When Jesus heard it, he marvelled, and said to them that followed, Verily I say unto you, I have not found so great faith, no, not in Israel.

11. And I say unto you, That many shall come from the east and west, and shall sit down with Abraham, and

Isaac, and Jacob, in the kingdom of heaven.

12. But the children of the kingdom shall he cast out into outer darkness : there shall be weeping and gnashing of teeth.

13. And Jesus said unto the centurion, Go thy way ; and as thou hast believed, so be it done unto thee.

And his servant was healed in the self-same hour.

M. XIII. 42. 50.
XXII. 13.
XXIV. 51.
XXV. 30.

See L. XIII., 28. 29. P. 41.

10. And they that were sent, returning to the house, found the servant whole that had been sick.

11. ¶ And it came to pass the day after, that he went into a city called Nain ; and many of his disciples went with him, and much people.

12. Now when he came nigh to the gate of the city, behold, there was a dead man carried out, the only son of his mother, and she was a widow : and much people of the city was with her.

13. And when the Lord saw her, he had compassion on her, and said unto her, Weep not.

14. And he came and touched the bier : and they that bare *him* stood still. And he said, Young man, I say unto thee, Arise.

15. And he that was dead sat up, and began to speak. And he delivered him to his mother.

16. And there came a fear on all : and they glorified God, saying, That a great prophet is risen up among us ; and, That God hath visited his people.

17. And this rumour of him went forth throughout all Judea, and throughout all the region round about.

Continued P. 58.

Chap. I. from P. 19.

29. And forthwith, when they were come out of the synagogue, they entered into the house of Simon and Andrew, with James and John.

14. ¶ And when Jesus was come into Peter's house,

he saw his wife's mother laid, and sick of a fever.

30. But Simon's wife's mother lay sick of a fever, and anon they tell him of her.

Chap. IV. from P. 19.

38. ¶ And he arose out of the synagogue, and entered into Simon's house. And Simon's wife's mother was taken with a great fever ; and they besought him for her.

15. And he touched her hand, and the fever left her : and she arose, and ministered unto them.

31. And he came and took her by the hand, and lifted her up ; and immediately the fever left her, and she ministered unto them.

39. And he stood over her, and rebuked the fever ; and it left her : and immediately she arose and ministered unto them.

16. ¶ When the even was come, they brought unto him many that were possessed with devils :

and he cast out the spirits with *his* word,
and healed all that were sick.

32. And at even, when the sun did set, they brought unto him all that were diseased, and them that were possessed with devils.

33. And all the city was gathered together at the door.

34. And he healed many that were sick of divers diseases, and cast out many devils ; and suffered not the devils to speak,

40. ¶ Now when the sun was setting, all they that had any sick with divers diseases brought unto him ; and he laid his hands on every one of them, and healed them.

41. And devils also came out of many, crying out, and saying, Thou art Christ the Son of God. And he rebuking *them* suffered them not to speak :

ST. MATTHEW, VIII.   ST. MARK, II. IV.   ST. L., IV., VIII., IX., VIII.   ST. JOHN VI.

17. That it might be fulfilled which was spoken by Esaias the prophet, saying, Himself took our infirmities, and bare our sicknesses.

18. ¶ Now when Jesus saw great multitudes about him, he gave commandment to depart unto the other side.

19. And a certain scribe came and said unto him, Master, I will follow thee whithersoever thou goest.

20. And Jesus saith unto him, The foxes have holes, and the birds of the air have nests ; but the Son of man hath not where to lay his head.

21. And another of his disciples said unto him, Lord, suffer me first to go and bury my father.

22. But Jesus said unto him, Follow me ; and let the dead bury their dead.

23. ¶ And when he was entered into a ship, his disciples followed him.

24. And, behold, there arose a great tempest in the sea, insomuch that the ship was covered with the waves : but he was asleep.

25. And his disciples came to him, and awoke him, saying, Lord, save us ; we perish.

26. And he saith unto them, Why are ye fearful, O ye of little faith ? Then he arose, and rebuked the winds and the sea ; and there was a great calm.

27. But the men marvelled, saying,

---

because they knew him.
Continued at P. 19.

Chap. IV. from P. 70.
35. ¶ And the same day, when the even was come, he saith unto them, Let us pass over unto the other side.

36. And when they had sent away the multitude, they took him even as he was in the ship. And there were also with him other little ships.

37. And there arose a great storm of wind, and the waves beat into the ship, so that it was now full.

38. And he was in the hinder part of the ship, asleep on a pillow : and they awake him, and say unto him, Master, carest thou not that we perish ?

39. And he arose, and rebuked the wind, and said unto the sea, Peace, be still. And the wind ceased, and there was a great calm.

40. And he said unto them, Why are ye so fearful ? how is it that ye have no faith ?

---

for they knew that he was Christ.
Continued P. 19.

Chap. VIII. from P. 66.
22. ¶ Now it came to pass on a certain day, that he went into a ship with his disciples : and he said unto them, Let us go over unto the other side of the lake. And they launched forth.

Continued below.

Chap. IX. from P. 118.
57. ¶ And it came to pass, that as they went in the way, a certain man said unto him, Lord, I will follow thee whithersoever thou goest.

58. And Jesus said unto him, Foxes have holes, and birds of the air have nests : but the Son of man hath not where to lay his head.

59. And he said unto another, follow me. But he said, Lord, suffer me first to go and bury my father.

60. Jesus said unto him, Let the dead bury their dead : but go thou and preach the kingdom of God.

61. And another also said, Lord, I will follow thee ; but let me first go bid them farewell, which are at home at my house.

62. And Jesus said unto him, No man, having put his hand to the plough, and looking back, is fit for the kingdom of God.

For Chap. X. see P. 57.

Chap. VIII. from above.
23. But as they sailed he fell asleep : and there came down a storm of wind on the lake ; and they were filled with water, and were in jeopardy.

24. And they came to him, and awoke him, saying, Master, master, we perish. Then he arose, and rebuked the wind and the raging of the water : and they ceased, and there was a calm.

25. And he said unto them, Where is your faith ? and they, being afraid, won-

Sᴛ. MATTHEW, VIII.   Sᴛ. MARK, II., IV., V.   Sᴛ. LUKE, VIII.   Sᴛ. JOHN. VI.

What manner of man is this, that even the winds and the sea obey him?

41. And they feared exceedingly, and said one to another, What manner of man is this, that even the wind and the sea obey him?

dered, saying one to another, What manner of man is this for he commandeth even the winds and waters, and they obey him.

For Chap. III. see P. 62.

CHAP. V.

. 28 ¶ And when he was come to the other side into the country of the Gergesenes,

there met him two possessed with devils,

coming ont of the tombs, exceeding fierce, so that no man might pass by that way.

1. And they came over unto the other side of the sea, into the country of the Gadarenes.
2. And when he was come out of the ship, immediately there met him out of the tombs a man with an unclean spirit.
3. Who had *his* dwelling among the tombs : and no man could bind him, no, not with chains :
4. Because that he had been often bound with fetters and chains, and the chains had been plucked asunder by him, and the fetters brcken in pieces :*
neither could any *man* tame him.
5. And always, night and day, he was in the mountains, and in the tombs, crying and cutting himself with stones.
6. But when he saw Jesus afar off he ran and worshipped him,

26. ¶ And they arrived at the country of the Gadarenes, which is over against Galilee.
27. And when he went forth to land, there met him out of the city, a certain man which had devils long time,
and ware no clothes, neither abode in *any* house, but in the tombs.

* L. VIII., 20, *below*.

29. And, behold, they cried out, saying, What have we to do with thee, Jesus, thou Son of God? art thou come hither to torment us before the time?

7. And cried with a loud voice, and said, What have I to do with thee, Jesus *thou* Son to do with the most high God? I adjure thee by God, that thou torment me not.
8. For he said unto him, Come out of the man, *thou* unclean spirit.

28. When he saw Jesus, he cried out, and fell down before him, and with a loud voice said, What have I to do with thee, Jesus, *thou* Son of God most high? I beseech thee, torment me not.
29. (For he had commanded the unclean spirit to come out of the man. For oftentimes it had caught him ; and he was kept bound with chains and in fetters ; and he brake the bands, and was driven of the devil into the wilderness.)

Mk. V. 45. P. 46.

9. And he asked him, What *is* thy name? And he answered, saying, My name *is* Legion : for we are many.

30. And Jesus asked him, saying, What is thy name? And he said, Legion : beause many devils were entered into him.

10. And he besought him much that he would not send them away cut of the country.
11. Now there was nigh unto the mountains a great herd of swine feeding.
12. And all the devils besought him, saying, Send us into the swine, that we may enter into them.
13. And forthwith Jesus gave

31. And they besought him that he would not command them to go out into the deep.
32. And there was there an herd of many swine feeding on the mountain :
and they besought him that he would suffer them to enter into them.

And he suffered them.

30. And there was a good way off from them an herd of many swine feeding.
31. So the devils besought him, saying, If thou cast us out, suffer us to go away into the herd of swine.
32. And he said unto them, Go.

ST. MATTHEW, IX.	ST. MARK, II. V.	ST. LUKE, VIII. V.	ST. JOHN, VI.

And when they were come out, they went into the herd of swine : and behold, the whole herd of swine ran violently down a steep place into the sea, and perished in the waters.

33. And they that kept them fled, and went their ways into the city, and told every thing, and what was befallen to the possessed of the devils.

34. And, behold, the whole city came out to meet Jesus :

and when they saw him, they besought *him* that he would depart out of their coasts.

them leave. And the unclean spirits went out and entered into the swine : and the herd ran violently down a steep place into the sea, (they were about two thousand), and were choked in the sea.

14. And they that fed the swine fled, and told *it* in the city and in the country.
And they went out to see what it was that was done.

15. And they come to Jesus, and see him that was possessed with the devil, and had the legion, sitting, and clothed, and in his right mind.
And they were afraid.

16. And they that saw *it* told them how it befel to him that possessed with the devil, and *also* concerning the swine.

17. And they began to pray him to depart out of their coasts.

33. Then went the devils out of the man, and entered into the swine : and the herd ran violently down a steep place into the lake, and were choked.

34. When they that fed *them* saw what was done, they fled ; and went and told *it* in the city and in the country.

35. Then they went out to see what was done ;
and came to Jesus, and found the man, out of whom the devils were departed, sitting at the feet of Jesus, clothed, and in his right mind : and they were afraid.

36. They also which saw *it* told them by what means he that was possessed of the devil was healed.

37. ¶ Then the whole multitude of the country of the Gadarenes round about besought him to depart from them : for they were taken with great fear :

CHAP. IX.

1. And he entered into a ship.

and passed over,

and came into his own city.

18. And when he was come into the ship, he that had been possessed with the devil prayed him that he might be with him.

19. Howbeit Jesus suffered him not, but saith unto him, Go home to thy friends, and tell them how great things the Lord hath done for thee, and hath had compassion on thee.

20. And he departed, and began to publish in Decapolis how great things Jesus had done for him : and all *men* did marvel.

21. And when Jesus was passed over again by ship unto the other side, much people gathered unto him : and he was nigh unto the sea.
Continued P. 50.

and he went up into the ship, and returned back again.

38. Now the man out of whom the devils were departed besought him that he might be with him. But Jesus sent him away, saying,

39. Return to thine own house, and show how great things God hath done unto thee.
And he went his way, and published throughout the whole city how great things Jesus had done unto him.

40. And it came to pass, that, when Jesus was returned, the people *gladly* received him : for they were all waiting for him.
Continued P. 50.

CHAP. II.

From P. 43.
1. And again he entered into Capernaum after *some* days ; and it was noised that he was in the house.

2. And straightway many were gathered together, insomuch that there was no room

Chap. V. from P. 43.

17. And it came to pass on a certain day, as he was teaching, that there were Pharisees and doctors of the law sitting by, which were come out of every town of Galilee, and Judea, and

ST. MATTHEW, IX. | ST. MARK, II. | ST. LUKE, V. | ST. JOHN, VI.

to receive them, no, not so much as about the door : and he preached the word unto them.

3. And they come unto him, bringing one sick of the palsy, which was home of four.

4. And when they could not come nigh unto him for the press, they uncovered the roof where he was : and when they had broken it up, they let down the bed wherein the sick of the palsy lay.

Jerusalem ; and the power of the Lord was *present* to heal them.

18. ¶ And, behold, men V. brought in a bed a man which was taken with a palsy : and they sought *means* to bring him in, and to lay *him* before him.

19. And when they could not find by what *way* they might bring him in, because of the multitude, they went upon the housetop and let him down through the tiling with *his* couch into the midst, before Jesus.

2. And behold, they brought to him a man sick of the palsy, lying on a bed :

and Jesus seeing their faith said unto the sick of the palsy : Son, be of good cheer : thy sins be forgiven thee.

5. When Jesus saw their faith, he said unto the sick of the palsy, Son, thy sins be forgiven thee.

20. And when he saw their faith, he said unto him, Man, thy sins are forgiven thee.

3. And behold certain of the scribes said within themselves,

This *man* blasphemeth.

6. But there were certain of the scribes sitting there, and reasoning in their hearts,

7. Why doth this *man* thus speak blasphemies ? who can forgive sins but God only ?

21. And the scribes and the Pharisees began to reason, saying, Who is this which speaketh blasphemies ? Who can forgive sins but God alone ?

4. And Jesus knowing their thoughts said,

wherefore think ye evil in your hearts ?

8. And immediately when Jesus perceived in his spirit that they so reasoned within themselves, he said unto them, Why reason ye these things in your hearts ?

22. But when Jesus perceived their thoughts, he, answering, said unto them,

What reason ye in your hearts ?

5. For whether is easier to say, *Thy* sins be forgiven thee, or to say, Arise, and walk ?

9. Whether is it easier to say to the sick of the palsy, *Thy* sins he forgiven thee ; or to say, Arise, and take up thy bed, and walk ?

23. Whether is easier, to say, Thy sins be forgiven thee : or to say, Rise up and walk ?

6. But that ye may know that the Son of man hath power on earth to forgive sins, (then saith he to the sick of the palsy,) Arise, take up thy bed, and go unto thine house.

10. But that ye may know that the Son of man hath power on earth to forgive sins, (he saith to the sick of the palsy,)

11. I say unto thee, Arise, and take up thy bed, and go thy way into thine house.

24. But that ye may know that the Son of man hath power upon earth to forgive sins, (he said unto the sick of the palsy,) I say unto thee, Arise, and take up thy couch, and go unto thine house.

7. And he arose, and departed to his house.

8 But when the multitude saw *it*, they marvelled, and glorified God, which had given such power unto men.

12. And immediately he arose, took up the bed, and went forth before them all : insomuch that they were all amazed, and glorified God, saying, We never saw it on this fashion.

25. And immediately he rose up before them, and took up that whereon he lay, and departed to his own house, glorifying God.

26. And they were all amazed, and they glorified God, and were filled with fear, saying, We have seen strange things to day.

9. And as Jesus passed forth from thence

13. And he went forth again by the seaside : and all the multitude resorted unto him, and he taught them.

27. ¶ And after these things he went forth,

he saw a man, named Matthew, sitting at the receipt of custom ; and he saith unto him, Follow me. And he arose and followed him.

14. And as he passed by, he saw Levi, the *son* of Alphæus sitting at the receipt of custom, and said unto him, Follow me. And he arose and followed him.

and saw a publican, named Levi, sitting at the receipt of custom : and he said unto him, Follow me.

28. And he left all, rose up, and followed him.

ST. MATTHEW, IX.   ST. MARK, II.   ST. LUKE, V.   ST. JOHN, VI.

10. ¶ And it came to pass, as Jesus sat at meat in the house, behold, many publicans and sinners came and sat down with him and his disciples.

11. And when the Pharisees saw *it*,

they said unto his disciples, Why eateth your Master with publicans and sinners?
12. But when Jesus heard *that*, he said unto them, They that be whole need not a physician, but they that are sick.

13. But go ye and learn what *that* meaneth, I will have mercy and not sacrifice :
for I am not come to call the righteous but sinners to repentance.

14. ¶ Then came to him the disciples of John, saying, Why do we and the Pharisees fast oft, but thy disciples fast not?
15. And Jesus said unto them, Can the children of the bridechamber mourn, as long as the bridegroom is with them?

but the days will come when the bridegroom shall be taken from them, and then shall they fast.

16. No man putteth a piece of new cloth unto an old garment ; for that which is put in to fill it up taketh from the garment, and the rent is made worse.
17. Neither do men put new wine into old bottles : else the bottles break, and the wine runneth out, and the bottles perish : but they put new wine into new bottles, and both are preserved.

15. And it came to pass, that, as Jesus sat at meat in his house, many publicans and sinners sat also together with Jesus and his disciples : for there were many,
and they followed him.
16. And when the scribes and Pharisees saw him eat with publicans and sinners, they said unto his disciples, How is it that he eateth and drinketh with publicans and sinners?
17. When Jesus heard *it* he saith unto them, They that are whole have no need of the physician, but they that are sick :

I came not to call the righteous, but sinners to repentance.

18. And the disciples of John and of the Pharisees used to fast : and they come and say unto him, Why do the disciples of John and of the Pharisees fast, but thy disciples fast not?
19. And Jesus said unto them, Can the children of the bridechamber fast, while the bridegroom is with them?
as long as they have the bridegroom with them, they cannot fast.
20. But the days will come when the bridegroom shall be taken away from them, and then shall they fast in those days.

21. No man also seweth a piece of new cloth on an old garment : else the new piece that filled it up taketh away from the old ; and the rent is made worse.
22. And no man putteth new wine into old bottles : else the new wine doth burst the bottles, and the wine is spilled ; and the bottles will be marred : but new wine must be put into new bottles.

Continued P. 61.

29. And Levi made him a great feast in his own house : and there was a great company of publicans, and of others that sat down with them.

30. But their scribes and Pharisees murmured against his disciples, saying, Why do ye eat and drink with publicans and sinners?

31. And Jesus answering said unto them, They that are whole need not a physician ; but they that are sick.

32. I came not to call the righteous but sinners to repentance.

33. ¶ And they said unto him, Why do the disciples of John fast often and make prayers ; and likewise *the disciples* of the Pharisees ; but thine eat and drink?
34. And he said unto them, Can ye make the children of the bridechamber fast, while the bridegroom is with them?

35. But the days will come, when the bridegroom shall be taken away from them, and then shall they fast in those days.
36. ¶ And he spake also a parable unto them ;
No man putteth a piece of a new garment upon an old ; if otherwise, then both the new maketh a rent, and the piece that was *taken* out of the new agreeth not with the old.
37. And no man putteth new wine into old bottles : else the new wine will burst the bottles, and be spilled, and the bottles shall perish.
38. But new wine must be put into new bottles ; and both are preserved.
39. No man also having drunk old *wine* straightway desireth new : for he saith, The old is better.

For Chap. VI. see P. 61.

ST. MATTHEW, IX.   ST. MARK IL, V.   ST. LUKE, VIII.   ST. JOHN, VI.

Chap. V. from P. 47.   *Chap. VIII. from P. 47.*

18. ¶ While he spake these things unto them, behold, there came a certain ruler,

and worshipped him

saying, My daughter is even now dead: but come and lay thy hand upon her, and she shall live.

22. And, behold, there cometh one of the rulers of the synagogue, Jairus by name: and when he saw him, he fell at his feet,

23. And besought him greatly, saying, My little daughter lieth at the point of death: *I pray thee*, come and lay thy hands on her, that she may be healed and she shall live.

41. ¶ And, behold, there came a man named Jairus, and he was a ruler of the synagogue: and he fell down at Jesus' feet, and besought him that he would come into his house:

42. For he had one only daughter, about twelve years of age, and she lay a dying.

19. And Jesus arose, and followed him, and *so did* his disciples.

24. And Jesus went with him; and much people followed him; and thronged him.

But as he went the people thronged him.

20. ¶ And, behold, a woman which was diseased with an issue of blood twelve years,

25. And a certain woman, which had an issue of blood twelve years,

26. And had suffered many things of many physicians, and had spent all that she had, and was nothing bettered, but rather grew worse.

43. ¶ And a woman having an issue of blood twelve years,

which had spent all her living upon physicians, neither could be healed of any,

came behind *him*, and touched the hem of his garment:

27. When she had heard of Jesus, came in the press behind, and touched his garment.

44. Came behind *him*, and touched the border of his garment:

21. For she said within herself, If I may but touch his garment, I shall be whole.

28. For she said, If I may touch but his clothes, I shall be whole.

29. And straightway the fountain of her blood was dried up; and she felt in *her* body that she was healed of that plague.

and immediately her issue of blood stanched.

45. And Jesus said, Who touched me? When all denied, Peter and they that were with him, said, Master, the multitude throng thee and press *thee*, and sayest thou, Who touched me?

30. And Jesus, immediately knowing in himself that virtue had gone out of him, turned him about in the press, and said, Who touched my clothes?

22. But Jesus turned him about,

31. And his disciples said unto him, Thou seest the multitude thronging thee, and sayest thou, Who touched me?

32. And he looked round about to see her that had done this thing.

33. But the woman fearing and trembling, knowing what was done in her, came and fell down before him; and told him all the truth.

46. And Jesus said, Somebody hath touched me: for I perceive that virtue is gone out of me.

47. And when the woman saw that she was not hid, she came trembling, and falling down before him, she declared unto him before all the people for what cause she had touched him, and how she was healed immediately.

48. And he said unto her, Daughter, be of good comfort: thy faith hath made thee whole.* Go in peace.

and when he saw her, he said, Daughter, be of good comfort: thy faith hath made thee whole. And the woman was made whole from that hour.

34. And he said unto her, Daughter, thy faith hath made thee whole * Go in peace, and be whole of thy plague.

* [literally "hath saved thee."— Alford.]

35. While he yet spake there came from the ruler of the synagogue's house certain, which said, Thy daughter is dead.

49. ¶ While he yet spake, there cometh one from the ruler of the synagogue's *house*, saying to him, Thy daughter is dead.

* ["Hath saved thee."—Alford.]

why troublest thou the master any further?

36. As soon as Jesus heard the word that was spoken, he saith unto the ruler of the synagogue, Be not afraid. Only believe.

trouble not the master.

50. But when Jesus heard it, he answered him, saying, Fear not. Believe only.
and she shall be made whole.

37. And he suffered no man to follow him, save Peter, and James and John the brother of James.

51. And when he came into the house, he suffered no man to go in save Peter and James and John and the father and the mother of the maiden.

23. And when Jesus came into the ruler's house, and saw the minstrels and the people making a noise,

38. And he cometh to the house of the ruler of the synagogue, and seeth the tumult, and them that wept and wailed greatly.

52. And all wept and bewailed her.

24. He said unto them, Give place;
for the maid is not dead, but sleepeth.
And they laughed him to scorn.

39. And when he was come in, he saith unto them, Why make ye this ado, and weep? The damsel is not dead, but sleepeth.
40. And they laughed him to scorn.

But he said, Weep not;

she is not dead, but sleepeth.
53. And they laughed him to scorn,
knowing that she was dead.

25. But when the people were put forth,

But when he had put them all out, he taketh the father and the mother of the damsel, and them that were with him, and entereth in where the damsel was lying.

54. And he put them all out,

he went in,
and took her by the hand,

41. And he took the damsel by the hand, and said unto her, Talitha cumi: which is, being interpreted, Damsel, I say unto thee, arise.

and took her by the hand,
and called, saying;

Maid, arise.

and the maid arose.

42. And straightway the damsel arose, and walked;
for she was of the age of twelve years. And they were astonished with a great astonishment.
43. And he charged them straitly that no man should know it; and commanded that something should be given her to eat.

55. And her spirit came again; and she rose straightway:

and he commanded to give her meat.
56. And her parents were astonished: but he charged them that they should tell no man what was done.

26. And the fame hereof went abroad into all that land.

27. ¶ And when Jesus departed thence, two blind men followed him, crying, and saying, Thou son of David, have mercy on us. (1)
28. And when he was come into the house, the blind men came to him: and Jesus saith unto them, Believe ye that I am able to do this? They said unto him, Yea, Lord.
29. Then touched he their eyes, saying, According to your faith be it unto you.
30. And their eyes were opened: and Jesus straitly charged them, saying, See that no man know it.

(1) M. XX. 30.

For Chap. VI. see P. 71.

For Chap. IX. see P. 52.

ST. MATTHEW, X.   ST. MARK II, III.   ST. LUKE, IX., VI., IX.   ST. JOHN, VI.

31. But they, when they were departed spread abroad his fame in all that country.

32. As they went out, behold, they brought to him a dumb man possessed with a devil.

33. And when the devil was cast out, the dumb spake : and the multitude marvelled saying, It was never so seen in Israel.

34. But the Pharisees said, He casteth out devils through the prince of the devils.

M. XII. 23, 24.

L. XI. 14, 15, P. 6.

35. And Jesus went about all the cities and villages, teaching in their synagogues, and preaching the Gospel of the kingdom, and healing every sickness and every disease among the people.

36. But when he saw the multitudes, he was moved with compassion on them, because they fainted and were scattered abroad, as sheep having no shepherd.

M. XIV. 14.
Mk. VI. 34. P. 74.

37. Then saith he unto his disciples, The harvest truly is plenteous, but the laborers are few.

See Mk. VI. 34. P. 74.

38. Pray ye therefore the Lord of the harvest that he will send forth laborers into his harvest.

See L. X. 2, P. 57.

CHAP. X.

1. And when he had called unto him his twelve disciples, he gave them power against unclean spirits, to cast them out, and to heal all manner of sickness, and all manner of disease.

Chap. III. from P. 63.

13. And he goeth up into a mountain, and calleth unto him whom he would : and they came unto him.

14. And he ordained twelve, that they should be with him, and that he might send them forth to preach,

15. And to have power to heal sicknesses and to cast out devils.

CHAP. IX.

1. Then he called his twelve disciples together, and gave them power and authority over all devils, and to cure diseases.
Continued below.

Chap. VI. from P. 63.

12. And it came to pass in those days that he went out into a mountain to pray, and continued all night in prayer to God.

13. And when it was day he called unto him his disciples : and of them he chose twelve, whom also he named apostles ;

2. Now the names of the twelve apostles are these : The first Simon, who is called Peter : and Andrew his brother : James the son of Zebedee : and John his brother :

3. Philip : and Bartholomew : Thomas : and Matthew the publican : James the son of Alpheus : and Lebbeus, whose surname was Thaddeus :

4. Simon the Canaanite : and Judas Iscariot : who also betrayed him.

5. These twelve Jesus sent forth, and commanded them, saying, Go not into the way of the Gentiles, and into any city

16. And Simon he surnamed Peter ;

17. And James the son of Zebedee : and John, the brother of James ; and he surnamed them Boanerges ; which is the sons of thunder :

18. And Andrew and Philip : and Bartholomew : and Matthew : and Thomas : and James the son of Alpheus : and Thaddeus : and Simon the Canaanite :

19. And Judas Iscariot, which also betrayed him : and they went into an house.
Continued P. 63.

14. Simon, (whom he also named Peter) and Andrew his brother ; James, and John : Philip, and Bartholomew :

15. Matthew, and Thomas : James the son of Alpheus : and Simon called Zelotes :

16. And Judas, the brother of James : and Judas Iscariot, which also was the traitor.
Continued P. 63.

Chap. IX. continued,

2. And he sent them to

ST. MATTHEW, X. | ST. MARK, II., VI. | ST. LUKE, IX., XII. | ST. JOHN, VI.

preach the kingdom of God.

of the Samaritans enter ye not :

6. But go rather to the lost sheep of the house of Israel.

7. And as ye go, preach, saying, The kingdom of heaven is at hand. (1)

Chap. VI. from P. 72.

7. And he called unto him the twelve and began to send them forth by two and two,

8. Heal the sick : cleanse the lepers : raise the dead : cast out devils : freely ye have received, freely give.

and gave them power over unclean spirits,

and to heal the sick.

L. X. 9, 1. P. 57.

9. Provide neither gold, nor silver, nor brass in your purses, (2)

8. And commanded them that they should take nothing for *their* journey, save a staff only, no scrip, no bread, no money in *their* purse :

3. And he said unto them, Take nothing for *your* journey, neither staves, nor scrip, neither bread, neither money ;

X. 4. P. 57.

10. Nor scrip *for your* journey, neither two coats, neither shoes, nor yet staves : for the workman is worthy of his meat.

9. But *be* shod with sandals ; and not put on two coats.

neither have two coats apiece.

11. And into whatsoever city or town ye shall enter, enquire who in it is worthy : and there abide till ye go thence.

12. And when ye come into an house salute it. (3)

13. And if the house be worthy, let your peace come upon it : but if it be not worthy let your peace return to you. (4)

10. And he said unto them, In what place soever ye enter into an house, there abide till ye depart from that place.

4. And whatsoever house ye enter into, there abide, and thence depart.

X. 7. P. 57.

See L. X. 1, & 5, 6. P. 57.

14. And whosoever shall not receive you nor hear your words, when ye depart out of that house or city, shake off the dust of your feet. (5)

11. And whosoever shall not receive you, nor hear you ; when ye depart thence, shake off the dust under your feet ; for a testimony against them. [Verily I say unto you, It shall be more tolerable for Sodom and Gomorrha in the day of judgment, than for that city.]*
Continued P. 56.

5. And whoever will not receive you, when ye go out of that city, shake off the very dust from your feet for a testimony against them.
Continued P. 56.

X. 10, 11. P. 57.

15. Verily I say unto you, It shall be more tolerable for the land of Sodom and Gomorrha in the day of judgment, than for that city.

See L. X. 1, & 12. P. 57.

16. Behold, I send you forth as sheep in the midst of wolves : be ye therefore wise as serpents, and harmless as doves.

See L. X. 1, 3. P. 57.

17. But beware of men ; for they will deliver you up to the councils, and they will scourge you in their synagogues :

18. And ye shall be brought before governors and kings for my sake, for a testimony against them and the gentiles. (6)

19. But when they deliver you up, take no thought how, or what ye shall speak : for it shall be given you in that same hour what ye shall speak.

See Mk. XIII. 9, 11. P. 130.

Chap. XII. from P. 64.

11. And when they bring you into the synagogues ; and *unto* magistrates, and powers, take ye no thought how or what thing ye shall answer ; or what ye shall say :

12. For the Holy Ghost shall teach you in the same hour what ye ought to say.

20. For it is not ye that speak, but the spirit of your Father which speaketh in you.

21. And the brother shall deliver up the brother to death, and the father the child : and

13. And one of the company said unto him, Master, speak

(1) L. X. 9 & 1, P. 57. (2) L. X. 4, P. 57.
(3) L. X. 8, 7, P. 57. (4) 5, 6.
(5) X. 10, P. 57.
(6) L. XXI. 12, P. 139.

* *Wanting in almost all the ancient MSS.—Alford.*

ST. MATTHEW, X.   ST. MARK, II.   ST. LUKE, XII., VI., XII.   ST. JOHN, VI.

the children shall rise up against their parents ; and cause them to be put to death.*

*["Shall put them to death."—Alford]

to my brother that he divide the inheritance with me.

14. And he said unto him, Man, who made me a judge or a divider over you?

15. And he said unto him, Take heed and beware of covetousness : for a man's life consisteth not in the abundance of the things which he possesseth.

16. And he spake a parable unto them, saying, The ground of a certain rich man brought forth plentifully :

17. And he thought within himself saying, What shall I do, because I have no room where to bestow my fruits.

18. And he said, This will I do : I will pull down my barns, and build greater : and there will I bestow all my fruits and my goods.

19. And I will say to my soul, Soul, thou hast much goods laid up for many years, Take thine ease ; eat, drink, *and* be merry.

20. But God said unto him, *Thou* fool : this night thy soul shall be required of thee : Then whose shall those things be which thou hast provided?

21. So *is* he that layeth up treasure for himself, and is not rich toward God.

Continued P. 38.

22. And ye shall be hated of all *men* for my name's sake : but he that endureth to the end shall be saved.

23. But when they persecute you in this city, flee ye into another : for verily I say unto you, Ye shall not have gone over the cities of Israel, till the Son of man be come.

24. The disciple is not above *his* master, nor the servant above his Lord.

25. It is enough for the disciple that he be as his master, and the servant as his Lord. If they have called the master of the house Beelzebub, how much more *shall they call* them of his household?

26. Fear them not therefore :

Chap. VI. from 80.

40. The disciple is not above his master ;
but every one that is perfect shall be as his master.
Continued P. 39.

CHAP. XII.
From P. 137.

1. In the meantime, when there were gathered together an innumerable multitude of

ST. MATTHEW, X.　　　ST. MARK, II., IV.　　　ST. LUKE, XII., XIV.　　　ST. JOHN, VI.

people, in so much that they
trod one upon another, he began
to say unto his disciples first of
of all, Beware of the leaven of the
Pharisees, which is hypocrisy.

for there is nothing covered
that shall not be revealed and
hid, that shall not be known.

Chap. IV. from P. 33.
22. For there is nothing hid,
which shall not be manifested;
neither was anything kept
secret, but that it should come
abroad.
Continued P. 68.

2. For there is nothing
covered that shall not be revealed : neither hid that shall
not be known.

L. VIII. 17., P. 33.

27. What I tell you in darkness *that* speak ye in light : and
what ye hear in the ear, *that*
preach ye upon the housetops.

3. Therefore whatsoever ye
have spoken in darkness shall
be heard in the light ; and that
which ye have spoken in the
ear in closets shall be pro-
claimed upon the house tops.

28. And fear not them which
kill the body, but are not able
to kill the soul.

4. And I say unto you my
friends, Be not afraid of them
that kill the body, and after that
have no more that they can do.

but rather fear him which is
able to destroy both soul and
body in hell.

5. But I will forewarn you
whom ye shall fear : Fear him
which after he hath killed, hath
power to cast into hell. Yea,
I say unto you, Fear him.

29. Are not two sparrows
sold for a farthing ? and one of
them shall not fall on the
ground without your Father.
30. But the very hairs of
your head are all numbered.
31. Fear ye not therefore ;
Ye are of more value than many
sparrows.
32. Whosoever therefore shall
confess me before men, him will
I confess also before my Father
which is in heaven.
33. But whosoever shall deny
me before men, him will I also
deny before my Father which
is in heaven.

6. Are not five sparrows sold
for two farthings ? and not one
of them is forgotten before
God.
7. But even the very hairs of
your head are all numbered.
Fear not, therefore : Ye are
of more value than many sparrows.
8. Also I say unto you,
Whosoever shall confess me
before men, him shall the Son
of man also confess before the
angels of God.
9. But he that denieth me
before men shall be. denied
before the angels of God.
Continued P. 64.

34. Think not that I am
come to send peace on earth :
I came not to send peace but a
sword.

Chap. XII. from P. 144.
*
51. Suppose ye that I am
come to give peace on earth ? I
tell you nay: but rather division.
52. For from henceforth there
shall be five in one house divided ;
three against two, and two
against three.
53. The father shall be divided
against the son : and the son
against the father : the mother
against the daughter : and the
daughter against the mother :
the mother-in-law against her
daughter in law : and the
daughter in law against her
mother in law.
Continued P. 83.

* *Quere. V. 49, 50, also ? See P. 144.*

35. For I am come to set a
man at variance against his
father ; and the daughter
against her mother ; and the
daughter in law against her
mother in law.

36. And a man's foes *shall
be* they of his own household.

Chap. XIV. from P. 130.
25. And there went out great
multitudes with him : and he

ST. MATTHEW, X.   ST. MARK. II., IX., VI.   ST. LUKE, XIV., IX.   ST. JOHN, VI.

37. He that loveth father or mother more than me is not worthy of me : and he that loveth son or daughter more than me is not worthy of me.

38. And he that taketh not his cross, and followeth after me, is not worthy of me.

turned, and said unto them,

26. If any *man* come to me, and hate not his father, and mother, and wife, and children, and brethren, and sisters, yea, and his own life also, he cannot be my disciple.

27. And whosoever doth not bear his cross, and come after me, cannot be my disciple.

28. For which of you, intending to build a tower, sitteth not down first, and counteth the cost, whether he have *sufficient* to finish *it* ?

29. Lest haply, after he hath laid the foundation, and is not able to finish *it* all that behold *it* begin to mock him,

30. Saying, This man began to build, and was not able to finish.

31. Or what king, going to make war against another king, sitteth not down first, and consulteth whether he be able with ten thousand, to meet him that cometh against him with twenty thousand ?

32. Or else, while the other is yet a great way off, he sendeth an ambassage, and desireth conditions of peace.

33. So likewise, whosoever he be of you that forsaketh not all that he hath, he cannot be my disciple.

Continued P. 33.

L. XVII. 33. *P.* 140.

39. He that findeth his life shall lose it : and he that loseth his life for my sake shall find it.

40. He that receiveth you receiveth me, and he that receiveth me receiveth him that sent me.

41. He that receiveth a prophet in the name of a prophet shall receive a prophet's reward ; and he that receiveth a righteous man in the name of a righteous man shall receive a righteous man's reward.

42. And whosoever shall give to drink unto one of these little ones a cup of cold *water* only in the name of a disciple, verily I say unto you, He shall in no wise lose his reward.

L X. 1 & 16, *P.* 57, 60.

Chap. IX. from P. 90.
41. For whosoever shall give you a cup of water to drink in my name, because ye belong to Christ, verily I say unto you, He shall not lose his reward.
Continued P. 90.

Chap. VI. from P. 53.
12. And they went out and preached that men should repent.

13. And they cast out many devils, and anointed with oil many that were sick, and healed them.   *Continued P. 72.*

Chap. IX. from P. 53.
6. And they departed, and went through the towns, preaching the Gospel, and healing every where.
Continued P. 72.

CHAP. X. *(from P. 45.)*

1. After these things the Lord appointed other seventy also, and sent them two and two before his face into every city and place, whither he himself would come.

2. Therefore said he unto them, The harvest truly *is* great, but the laborers *are* few: pray ye therefore the Lord of the harvest, that he would send forth laborers into his harvest.   M. IX. 37, 38.

3. Go your ways: behold, I send you forth as lambs among wolves.   M. X. 16.

4. Carry neither purse, nor scrip, nor shoes: and salute no man by the way.   M. X. 9, 10.

5. And into whatsoever house ye enter, first say, Peace *be* to this house.   12.

6. And if the son of peace be there, your peace shall rest upon it: if not it shall turn to you again.   13.

7. And in the same house remain, eating and drinking such things as they give: for the laborer is worthy of his hire. Go not from house to house.   X., 11.

8. And into whatsoever city ye enter, and they receive you, eat such things as are set before you:

9. And heal the sick that are therein, and say unto them, The kingdom of God is come nigh unto you.   X., 7, 8.

10. But into whatsoever city ye enter, and they receive you not, go your ways out into the streets of the same, and say,

11. Even the very dust of your city, which cleaveth on us, we do wipe off against you: notwithstanding be ye sure of this, that the kingdom of God is come nigh unto you.   14.

12. But I say unto you, That it shall be more tolerable in that day for Sodom, than for that city.   15.
Continued P. 59.

CHAP. XI.
1. And it came to pass, when Jesus had made an end of commanding his twelve disciples, he departed thence to teach and to preach in their cities.

Chap. X., from P. 60.
17. And the seventy returned again with joy, saying, Lord, even the devils are subject unto us through thy name.

18. And he said unto them, I beheld Satan as lightning fall from heaven.

19. Behold, I give unto you power to tread on serpents and scorpions, and over all the power

St. MATTHEW, XI.　　St. MARK, II.　　St. LUKE, X., VII.　　St. JOHN, VI.

of the enemy : and nothing shall by any means hurt you.

20. Notwithstanding in this rejoice not, that the spirits are subject unto you ; but rather rejoice, because your names are written in heaven.

Continued P. 60.

Chap. VII. from P. 44.

18. And the disciples of John shewed him of all these things.

2. Now when John had heard in the prison the works of Christ, he sent two of his disciples,

3. And said unto him, Art thou he that should come, or do we look for another?

M. III. 11 to 15. C. I. 20 to 34. J. 15, 16.

19. And John calling *unto him* two of his disciples sent *them* to Jesus, saying, Art thou he that should come? Or look we for another?

J. I. 20, 33, 34.　P. 15, 16.

20. When the men were come unto him, they said, John Baptist hath sent us unto thee, saying, Art thou he that should come? Or look we for another?

21. And in that same hour he cured many of *their* infirmities and plagues, and of evil spirits ; and unto many *that were* blind he gave sight.

22. Then Jesus answering said unto them, Go your way, and tell John what things ye have seen and heard ; how that the blind see, the lame walk, the lepers are cleansed, the deaf hear, the dead are raised, to the poor the Gospel is preached.

23. And blessed is *he*, whosoever shall not be offended in me.

4. Jesus answered and said unto them, Go and show John again those things which ye do hear and see :

5. The blind receive their sight, and the lame walk, the lepers are cleansed, and the deaf hear, the dead are raised up, and the poor have the Gospel preached to them.

6. And blessed is *he*, whosoever shall not be offended in me.

7. And as they departed, Jesus began to say unto the multitudes concerning John, What went ye out into the wilderness to see? A reed shaken with the wind?

8. But what went ye out for to see? A man clothed in soft raiment? behold, they that wear soft *clothing* are in kings' houses.

9. But what went ye out for to see? A prophet? yea, I say unto you, And more than a prophet.

10. For this is *he*, of whom it is written, Behold, I send my messenger before thy face which shall prepare thy way before thee.

11. Verily I say unto you, Among them that are born of

24. And when the messengers of John were departed, he began to speak unto the people concerning John. What went ye out into the wilderness for to see? A reed shaken with the wind?

25. But what went ye out for to see? A man clothed in soft raiment? Behold, they which are gorgeously apparelled, and live delicately, are in kings' courts.

26. But what went ye out for to see? a prophet? yea I say unto you, And much more than a prophet.

27. This is *he*, of whom it is written, Behold, I send my messenger before thy face, which shall prepare thy way before thee.

28. For I say unto you, Among those that are born of

women there hath not risen a greater than John the Baptist: notwithstanding he that is least in the kingdom of heaven is greater than he.

12. And from the days of John the Baptist until now the kingdom of heaven suffereth violence, and the violent take it by force.

13. For all the prophets and the law prophesied unto John.

14. And if ye will receive *it*, this is Elias, which was for to come.

15. He that hath ears to hear, let him ear.

16. But whereunto shall I liken this generation?
It is like unto children sitting in the markets, and calling unto their fellows,

17. And saying, We have piped unto you, and ye have not danced; we have mourned unto you, and ye have not lamented.

18. For John came neither eating nor drinking, and they say, He hath a devil.

19. The Son of man came eating and drinking, and they say; Behold a man gluttonous, and a winebibber, a friend of publicans and sinners. But wisdom is justified of her children.

20. Then began he to upbraid the cities wherein most of his mighty works were done, because they repented not:

21. Woe unto thee, Chorazin! Woe unto thee, Bethsaida! For if the mighty works, which were done in you, had been done in Tyre and Sidon, they would have repented long ago in sackcloth and ashes.

22. But I say unto you, It shall be more tolerable for Tyre and Sidon at the day of judgment, than for you.

23. And thou, Capernaum, which art exalted unto heaven, shalt be brought down to hell: for if the mighty works, which have been done in thee, had been done in Sodom, it would have remained until this day.

M. XVII. 12—contra J. I. 21. P. 15.

L. VIII. 8. P. 67.

women there is not a greater prophet than John the Baptist; but he that is least in the kingdom of God is greater than he.

See L. XVI. 16, P. 94,

29. And all the people that heard *him* and the publicans, justified God, being baptised with the baptism of John.

30. But the Pharisees and lawyers rejected the counsel of God against themselves, being not baptised of him.

31. And the Lord said, Whereunto then shall I liken the men of this generation? and to what are they like?

32. They are like unto children sitting in the market place, and calling one to another, and saying, We have piped unto you, and ye have not danced; We have mourned to you, and ye have not wept.

33. For John the Baptist came neither eating bread nor drinking wine; and ye say, He hath a devil.

34. The Son of man is come eating and drinking; and ye say, Behold a gluttonous man, and a winebibber, a friend of publicans and sinners!

35. But wisdom is justified of all her children.

Continued P. 149.

Chap. X. from P. 57.

13. Woe unto thee, Chorazin! Woe unto thee, Bethsaida! For if the mighty works had been done in Tyre and Sidon, which have been done in you, they had a great while ago repented, sitting in sackcloth and ashes.

14. But it shall be more tolerable for Tyre and Sidon at the judgment, than for you.

15. And thou, Capernaum, which art exalted to heaven, shalt be thrust down to hell.

St. MATTHEW, XI.   St. MARK, II.   St. LUKE, X., XIII.   St. JOHN, VI.

24. But I say unto you, That it shall be more tolerable for the land of Sodom in the day of judgment than for thee.

16. He that heareth you heareth me ; and he that despiseth you, despiseth me ; and he that despiseth me despiseth him that sent me.
Continued P. 57.

25. At that time Jesus answered and said, I thank thee, O Father, Lord of heaven and earth, because thou hast hid these things from the wise and prudent, and hast revealed them unto babes.
26. Even so, Father : for so it seemed good in thy sight.
27. All things are delivered unto me of my Father : and no man knoweth the Son, but the Father ; neither knoweth any man the Father, save the Son, and *he* to whomsoever the Son will reveal *him.*
28. Come unto me, all *ye* that labor and are heavy laden, and I will give you rest.
29. Take my yoke upon you, and learn of me ; for I am meek and lowly in heart : and ye shall find rest unto your souls.
30. For my yoke *is* easy, and my burden is light.

From P. 58.
21. In that hour Jesus rejoiced in spirit, and said, I thank thee, O Father, Lord of heaven and earth, that thou hast hid these things from the wise and prudent, and hast revealed them unto babes : even so, Father ; for so it seemed good in thy sight.
22.* All things are delivered to me of my Father : and no man knoweth who the Son is, but the Father ; and who the Father is, but the Son, and *he* to whom the Son will reveal *him.*
Continued P. 67.

[*I "confess" to thee, O Father.—Alford.*]

* [*"Turning to his disciples he said," All things are delivered. Alford.*]

CHAP. XIII.

From P. 34.

1. There were present at that season some that told him of the Galileans, whose blood Pilate had mingled with their sacrifices.
2. And Jesus answering said unto them, Suppose ye that these Galileans were sinners above all the Galileans, because they suffered such things ?
3. I tell you, nay ; but, except ye repent, ye shall all likewise perish.
4. Or those eighteen, upon whom the tower in Siloam fell, and slew them, think ye that they were sinners above all men that dwelt in Jerusalem ?
5. I tell you, nay : but, except ye repent, ye shall all likewise perish.
6. He spake also this parable ; A certain *man* had a fig tree planted in his vineyard ; and he came and sought fruit thereon, and found none.
7. Then said he unto the dresser of his vineyard, Behold,

these three years I come seeking fruit on this fig tree, and find none : cut it down ; why cumbereth it the ground ?

8. And he answering said unto him, Lord, let it alone this year also, till I shall dig about it, and dung *it :*

9. And if it bear fruit *well :* and if not *then*, after that, thou shalt cut it down.

10. And he was teaching in one of the synagogues on the sabbath.

11. And behold, there was a woman which had a spirit of infirmity eighteen years, and was bowed together, and could in no wise lift up *herself.*

12. And when Jesus saw her, he called *her to him*, and said unto her, Woman, thou art loosed from thine infirmity.

13. And he laid *his* hands on her, and immediately she was made straight, and glorified God.

14. And the ruler of the synagogue answered with indignation, because that Jesus had healed on the sabbath day : and said unto the people, There are six days in which men ought to work : in them therefore come and be healed ; and not on the sabbath day.

15. The Lord then answered him and said, *Thou* hypocrite ; doth not each one of you on the sabbath loose his ox or *his* ass from the stall, and lead *him* away to watering ?

16. And ought not this woman being a daughter of Abraham, whom Satan hath bound, lo, these eighteen years, be loosed from this bond on the sabbath day ?

17. And when he had said these things, all his adversaries were ashamed : and all the people rejoiced, for all the glorious things that were done by him.

Continued P. 69.

CHAP. XII.

1. At that time Jesus went on the sabbath day through the corn ; and his disciples were an hungred, and began to pluck the ears of corn, and to eat.

2. But when the Pharisees saw *it*, they said unto him, Behold, thy disciples do that which is not lawful to do upon the sabbath day.

Chap. II. from P. 49.

23. And it came to pass, that he went through the corn fields on the sabbath day ; and his disciples began, as they went, to pluck the ears of corn.

24. And the Pharisees said unto him, Behold, why do they on the sabbath day that which is not lawful ?

CHAP. VI.

From P. 49.

1. And it came to pass on the second sabbath after the first, that he went through the corn fields : and his disciples plucked the ears of corn and did eat, rubbing *them* in *their* hands.

2. And certain of the Pharisees said unto them, Why do ye that

ST. MATTHEW, XII. | ST. MARK, III. | ST. LUKE, VI. | ST. JOHN, VI.

3. But he said unto them, Have ye not read what David did when he was an hungered, and they that were with him?
4. How he entered into the house of God, and did eat the shew bread, which was not lawful for him to eat, neither for them which were with him; but only for the priests?

5. Or have ye not read in the law, how that on the sabbath days the priests in the temple profane the sabbath, and are blameless?
6. But I say unto you, That in this place is *one* greater than the temple.
7. But if ye had known what *this* meaneth; I will have mercy, and not sacrifice; ye would not have condemned the guiltless.

8. For the Son of man is Lord even of the sabbath day.

9. And when he was departed thence, he went into their synagogue.
10. And behold there was a man which had *his* hand withered.
And they asked him, saying, Is it lawful to heal on the sabbath days? That they might accuse him. (1)
11. And he said unto them, What man shall there be among you, that shall have one sheep, and if it fall into a pit on the sabbath day, will he not lay hold on it, and lift *it* out?
12. How much then is a man better than a sheep?

wherefore it is lawful to do well on the sabbath days.

13. Then saith he to the man, stretch forth thine hand. And he stretched *it* forth: and it was restored whole, like as the other.

25. And he said unto them, Have ye never read what David did, when he had need, and was an hungered, he and they that were with him?
26. How he went into the house of God in the days of Abiathar, the high Priest, and did eat the shew bread, which is not lawful to eat but for the priests, and gave also to them which were with him?

27. And he said unto them, The sabbath was made for man, and not man for the sabbath.
28. Therefore the Son of man is Lord also of the sabbath.

CHAP. III. *(from P. 46.)*

1. And he entered again into the synagogue: and there was a man there which had a withered hand.
2. And they watched him, whether he would heal him on the sabbath day; that they might accuse him.

3. And he saith unto the man which had the withered hand, stand forth.

4. And he saith unto them, Is it lawful to do good on the sabbath days, or to do evil? To save life, or to kill?
But they held their peace.
5. And when he had looked round about on them with anger, being grieved for the hardness of their hearts, he saith unto the man, stretch forth thine hand. And he stretched *it* out. And his hand was restored whole as the other.

which is not lawful to do on the sabbath days?
3. And Jesus answering them, said, Have ye not read so much as this, what David did, when himself was an hungred, and they which were with him;
4. How he went into the house of God, and did take and eat the shew bread, and gave also to them that were with him; which it is not lawful to eat but for the priests alone?

5. And he said unto them that the Son of man is Lord also of the sabbath.

6. And it came to pass also on another sabbath; that he entered into the synagogue and taught: and there was a man whose right hand was withered.
7. And the Scribes and Pharisees watched him, whether he would heal on the sabbath day: that they might find an accusation against him.

L. XIV. 5, P. 129.

8. But he knew their thoughts, and said to the man which had the withered hand, Rise up, and stand forth in the midst. And he arose, and stood forth.
9. Then said Jesus unto them, I will ask you one thing, Is it lawful on the sabbath days to do good, or to do evil? To save life, or to destroy *it?*

10. And looking round about upon them all

he said unto the man. Stretch forth thy hand.
And he did so.
And his hand was restored whole as the other.

(1) J. VII., 23, P. 99

St. MATTHEW, XII. St. MARK, III. St. LUKE, VI., XI. St. JOHN, VI.

14. Then the Pharisees went out and held a council against him, how they might destroy him.

15. But when Jesus knew *it*, he withdrew himself from thence :

and great multitudes followed him,

and he healed them all ;

16. And charged them that they should not make him known :

17. That it might be fulfilled which was spoken by Esaias the prophet, saying,

18. Behold my servant, whom I have chosen ; my beloved, in whom my soul is well pleased : I will put my spirit upon him ; and he shall shew judgment to the Gentiles.

19. He shall not strive, nor cry, neither shall any man hear his voice in the streets.

20. A bruised reed shall he not break, and smoking flax shall he not quench, till he send forth judgment unto victory.

21. And in his name shall the Gentiles trust.

22. Then was brought unto him one possessed with a devil, blind and dumb ; and he healed him, insomuch that the blind and dumb both spake and saw.

23. And all the people were amazed ; and said, Is not this the Son of David ?

24. But when the Pharisees heard *it*, they said, This *fellow* doth not cast out devils, but by Beelzebub, the Prince of the devils.

6. And the Pharisees went forth, and straightway took counsel with the Herodians against him, how they might destroy him.

7. But Jesus withdrew himself with his disciples to the sea :

and a great multitude from Galilee followed him, and from Judea,

8. And from Jerusalem, and from Idumea, and *from* beyond Jordan ; and they about Tyre and Sidon, a great multitude, when they had heard what great things he did, came unto him.

9. And he spake to his disciples, that a small ship should wait on him because of the multitude, lest they should throng him.

10. For he had healed many; insomuch that they pressed upon him for to touch him, as many as had plagues.

11. And unclean spirits, when they saw him, fell down before him, and cried, saying, Thou art the Son of God.

12. And he straitly charged them that they should not make him known.

Continued P. 52.

From P. 52.

20. And the multitude cometh together again, so that they could not so much as eat bread.

21. And when his friends heard *of it*, they went out to lay hold on him : for they said, He is beside himself.

22. And the Scribes which came down from Jerusalem, said, He hath Beelzebub, and by the prince of the devils casteth he out devils.

11. And they were filled with madness ; and communed one with one another what they might do to Jesus.

Continued at P. 52.

From P. 52.

17. And he came down with them and stood in the plain, and the company of his disciples, and a great multitude of people out of all Judea and Jerusalem, and from the sea coast of Tyre and Sidon which came to hear him, and to be healed of their diseases ;

18. And they that were vexed with unclean spirits : and they were healed.

19. And the whole multitude sought to touch him, for there went virtue out of him, and healed *them* all.

Continued P. 52.

Chap. XI. from P. 40.

14. And he was casting out a devil, and it was dumb. And it came to pass, when the devil was gone out, the dumb spake, and the people wondered.

15. But some of them said, He casteth out devils through Beelzebub, the chief of the devils.

Continued P. 65.

St. MATTHEW, XII.

St. MARK, III.

St. LUKE, XI., XII.

St. JOHN, VI.

25. And Jesus knew their thoughts, and said unto them Every kingdom divided against itself is brought to desolation : and every city or house divided against itself shall not stand.

26. And if Satan cast out Satan, he is divided against himself. How shall then his kingdom stand ?

27. And if I by Beelzebub cast out devils, by whom do your children cast them out? Therefore they shall be your judges.
28. But if I cast out devils by the Spirit of God, then the kingdom of God is come unto you.
29. Or else how can one enter into a strong man's house, and spoil his goods, except he first bind the strong man? and then he will spoil his house.

30. He that is not with me is against me : and he that gathereth not with me scattereth abroad.
31. Wherefore I say unto you, All manner of sin and blasphemy shall be forgiven unto men : but the blasphemy *against* the Holy Ghost shall not be forgiven unto men.
32. And whosoever speaketh a word against the Son of man it shall be forgiven him : but whosoever speaketh against the Holy Ghost, it shall not be forgiven him neither in this world neither in the *world* to come.

33. Either make the tree good, and his fruit good ; or else make the tree corrupt, and his fruit corrupt : for the tree is known by *his* fruit.
34. O generation of vipers, how can ye, being evil, speak good things? For out of the abundance of the heart the mouth speaketh.
35. A good man out of the good treasure of the heart bringeth forth good things : and an evil man out of the evil treasure bringeth forth evil things.
36. But I say unto you, That every idle word that men shall speak, they shall give account thereof in the day of judgment.
37. For by thy words thou

23. And he called them *unto him*, and said unto them in parables, How can Satan cast out Satan ?
24. And if a kingdom be divided against itself, that kingdom cannot stand.
25. And if a house be divided against itself, that house cannot stand.
26. And if Satan rise up against himself and be divided, he cannot stand, but hath an end.

27. No man can enter into a strong man's house, and spoil his goods, except he will first bind the strong man ; and then he will spoil his house.

28. Verily I say unto you, All sins shall be forgiven unto the sons of men, and blasphemies wherewith soever they shall blaspheme ;

29. But he that shall blaspheme against the Holy Ghost hath never forgiveness : but is in danger of eternal damnation.

30. Because they said, He hath an unclean spirit.

From P. 65.
17. But he knowing their thoughts, said unto them, Every kingdom divided against itself is brought to desolation : and a house *divided* against a house falleth.

18. If Satan also be divided against himself, how shall his kingdom stand ?
Because ye say that I cast out Mk. III. 30. devils through Beelzebub.
19. And if I by Beelzebub cast out devils, by whom do your sons cast *them* out? Therefore shall they be your judges.
20. But if I with the finger of God cast out devils, no doubt the kingdom of God is come upon you.
21. When a strong man armed keepeth his palace, his goods are in peace :
22. But when a stronger than he shall come upon him and overcome him, he taketh from him all his armour wherein he trusted and divideth his spoils.
23. He that is not with me is against me : and he that gathereth not with me, scattereth.
Continued P. 65.

Chap. XII., from P. 55.

10. And whosoever shall speak a word against the Son of man, it shall be forgiven him : but unto him that blasphemeth against the Holy Ghost it shall not be forgiven.

Continued P. 53.

shalt be justified ; and by thy words thou shalt be condemned.

38. Then certain of the Scribes and of the Pharisees answered, saying, Master, we would see a sign from thee.

Mk. VIII., 11, 12, P. 83.

39. But he answered and said unto them, An evil and adulterous generation seeketh after a sign ; and there shall no sign be given to it, but the sign of the prophet Jonas.

40. For as Jonas was three days and three nights in the whale's belly : so shall the Son of man be three days and three nights in the heart of the earth.

41. The men of Nineveh shall rise in judgment with this generation and shall condemn it : because they repented at the preaching of Jonas ; and, behold, a greater than Jonas is here.

42. The queen of the south shall rise up in the judgment with this generation, and shall condemn it : for she came from the nttermost parts of the earth to hear the wisdom of Solomon : and, behold, a greater than Solomon is here.

. 43. When the unclean spirit is gone out of a man, he walketh through dry places, seeking rest, and findeth none.

44. Then he saith, I will return into my house from whence I came out : and when he is come, he findeth it empty, swept, and garnished.

45. Then goeth he, and taketh with himself seven other spirits more wicked than himself ; and they enter in and dwell there : and the last state of that man is worse than the first.

Even so shall it be also unto this wicked generation.

Chap. XI. from P. 63.

16. And others tempting *him* sought of him a sign from heaven.

Continued at P. 64.

From P. 60.

29. And when the people were gathered thick together, he began to say, This is an evil generation : they seek a sign : and there shall no sign be given it, but the sign of Jonas the prophet.

30. For as Jonas was a sign unto the Ninevites, so shall also the son of man be to this generation.

For v. 31 see below.

32. The men of Nineveh shall rise up in the judgment with the men of this generation, and condemn it : for they repented at the preaching of Jonas ; and, behold, a greater than Jonas is here.

Continued at P. 37.

31. The queen of the south shall rise up in the judgment with the men of this generation, and condemn them : for she came from the uttermost parts of the earth to hear the wisdom of Solomon ; and, behold a greater than Solomon is here.

Transposed.

From P. 64.

24. When the unclean spirit is gone out of a man, he walketh in dry places, seeking rest : and finding none, he saith, I will return unto my house whence I come out.

25. And when he cometh, he findeth it swept and garnished.

26. Then goeth he, and taketh to him seven other spirits more wicked that himself ; and they enter in, and dwell there : and the last state of that man is worse than the first.

27. And it came to pass as he spake these things, a certain woman of the company lifted up her voice, and said unto him, Blessed is the womb that bare thee, and the paps which thou hast sucked.

28. But he said, Yea, rather,

10

ST. MATTHEW, XIII.   ST. MARK, IV.   ST. LUKE, VIII.   ST. JOHN, VI.

blessed *are* they that hear the word of God, and keep it.
Continued P. 65.

Chap. VIII. from P. 67.

46. ¶ While he yet talked to the people, behold, *his* mother and his brethren stood without, desiring to speak with him.

47. Then one said unto him, Behold, thy mother and thy brethren stand without, desiring to speak with thee.

48. But he answered and said unto him that told him, Who is my mother? and who are my brethren?

49. And he stretched forth his hand toward his disciples, and said, Behold, my mother and my brethren!

50. For whosoever shall do the will of my Father which is in heaven, the same is my brother, and sister, and mother.

31. ¶ There came then his brethren and his mother, and, standing without, sent unto him, calling him.

32. And the multitude sat about him; and they said unto him, Behold, thy mother and thy brethren without seek for thee.

33. And he answered them, saying, Who is my mother? or my brethren?

34. And he looked round about on them which sat about him, and said, Behold my mother and my brethren

35. For whosoever shall do the will of God, the same is my brother, and my sister, and mother.

19. ¶ Then came to him *his* mother and his brethren, and could not come at him for the press.

20. And it was told him *by certain* which said, Thy mother and thy brethren stand without, desiring to see thee.

21. And he answered and said unto them,

my mother and my brethren are these which hear the word of God, and do it.

Continued P. 45.

CHAP. XIII.   CHAP. IV.   CHAP. VIII. *(from P. 150.)*

1. The same day went Jesus out of the house, and sat by the sea side.

1. And he began again to teach by the sea side:

1. And it came to pass afterward that he went throughout every city and village preaching, and showing the glad tidings of the kingdom of God; and the twelve *were* with him,

2. And certain women which had been healed of evil spirits and infirmities, Mary, called Magdalene, out of whom went seven devils;

3. And Joanna, the wife of Chuza, Herod's steward; and Susanna, and many others, which ministered unto him of their substance.

2. And great multitudes were gathered together unto him so that he went into a ship and sat: and the whole multitude stood on the shore.

3. And he spake many things unto them in parables, saying,

Behold, a sower went forth to sow:

4. And when he sowed, some *seeds* fell by the way side, and the fowls came, and devoured them up:

5. Some fell upon stony places,

and there was gathered unto him a great multitude, so that he entered into a ship, and sat in the sea: and the whole multitude was by the sea on the land.

2. And he taught them many things by parables, and said unto them in his doctrine,

3. Hearken; Behold, there went out a sower to sow.

4. And it came to pass, as he sowed, some fell by the way side, and the fowls of the air came, and devoured it up.

5. And some fell on stony

4. ¶ And when much people were gathered together, and were come to him out of every city,

he spoke by a parable:

5. A sower went out to sow his seed:

and as he sowed, some fell by the way side; and it was trodden down; and the fowls of the air devoured it.

6. And some fell upon a rock

St. MATTHEW, XIII.　　St. MARK, IV.　　St. LUKE, VIII., X.　　St. JOHN, VI.

where they had not much earth : and forthwith they sprung up; because they had no deepness of earth :

6. And when the sun was up, they were scorched ; and because they had no root, they withered away.

7. And some fell among thorns ; and the thorns sprang up and choked them :

8. But other fell into good ground ; and brought forth fruit, some an hundred fold, some sixty fold, some thirty fold.

9. Who hath ears to hear let him hear. (1)

10. And the disciples came, and said unto him, Why speakest thou unto them in parables ?

11. And he answered, and said unto them, Because it is given unto you to know the mysteries of the kingdom of heaven : but to them it is not given.

12. For whosoever hath, to him shall be given ; and he shall have more abundance : but whosoever hath not, from him shall be taken away even that he hath. (2)

13. Therefore speak I to them in parables : because they seeing see not : and hearing, they hear not ; neither do they understand.

14. And in them is fulfilled the prophecy of Esaias, which saith, By hearing ye shall hear, and shall not understand : and seeing ye shall see, and shall not perceive.

15. For this people's heart is waxed gross ; and *their* ears are dull of hearing : and their eyes they have closed : lest at any time they should see with *their* eyes, and hear with *their* ears ; and should understand with *their* heart ; and should be converted, and I should heal them.

16. But blessed are your eyes, for

they see : and your ears, for they hear.

(1) M. XI. 15 ; XIII. 43.　Mk. IV. 23, P. 68.
(2) M. XXV. 29.

ground, where it had not much earth, and immediately it sprang up, because it had no depth of earth :

6. But when the sun was up, it was scorched : and because it had no root it withered away.

7. And some fell among thorns ; and the thorns grew up and choked it ;
and it yielded no fruit.

8. And other fell on good ground, and did yield fruit that sprang up and increased and brought forth some thirty and some sixty, and some an hundred.

9. And he said unto them, He that hath ears to hear let him hear.

10. And when he was alone, they that were about him, with the twelve, asked of him the parable.

11. And he said unto them, Unto you it is given to know the mystery of the kingdom of God ; but unto them that are without, all *these* things are done in parables :
Continued below.

From P. 68.
24. And he saith unto them, Take heed what ye hear : with what measure ye mete, it shall be measured to you : and unto you that hear, shall more be given.

25. For he that hath, to him shall be given : and he that hath not, from him shall be taken even that which he hath.
Continued P. 69.

12. That seeing, they may see, and not perceive : and hearing they may hear, and not understand :

lest at any time they should be converted and *their* sins should be forgiven them.

and as soon as it was sprung up, it withered away because it lacked moisture.

7. And some fell among thorns ; and the thorns sprang up with it, and choked it.

8. And other fell on good ground ; and sprang up, and bare fruit, an hundred fold. And when he had said these things, he cried,

He that hath ears to hear, let him hear.

9. And his disciples asked him, saying, What might this parable be ?

10. And he said, Unto you it is given to know the mysteries of the kingdom of God, but to others in parables : that seeing, they might not see ; and hearing, they might not understand.
Continued P. 68.

From P. 33.
18. Take heed therefore how ye hear.

For whosoever hath, to him shall be given, and whosoever hath not, from him shall be taken even that which he seemeth to have.
Continued P. 66.

Chap. X. from P. 60.

23. ¶ And he turned him unto *his* disciples, and said privately,

Blessed *are* the eyes which see the things that ye see :

M. XIII. 13.
Mk. IV. 12.

St. MATTHEW, XIII.

17. For verily I say unto you, That many prophets and righteous men have desired to see *those things* which ye see, and have not seen *them;* and to hear *those things* which ye hear, and have not heard *them.*

18. ¶ Hear ye therefore the parable of the sower.
19. When any one heareth the word of the kingdom, and understandeth *it* not, then cometh the wicked *one*, and catches away that which was sown in his heart. This is he which received seed by the way side.
20. But he that received the seed into stony places, the same is he that heareth the word, and anon with joy receiveth it ;
21. Yet hath he not root in himself but dureth for a while : for when tribulation or persecution ariseth because of the word, by and by he is offended.
22. He also that received seed among the thorns is he that heareth the word ; and the care of this world and the deceitfulness of riches, choke the word, and he becometh unfruitful.

23. But he that received seed into the good ground is he that heareth the word, and understandeth *it;* which also beareth fruit, and bringeth forth, some an hundred fold, some sixty, some thirty.

24. ¶ Another parable put he forth unto them, saying, The kingdom of heaven is likened unto a man which sowed good seed in his field :
25. But while men slept, his enemy came, and sowed tares among the wheat, and went his way.
26. But when the blade was sprung up, and brought forth fruit, there appeared the tares also.
27. So the servants of the householder came, and said unto him, Sir, didst not thou sow good seed in thy field ? From whence then hath it tares ?
28. He saith unto them, An

St. MARK, IV.

13. And he said unto them, Know ye not this parable? and how then will ye know all parables ?

14. ¶ The sower soweth the word.
15. And these are they by the way side, where the word is sown : but when they have heard, Satan cometh immediately, and taketh away the word that was sown in their hearts.

16. And these are they likewise which are sown on stony ground : who, when they have heard the word, immediately receive it with gladness ;
17. And have no root in themselves ; and so endure but for a time : afterward, when affliction or persecution ariseth, for the word's sake, immediately they are offended.
18. And these are they which are sown among thorns : such as hear the word ;
19. And the cares of this world, and the deceitfulness of riches, and the lusts of other things entering in, choke the word and it becometh unfruitful.
20. And these are they which are sown on good ground : such as hear the word, and receive *it*, and bring forth fruit, some thirty fold, some sixty, and some an hundred.

Continued at P. 33.
23. If any man have ears to hear, let him hear. (I)

Continued P. 67.

St. LUKE, X., VIII.

24. For I tell you that many prophets and kings have desired to see those things which ye see, and have not seen *them;* and to hear those things which ye hear, and have not heard *them.*

Continued P. 132.

Chap. VIII. from p. 67.
11. Now the parable is this: The seed is the word of God.
12. Those by the way side are they that hear. Then cometh the devil, and taketh away the seed out of their hearts; lest they should believe and be saved.

13. They on the rock *are they* which, when they hear, receive the word with joy: and these have no root ; which for a time believe and in time of temptation fall away.

14. And that which fell among thorns *are they*, which when they have heard, go forth, and are choked with cares and riches and pleasures of *this* life, and bring no fruit to perfection.

15. But that on the good ground are they, which in an honest and good heart, having heard the word, keep *it*, and bring forth fruit with patience.

Continued P. 33.

St. JOHN VI.

St. MATTHEW, XIII.   St. MARK, IV.   St. LUKE, XIII.   St. JOHN, VI.

enemy hath done this. The servant said unto him, Wilt thou then that we go and gather them up?

29. But he said, Nay; lest while ye gather up the tares, ye root up the wheat with them.

30. Let both grow together until the harvest: and in the time of harvest, I will say to the reapers, Gather up together first the tares, and bind them together in bundles to burn them: but gather the wheat into my barn.

From P. 67.

26. ¶ And he said, so is the kingdom of God, as if a man should cast seed into the ground:

27. And should sleep, and rise night and day, and the seed should spring and grow up, he knoweth not how.

28. For the earth bringth forth fruit of herself; first the blade, then the ear, after that the full corn in the ear.

29. But when the fruit is brought forth, immediately he putteth in the sickle, because the harvest is come.

31. ¶ Another parable put he forth unto them, saying,

Chap. XIII. from P. 61.

30. ¶ And he said, Whereunto shall we liken the kingdom of God? or with what comparison shall we compare it?

18. ¶ Then saith he, Unto what is the kingdom of God like? And whereunto shall I resemble it?

The kingdom of heaven is like to a grain of mustard seed, which a man took, and hid in his field:

31. *It is* like a grain of mustard seed, which, when it is sown in the earth, is less than all the seeds that be in the earth:

19. It is like a grain of mustard seed, which a man took, and cast into his garden:

32. Which indeed is the least of all seeds:
but when it is grown, it is the greatest among herbs: and becometh a tree; so that the birds of the air come, and lodge in the branches thereof.

32. But when it is sown, it groweth up, and becometh greater than all herbs, and shooteth out great branches: so that the fowls of the air may lodge under the shadow of it.

and it grew, and waxed a great tree
and the fowls of the air lodged in the branches of it.

20. And again he said, Whereunto shall I liken the kingdom of God?

33. ¶ Another parable spake he unto them: The kingdom of heaven is like unto leaven, which a woman took, and hid in three measures of meal, till the whole was leavened.

21. It is like leaven, which a woman took, and hid in three measures of meal, till the whole was leavened.

33. And with many such parables spake he the word unto them; as they were able to bear *it.*

34. All these things spake Jesus unto the multitude in parables; and without a parable spake he not unto them:

34. But without a parable spake he not unto them:

Continued P. 40.

35. That it might be fulfilled which was spoken by the prophet, saying, I will open my mouth in parables; I will utter things which have been kept secret from the foundation of the world.

This verse concluded at P. 70.

36. Then Jesus sent the multitude away, and went into the house: and his disciples came unto him,

saying, Declare unto us the parable of the tares of the field.

37. He answered, and said unto them, He that soweth the good seed is the Son of man :

38. The field is the world : the good seed are the children of the kingdom : but the tares are the children of the wicked *one:*

39. The enemy that sowed them is the devil : the harvest is the end of the world : and the reapers are the angels.

40. As therefore the tares are gathered and burned in the fire, so shall it be in the end of this world.

41. The Son of man shall send forth his angels, and they shall gather, out of his kingdom, all things that offend, and them which do iniquity ;

42. And shall cast them into a furnace of fire ; there shall be wailing and gnashing of teeth. *See v. 50 below.*

43. Then shall the righteous shine forth as the sun, in the kingdom of their Father. Who hath ears to hear let him hear. *See v. 9.*

44. ¶ Again, the kingdom of heaven is like unto treasure hid in a field ; the which when a man hath found, he hideth, and for joy thereof goeth, and selleth all that he hath, and buyeth that field.

45. ¶ Again, the kingdom of heaven is like unto a merchantman seeking goodly pearls :

46. Who when he had found one pearl of great price, went and sold all that he had and bought it.

47. ¶ Again the kingdom of heaven is like unto a net that was cast into the sea, and gathered of every kind :

48. Which when it was full, they drew to shore, and sat down, and gathered the good into vessels ; but cast the bad away.

49. So shall it be at the end of the world : the angels shall come forth, and sever the wicked from among the just ;

50. And shall cast them into the furnace of fire : there shall be wailing and gnashing of teeth.*

51. Jesus saith unto them, Have ye understood all these things? they say unto him, Yea, Lord.

52. Then said he unto them, Therefore every scribe *which is* instructed unto the kingdom of heaven is like unto a man

and when they were alone he expounded all things to his disciples.

Continued P. 45.

* See M. VIII., 12 ; XIII., 42, 50 ; XXII., 13 ; XXIV., 15 ; XXV., 30.

St. MATTHEW, XIII.	St. MARK, V. VI.	St. LUKE, IV.	St. JOHN, VI.

that is an housebolder, which bringeth forth out of his treasure *things* new and old.

53. ¶ And it came to pass, *that* when Jesus had finished these parables,

CHAP. V.
1 to 21 see P. 46.
22 to 43 see P. 50.

———

Chap. IV. from P. 18.

he departed thence.

CHAP. VI. *(From P. 51.)*

16. ¶ And he came to Nazareth where he had been brought up :

54. And when he was come into his own country

1. And he went out from thence, and came into his own country ;
and his disciples follow him.

he taught them in their synagogue.

2. And when the sabbath day was come, he began to teach in the synagogue :

and, as his custom was, he went into the synagogue on the sabbath day, and stood up for to read.

17. And there was delivered unto him the book of the prophet Esaias. And when he had opened the book, he found the place where it was written,

18. The Spirit of the Lord *is* upon me, because he hath anointed me to preach the Gospel to the poor : he hath sent me to heal the brokenhearted : to preach deliverance to the captives and recovering of sight to the blind : to set at liberty them that are bruised :

19. To preach the acceptable year of the Lord.

20. And he closed the book, and he gave *it* again to the minister and sat down. And the eyes of all them that were in the synagogue were fastened on him.

21. And he began to say unto them, This day is this scripture fulfilled in your ears.

in so much that they were astonished ; and said, Whence hath this *man* this wisdom, and *these* mighty works ?

and many, hearing *him* were astonished : saying, From whence hath this *man* these things? and what wisdom *is* this which is given unto him, that even such mighty works are wrought by his hands ?

22. And all bear him witness, and wondered at the gracious words which proceeded out of his mouth.

55. Is not this the carpenter's son ? Is not his mother called Mary ? (1)
And his brethren, James, and Joses, and Simon, and Judas? (2)

3. Is not this the carpenter ; the son of Mary ; the brother of James, and Joses, and of Juda, and Simon ?

and they said, Is not this Joseph's son ?

J. VI. 42. P. 77.

56. And his sisters, are they not all with us ? Whence then hath this *man* all these things ?

and are not his sisters here with us ?

57. And they were offended in him. (3)

And they were offended at him.

23. And he said unto them,

(1) J. VI. 42., P. 77.
(2) M. XXVII. 56.
(3) L. IV. 28, P. 72.

St. MATTHEW, XIV. St. MARK, VI. St. LUKE, IV., IX. St. JOHN, VI.

Ye will surely say unto me this proverb,
Physician, heal thyself : whatsoever we have heard done in Capernaum, do also here in thy country.

But Jesus said unto them, A prophet is not without honour save in his own country,

4. But Jesus said unto them, A prophet is not without honour but in his own country; among his own kin : and in his own house.

24. And he said, Verily, I say unto you, No prophet is accepted in his own country.

and his own house.

25. But I tell you of a truth, Many widows were in Israel in the days of Elias, when the heaven was shut up three years and six months ; when great famine was throughout all the land :
26. But unto none of them was Elias sent, save unto Sarepta, *a city* of Sidon, unto a woman *that was* a widow.
27. And many lepers were in Israel in the time of Eliseus the prophet ; and none of them was cleansed saving Naaman, the Syrian.
28. And all they in the synagogue, when they heard these things, were filled with wrath,
29. And rose up, and thrust him out of the city ; and led him unto the brow of the hill whereon their city was built, that they might cast him down headlong.
30. But he, passing through the midst of them, went his way.

58. And he did not many mighty works there; because of their unbelief.

5. And he could there do no mighty work, save that he laid his hands upon a few sick folk, and healed *them*.
6. And he marvelled because of their unbelief : and he went round about the villages teaching.

Continued P. 53.
Chap. VI. from P. 56.

Chap. IX. from P. 56.

CHAP. XIV.

1. At that time Herod the Tetrarch* heard of the fame of Jesus.
2. And said unto his servants, This is John the Baptist ; He is risen from the dead ; and therefore many mighty works do show forth themselves in him.

14. And king Herod heard *of him*, (for his name was spread abroad :) and he said, That John the Baptist is risen from the dead: and therefore mighty works do show forth themselves in him.

7. ¶ Now Herod the Tetrarch heard of all that was done by him : and he was perplexed, because that it was said of some, That John was risen from the dead :

15. Others said, That it is Elias.
And others said, That it is a prophet ; or as one of the prophets.
16. But when Herod heard *thereof*, he said, It is John whom I have beheaded ; he is risen from the dead.

8. And of some that Elias had appeared : and of others that one of the old prophets was risen again.
9. And Herod said, John have I beheaded : But who is this, of whom I hear such things ?

* *2nd Herod. Archilaus.*
M. II, 22.

And he desired to see him
Continued P. 74.

Chap. III. from P. 15.

3. ¶ For Herod had laid hold on John, and bound him, and put *him* in prison, for Herodias' sake, his brother Philip's wife.

17. For Herod himself had sent forth and laid hold upon John, and bound him in prison, for Herodias' sake, his brother Philip's wife : for he had married her.

19. But Herod the Tetrarch, being reproved by him for Herodias his brother Philip's wife,
and for the evils Herod had done,

4. For John said unto him, It is not lawful for thee to have her.

18. For John had said unto Herod, It is not lawful for thee to have thy brother's wife.

20. Added yet this above all, that he shut up John in prison.
Continued P. 15.

19. Therefore Herodias had a quarrel against him, and would have killed him ; but she could not :

5. And when he would have put him to death, he feared the multitude, because they counted him as a prophet.

20. For Herod feared John, knowing that he was a just man, and an holy, and observed him :

and when he heard him, he did many things ; and heard him gladly.

6. But when Herod's birthday was kept,

21. And when a convenient day was come, that Herod on his birthday, made a supper to his lords, high captains, and chief *estates* of Galilee ;

the daughter of Herodias danced before them ; and pleased Herod.

22. And when the daughter of the said Herodias came in, and danced, and pleased Herod and them that sat with him ; the king said unto the damsel, Ask of me whatsoever thou wilt, and I will give *it* thee.

7. Whereupon he promised, with an oath, to give her whatsoever she would ask.

23. And he sware unto her, whatsoever thou shalt ask of me, I will give *it* thee, unto the half of my kingdom.

8. And she, being before instructed of her mother,

24. And she went forth, and said unto her mother, What shall I ask ? And she said, The head of John the Baptist.

said, Give me here John Baptist's head in a charger.

25. And she came in straightway with haste unto the king, and asked, saying, I will that thou give me by and by, in a charger, the head of John the Baptist.

9. And the king was sorry. Nevertheless for the oath's sake, and them which sat with him at meat,
he commanded *it* to be given *her*.

26. And the king was exceeding sorry ; *yet* for his oath's sake, and for their sakes which sat with him, he would not reject her.

27. And immediately the king sent an executioner ; and commanded his head to be brought : and he went and beheaded him in the prison,

10. And he sent, and beheaded John in the prison.

11. And his head was brought in a charger, and given to the damsel : and she brought *it* to her mother.

28. And brought his head in a charger, and gave it to the damsel : and the damsel gave it to her mother.

12. And his disciples came, and took up the body, and buried it,

29. And when his disciples heard *of it*, they came, and took up his corpse, and laid it in a tomb.

St. MATTHEW, XIV.

St. MARK, VI.

St. LUKE, IX.

St. JOHN, VI.

and went and told Jesus.

30. And the apostles gathered themselves together unto Jesus, and told him all things; both what they had done and what they had taught.
31. And he said unto them, Come ye yourselves apart into a desert place, and rest awhile : for there were many coming and going ; and they had no leisure, so much as to eat.

Chap. IX. from P. 73.

10. ¶ And the apostles, when they were returned, told him all that they had done.

And he took them, and went aside privately, into a desert place, belonging to the city called Bethsaida.

CH. VI.

1. After these things, Jesus went over the sea of Galilee, which is *the sea* of Tiberias.

13. ¶ When Jesus heard *of it*, he departed thence, by ship, into a desert place apart : and when the people had heard *thereof*, they followed him on foot out of the cities.

32. And they departed into a desert place by ship, privately.
33. And the people saw them departing, and many knew him, and ran afoot thither out of all cities ; and outwent them ; and came together unto him.

11. And the people, when they knew *it*, followed him ; and he received them ;

2. And a great multitude followed him, because they saw his miracles which he did on them that were diseased.
3. And Jesus went up into a mountain ; and there he sat with his disciples.
4. And the passover, a feast of the Jews, was nigh.
5. ¶ When Jesus then lifted up *his* eyes and saw a great company come unto him,

14. And Jesus went forth, and saw a great multitude, and was moved with compassion toward them,

34. And Jesus, when he came out, saw much people, and was moved with compassion toward them ; because they were as sheep not having a shepherd : and he began to teach them many things.

and he healed their sick.
15. ¶ And when it was evening his disciples came to him, saying, This is a desert place, and the time is now past : send the multitude away, that they may go into the villages and buy themselves victuals.

35. And when the day was now far spent, his disciples came unto him, and said,

This is a desert place, and now the time is far passed :
36. Send them away ; that they may go into the country round about and into the villages ; and buy themselves bread : for they have nothing to eat.

and spake unto them of the kingdom of God, And healed them that had need of healing.
12. And when the day began to wear away, then came the twelve, and said unto him,

send the multitude away that they may go into the towns, and country round about and lodge, and get victuals :

16. But Jesus said unto them, They need not depart : give ye them to eat.

37. He answered, and said unto them, Give ye them to eat.

for we are here in a desert place.
13. But he said unto them, Give ye them to eat.

he saith unto Philip, whence shall we buy bread, that these may eat ?

6. And this he said to prove him ; for he himself knew what he would do.
7. Philip answered him, Two hundred pennyworth of bread is not sufficient for them, that every one of them may take a little.

And they say unto him, Shall we go and buy two hundred pennyworth of bread, and give them to eat ?

17. And they said unto him, We have here but five loaves, and two fishes. (1)

38. He saith unto them, How many loaves have ye? Go and see. And when they knew they say, Five :
and two fishes.

and they said, We have no more but five loaves and two fishes ; except we should go and buy meat for all this people. (1)
14. For they were about five thousand men. (2)

8. One of his disciples, Andrew, Simon Peter's brother, saith unto him,
9. There is a lad here which hath five barley loaves, and two small fishes : but what are they among so many ?

(1) M. XV. 33 to 38.

(1) Mk. VI. 37.
(2) M. XIV. 21 ; J. VI. 10, P. 75.

St. MATTHEW, XIV.	St. MARK, VI.	St. LUKE, IX.	St. JOHN, VI.

St. MATTHEW, XIV.

18. He said, Bring them hither to me.

19. And he commanded the multitude to sit down on the grass,

and took the five loaves, and the two fishes, and looking up to heaven, he blessed, and brake, and gave the loaves to *his* disciples, and the disciples to the multitude. (1)

20. And they did all eat, and were filled :

and they took up of the fragments that remained twelve baskets full.

21. And they that had eaten were about five thousand men, beside women and children.

22. ¶ And straightway Jesus constrained his disciples to get into a ship, and to go before him unto the other side, while he sent the multitudes away.

23. And when he had sent the multitudes away, he went up into a mountain, apart, to pray. And when the evening was come he was there alone.

24. But the ship was now in the midst of the sea,

tossed with waves : for the wind was contrary.

25. And in the fourth watch of the night Jesus went unto them, walking on the sea.

26. And when the disciples saw him walking on the sea, they were troubled, saying, It is a spirit : and they cried out for fear.

27. But straightway Jesus spake unto them, saying, Be of good cheer :
It is I : be not afraid.

St. MARK, VI.

39. And he commanded them to make all sit down, by companies upon the green grass.

40. And they sat down in ranks by hundreds, and by fifties.

41. And when he had taken the five loaves and the two fishes, he looked up to heaven, and blessed, and brake the loaves, and gave *them* to his disciples to set before them : and the two fishes divided he among them all.

42. And they did all eat, and were filled.

43. And they took up twelve baskets full of fragments,

and of the two fishes.
44. And they that did eat of the loaves were about five thousand men.

45. And straightway he constrained his disciples to get into the ship, and to go to the other side, before, unto Bethsaida,* while he sent away the people.

46. And when he had sent them away, he departed into a mountain to pray.

47. And when even was come,

the ship was in the midst of the sea, and he alone on the land.

48. And he saw them toiling in rowing : for the wind was contrary unto them :

and about the fourth watch of the night he cometh unto them, walking upon the sea ; and would have passed by them.
49. But when they saw him walking upon the sea, they supposed it had been a spirit : and cried out :
50. For they all saw him, and were troubled. And immediately he talked with them ; and saith unto them, Be of good cheer : It is I : be not afraid.

St. LUKE, IX.

And he said to his disciples, Make them sit down by fifties in a company.
15. And they did so ; and made them all sit down.

16. Then he took the five loaves and the two fishes, and looking up to heaven he blessed them, and brake, and gave to the disciples to set before the multitude.

17. And they did eat, and were all filled :

and there was taken up of fragments that remained to them twelve baskets.

Continued P. 84.

* L. XIX. 38. P. 122.
  J. XII. 13. P. 122.
  M. XXVII. 11, 37.
  Mk. XV. 9, 18.
  J. XVIII. 37. P. 168.
  XIX. 19. P. 172.

* Mk. VI. 45.

St. JOHN, VI.

10. And Jesus said, Make the men sit down. Now there was much grass in the place. So the men sat down, in number about five thousand.

11. And Jesus took the loaves : and when he had given thanks, he distributed to the disciples, and the disciples to them that were set down :
and likewise of the fishes as much as they would.

12. When they were filled, he said unto his disciples, Gather up the fragments that remain, that nothing be lost.

13. Therefore they gathered *them* together, and filled twelve baskets with the fragments of the five barley loaves which remained over and above unto them that had eaten.

14. Then those men, when they had seen the miracle that Jesus did, said, This is of a truth that prophet that should come into the world.

15. ¶ When Jesus therefore perceived that they would come and take him by force, to make him a king,*

he departed again into a mountain himself alone.

16. And when even was *now* come, his disciples went down unto the sea,

17. And entered into a ship, and went over the sea toward Capernaum.*
And it was now dark, and Jesus was not come to them.

18. And the sea arose by reason of a great wind that blew.

19. So when they had rowed about five and twenty or thirty furlongs,

they see Jesus walking on the sea, and drawing nigh unto the ship :

and they were afraid.

20. But he saith unto them. It is I : be not afraid.｝

---

(1) See M. XV. 32 to 39.   * J. VI. 17.

ST. MATTHEW, XIV.   ST. MARK, VI.   ST. LUKE.   S. JOHN, VI.

28. And Peter answered him, and said, Lord, if it be thou, bid me come unto thee on the water.

29. And he said, Come. And when Peter was come down out of the ship, he walked on the water, to go Jesus.

30. But when he saw the wind boisterous, he was afraid : and beginning to sink, he cried, saying, Lord save me.

31. And immediately Jesus stretched forth *his* hand, and caught him ; and said unto him, O thou of little faith ; wherefore didst thou doubt ?

32. And when they were come into the ship the wind ceased.

51. And he went up unto them into the ship ; and the wind ceased.

And they were sore amazed in themselves beyond measure, and wondered.

52. For they considered not *the miracle* of the loaves : for their heart was hardened.

21. Then they willingly received him into the ship :

33. Then they that were in the ship came and worshipped him ; saying, Of a truth thou art the Son of God.

34. ¶ And when they were gone over, they came into the land of Gennesaret. (1)

54. And when they were come out of the ship, straightway they knew him ;

53. And when they had passed over, they came into the land of Gennesaret, and drew to the shore.

and immediately the ship was at the land whither they went.

22. ¶ The day following, when the people which stood on the other side of the sea saw that there was none other boat there save that one whereinto his disciples were entered ; and that Jesus went not with his disciples into the boat ; but *that* his disciples were gone away alone ;

23. (Howbeit there came other boats from Tiberias nigh unto the place where they did eat bread, after that the Lord had given thanks :)

24. When the people therefore saw that Jesus was not there, neither his disciples, they also took shipping, and came to Capernaum, seeking for Jesus.

25. And when they had found him on the other side of the sea, they said unto him, Rabbi, When camest thou hither ?

35. And when the men of that place had knowledge of him, they sent out into all that country round about and brought unto him all that were diseased

55. And ran through that whole region round about, and began to carry about in beds those that were sick, where they heard he was.

56. And whithersoever he entered, into villages, or cities, or country, they laid the sick in the streets ; and besought him that they might touch if it were but the border of his garment : and as many as touched him were made whole.

26. Jesus answered them, and said, Verily, verily, I say unto you ye seek me, not because ye saw the miracles ; but because ye did eat of the loaves, and were filled.

27. Labor not for the meat which perisheth, but for that meat which endureth unto everlasting

36. And besought him that they might only touch the hem of his garment, and as many as touched were made perfectly whole. *Continued P. 79.*

(1) M. XV, 39.

For Chap. VII. see P. 79.

77

St. MATTHEW, XIV., XV.   St. MARK, VI., VII.   St. LUKE.   St. JOHN, VI.

life, which the Son of man shall give unto you : for him hath God the Father sealed.

28. Then said they unto him, What shall we do, that we might work the works of God ?

29. Jesus answered, and said unto them, This is the work of God, that ye believe on him whom he hath sent.

* M. XVI. 1.

30. They said therefore unto him, What sign* showest thou then, that we may see, and believe thee ? What dost thou work ?

31. Our fathers did eat manna in the desert; as it is written, He gave them bread from heaven to eat.

32. Then Jesus said unto them, Verily, verily, I say unto you, Moses gave you not that bread from heaven : But my Father giveth you the true bread from heaven.

33. For the bread of God is he which cometh down from heaven, and giveth life unto the world.

34. Then said they unto them, Lord, evermore give us this bread.

35. And Jesus said unto them, I am the bread of life : he that cometh to me shall never hunger, and he that believeth on me shall never thirst.

36. But I said unto you, That ye also have seen me, and believe not.

37. All that the Father giveth me shall come to me : and him that cometh to me I will in no wise cast out.

38. For I came down from heaven, not to do mine own will, but the will of him that sent me.

39. And this is the Father's will which hath sent me, that of all which he hath given me I should lose nothing; but should raise it up again at the last day.

40. And this is the will of him that sent me, that every one which seeth the Son, and believeth on him, may have everlasting life : and I will raise him up at the last day.

41. The Jews then murmured at him, because he said, I am the bread which came down from heaven.

42. And they said, Is not this Jesus, the son of Joseph, whose father and mother we know ? M. XIII. 55. How is it then that he saith, I came down from heaven ?

43. Jesus therefore answered, and said unto them, Murmur not among yourselves.

44. No man can come to me,

except the Father which hath
sent me draw him : and I will
raise him up at the last day.

45. It is written in the prophets, and they shall be all
taught of God. Every man therefore that hath heard, and hath
learned of the Father, cometh
nnto me.

46. Not that any man hath
seen the Father, save he which is
M. XI. 27. of God ; he hath seen the Father.

47. Verily, verily, I say unto
you, He that believeth on me
hath everlasting life.

48. I am that bread of life.

49. Your fathers did eat manna
in the wilderness, and are dead.

50. This is the bread which
cometh down from heaven, that
a man may eat thereof and not
die.

51. I am the living bread which
came down from heaven : if any
man eat of this bread he shall
live for ever : and the bread that
I will give is my flesh, which
I will give for the life of the
world.

52. The Jews therefore strove
among themselves, saying, How
can this man give us *his* flesh to
eat ?

53. Then Jesus said unto them,
Verily, verily, I say unto you,
Except ye eat the flesh of the Son
of man, and drink his blood, ye
have no life in you.

54. Whoso eateth my flesh, and
drinketh my blood, hath eternal
life, and I will raise him up at
the last day.

55. For my flesh is meat indeed,
and my blood is drink indeed.

56. He that eateth my flesh,
and drinketh my blood, dwelleth
in me, and I in him.

57. As the living Father hath
sent me, and I live by the Father ;
so he that eateth me, even he
shall live by me.

58. This is that bread which
came down from heaven : not as
your fathers did eat manna, and
are dead : but he that eateth of
this bread shall live for ever.

59. These things said he in the
synagogue as he taught at Capernaum.

60. Many therefore of his disciples, when they heard *this;*
said, This is an hard saying :
Who can hear it?

61. When Jesus knew in himself that his disciples murmured
at it, he said unto them, Doth

St. MATTHEW, XV.   St. MARK, VII.   St. LUKE.   St. JOHN, VI.

this offend you?

62. *What* and if ye shall see the Son of man ascend up where he was before?

63. It is the spirit that quick-eneth; the flesh profiteth nothing: the words that I speak unto you, *they* are spirit, and *they* are life.

64. But there are some of you that believe not. For Jesus knew from the beginning who they were that believed not, and who should betray him.

65. And he said, Therefore said I unto you, That no man can come unto me except it were given unto him of my Father.

66. ¶ From that *time* many of his disciples drew back, and walked no more with him.

67. Then said Jesus unto the twelve, Will ye also go away?

68. Then Simon Peter answered him, Lord, To whom shall we go? Thou hast the words of eternal life.

M. XVI. 16. Mk. VIII. 29. L. IX. 20.

69. And we believe and are sure that thou art that Christ, the son of the living God.

70. Jesus answered them, Have not I chosen you twelve? and one of you is a devil.

L. VII. 40. J. XII. 4. P. 149.

71. He spake of Judas Iscariot, *the son* of Simon: for he it was that should betray him, being one of the twelve.

For Chap. VII. see P. 81.

CHAP. XV.

1. Then came to Jesus Scribes and Pharisees which were of Jerusalem, saying,

CHAP. VII. *(From P. 76.)*

1. Then came together unto him the Pharisees, and certain of the Scribes which came from Jerusalem.

2. And when they saw some of his disciples eat bread with defiled, that is to say with unwashen hands, they found fault.

3. For the Pharisees, and all the Jews, except they wash *their* hands oft, eat not, holding the tradition of the elders.

4. And *when they come* from the market, except they wash, they eat not. And many other things there be, which they have received to hold, *as* the washing of cups, and pots, brazen vessels, and of tables.

2. Why do thy disciples transgress the tradition of the elders? For they wash not their hands when they eat bread.

5. Then the Pharisees and Scribes asked him, Why walk not thy disciples according to the tradition of the elders, but eat bread with unwashen hands?

L. XI. 37—39. P. 13

3. But he answered and said unto them,

6. He answered and said unto them,
Residue of vs. 6 & 7, P. 80.
From P. 80.

8. For laying aside the commandment of God, ye hold the tradition of men, [as the washing of pots and cups: and many other such like things ye do.]†

9. And he said unto them, Full well ye reject the commandment of God, that ye may keep your own tradition.

Why do ye also transgress the commandment of God [by]* your tradition?

* ["*For sake of.*"—*Alford.*]

† [*Wanting in several of the most ancient MSS,—Alford.*)

ST. MATTHEW, XV.

ST MARK, VII.

ST. LUKE, VI.

ST. JOHN, VII.

4. For God commanded, saying, Honour thy father and mother : and he that curseth father and mother, let him die the death.

5. But ye say, Whosoever shall say to *his* father, or *his* mother, *it is* a gift, by whatsoever thou mightest be profited by me ;

6. And honour not his father or his mother, *he shall be free.*

Thus have ye made the commandment of God of none effect by your tradition.

7. *Ye* hypocrites. Well did Esaias prophesy of you, saying,

8. This people draweth nigh unto me with their mouth, and honoureth me with *their* lips ; but their heart is far from me.

9. But in vain they do worship me, teaching *for* doctrines the commandments of men.

10. ¶ And he called the multitude, and said unto them, Hear and understand :

11. Not that which goeth into the mouth defileth a man : but that which cometh out of the mouth, this defileth a man.

12. Then came his disciples, and said unto him, Knowest thou that the Pharisees were offended, after they heard this saying?

13. But he answered, and said, Every plant which my heavenly Father hath not planted, shall be rooted up.

14. Let them alone : they be blind leaders of the blind : and if the blind lead the blind, both shall fall into the ditch.

15. Then answered Peter, and said unto him, Declare unto us this parable.

16. And Jesus said, Are ye also yet without understanding?

17. Do not ye yet understand, that whatsoever entereth in at the mouth

goeth into the belly, and is cast out into the draught?

18. But those things which proceed out of the mouth come forth from the heart ; and they defile the man.

19. For out of the heart

10. For Moses said, Honour thy father and thy mother : and whoso curseth his father or mother, let him die the death.

11. But ye say, If a man shall say to his father or mother, *It is* Corban, that is to say, a gift, by whatsoever thou mightest be profited by me, *he shall be free.*

12. And ye suffer him no more to do aught for his father or his mother ;

13. Making the word of God of none effect through your tradition which ye have delivered: and many such like things do ye.

Continued below.

From P. 79.

6. Well hath Esaias prophesied of you hypocrites, as it is written, This people honoureth me with *their* lips, but their heart is far from me.

7. Howbeit in vain do they worship me, teaching *for* doctrines the commandments of men.

Continued at P. 79.

14. And when he had called all the people *unto him,* he said unto them, Hearken unto me every one *of you,* and understand :

15. There is nothing from without a man, that entering into him can defile him : but the things which come out of him, those are they that defile the man.

16. [If any man have ears to hear, let him hear.]*

17. And when he was entered into the house from the people, his disciples asked him concerning the parable.

18. And he saith unto them, Are ye so without understanding also ? Do ye not perceive that whatsoever thing from without entereth into the man, it cannot defile him ;

19. Because it entereth not into his heart, but into the belly, and goeth out into the draught : purging all meats?

20. And he said, That which cometh out of the man, that defileth the man.

21. For from within, out of the

Chap. VI. from P. 39.

39. And he spake a parable unto them ; Can the blind lead the blind? Shall they not both fall into the ditch?

Continued P. 54.

* [*Wanting in several most ancient MSS. —Alford.*]

proceed evil thoughts, murders, adulteries, fornications,

thefts, false witness, blasphemies :

20. These are the things which defile a man : but to eat with unwashen hands defileth not a man.

21. ¶ Then Jesus went thence, and departed into the coasts of Tyre and Sidon.

22. And, behold, a woman of Canaan* came out of the same coasts ; and cried unto him, saying, Have mercy on me ; O Lord, thou Son of David ; my daughter is grievously vexed with a devil.

23. But he answered her not a word. And his disciples came and besought him, saying, Send her away ; for she crieth after us.

24. But he answered and said, I am not sent but unto the lost sheep of the house of Israel.

25. Then came she and worshipped him, saying, Lord help me.

26. But he answered and said,

It is not meet to take the children's bread, and to cast it to dogs.

27. And she said, Truth, Lord, yet the dogs eat of the crumbs which fall from their master's table.

28. Then Jesus answered, and said unto her, O woman, great is thy faith : be it unto thee even as thou wilt.

And her daughter was made whole, from that very hour.

29. And Jesus departed from thence, and came nigh unto the sea of Galilee ; and

went up into a mountain, and sat down there.

30. And great multitudes came unto him ; having with them those that were lame, blind, dumb, maimed, and many others, and cast them down

* See Mk. VII. 26.

---

heart of men, proceed evil thoughts, adulteries, fornications, murders,

22. Thefts, covetousness, wickedness, deceit, lasciviousness, an evil eye, blasphemy, pride, foolishness :

23. All these evil things come from within, and defile the man.

24. ¶ And from thence he arose, and went into the borders of Tyre and Sidon ; and entered into an house, and would have no man know it : but he could not be hid.

25. For a certain woman, whose young daughter had an unclean spirit, heard of him, and came and fell at his feet :

26. The woman was a Greek, a Syrophenician by nation ;*

and she besought him that he would cast forth the devil out of her daughter.

27. But Jesus said unto her, Let the children first be filled : for it is not meet to take the children's bread, and to cast it unto the dogs.

28. And she answered, and said unto him, Yes, Lord ; yet the dogs under the table eat of the children's crumbs.

29. And he said unto her, For this saying go thy way : The devil is gone out of thy daughter.

30. And when she was come to her house, she found the devil gone out, and her daughter laid upon the bed.

31. ¶ And again, departing from the coasts of Tyre and Sidon, he came unto the sea of Galilee, through the midst of the coasts of Decapolis.

32. And they bring unto him one that was deaf, and had an impediment in his speech ; and they beseech him to put his hands upon him.

* See M. XV. 22.

CHAP. VII.

1. After these things Jesus walked in Galilee : for he would not walk in Jewry, because the Jews sought to kill him.

Continued P. 97.

at Jesus' feet ;

and he healed them :

31. Insomuch that the multitude
wondered, when they saw the dumb
to speak, the maimed to be whole,
the lame to walk, and the blind to
see : and they glorified the God of
Israel.

33. And he took him aside from
the multitude, and put his fingers
into his ears ; and he spit, and
touched his tongue ;
34. And looking up to heaven, he
sighed, and saith unto him, Eph-
phatha, that is, Be opened.
35. And straightway his ears
were opened and the string of his
tongue was loosed, and he spake
plain.
36. And he charged them that
they should tell no man : but the
more he charged them, so much the
more a great deal they published it ;
37. And were beyond measure
astonished, saying, He hath done
all things well : he maketh both the
deaf to hear, and the dumb to speak.

CHAP. VIII.

32. ¶ Then Jesus called his disciples unto him, and said,
I have compassion on the multitude
because they continue with me
now three days ; and have nothing
to eat :
and I will not send them away
fasting lest they faint in the way.

1. In those days the multitude
being very great, and having nothing
to eat, Jesus called his disciples
unto him, and saith unto them,
2. I have compassion on the multitude, because they have now been
with me three days, and have
nothing to eat :

33. And his disciples say unto
him, Whence should we have so
much bread in the wilderness as
to fill so great a multitude ?

3. And if I send them away
fasting to their own houses, they
will faint by the way : for divers of
them came from far.
4. And his disciples answered
him, From whence can a man satisfy
these men with bread here in the
wilderness ?

34. And Jesus saith unto them,
How many loaves have ye ? and
they said, Seven,
and a few little fishes.
35. And he commanded the multitude to sit down on the ground.
36. And he took the seven loaves
and the fishes,
and gave thanks, and brake them,
and gave them to his disciples, and
the disciples to the multitude.

5. And he asked them, How
many loaves have ye ? And they
said, Seven.
6. And he commanded the people
to sit down on the ground :
and he took the seven loaves,

and gave thanks, and brake, and
gave to his disciples to set before
them ; and they did set them before
the people.
7. And they had a few small
fishes : and he blessed, and commanded to set them also before
them.

37. And they did all eat, and were
filled : and they took up of the
broken meat that was left, seven
baskets full.
38. And they that did eat were
four thousand men,
beside women and children. (1)
39. And he sent away the multi-

8. So they did eat, and were
filled : and they took up of the
broken meat that was left, seven
baskets.
9. And they that had eaten were
about four thousand :

and he sent them away.

(1) Compare M. XIV. 14 to 21, with M.
   XV. 32 to 38.

Compare Mk. VI. 34 to 44, P. 74, 75, with
   Mk. VIII. 2 to 9.

tude, and took ship (1) and

came into the coasts of Magdala. (2)

10. ¶ And straightway he entered into a ship with his disciples and came into the parts of Dalmanutha. (1)

Chap. XVI.

1. The Pharisees also with the Sadducees came, and tempting, desired him that he would show them a sign (3) from heaven.

2. He answered and said unto them, When it is evening, ye say, *It will be* fair weather, for the sky is red.

3. And in the morning, *It will be* foul weather to-day; for the sky is red and lowering.
O, ye hypocrites, ye can discern the face of the sky; but can ye not *discern* the signs of the times?

11. And the Pharisees came forth, and began to question with him, seeking of him a sign from heaven, tempting him.

Omitted by some of the most ancient MSS.— Alford.

Chap. XII., from P. 55.

54. ¶ And he said also to the people, When ye see a cloud rise out of the west straightway ye say there cometh a shower: and so it is.

55. And when *ye see* the south wind blow ye say, There will be heat; and it cometh to pass.

56. *Ye* hypocrites, ye can discern the face of the sky and of the earth; but how is it that ye do not discern this time?

57. Yea, and why even of yourselves judge ye not what is right?

Continued P. 34.

4. A wicked and adulterous generation seeketh after a sign: and there shall no sign be given unto it but the sign of the prophet Jonas. (4)
And he left them and departed.

5. And when his disciples were come to the other side, they had forgotten to take bread.

6. ¶ Then Jesus said unto them, Take heed, and beware of the leaven of the Pharisees, and of the Sadducees.

7. And they reasoned among themselves, saying, *It is* because we have taken no bread.

8. *Which* when Jesus perceived, he said unto them, O, ye of little faith! Why reason ye among yourselves because ye have brought no bread?

9. Do ye not yet understand,

neither remember
the five loaves of the five thousand, and how many baskets ye took up?

12. And he sighed deeply in his spirit, and saith, Why doth this generation seek after a sign? Verily, I say unto you, there shall no sign be given unto this generation.

13. And he left them; and entering into the ship, again departed to the other side.

14. ¶ Now *the disciples* had forgotten to take bread:

neither had they in the ship with them more than one loaf.

15. And he charged them, saying, Take heed, beware of the leaven of Herod.

16. And they reasoned among themselves, saying, *It is* because we have no bread.

17. And when Jesus knew *it*, he said unto them,
Why reason ye, because ye have no bread? perceive ye not yet, neither understand?

have ye your heart yet hardened?
18. Having eyes, see ye not? and having ears, hear ye not?
And do ye not remember?
19. When I brake the five loaves among five thousand, how many

1) M. XIV. 22.   (2) M. XIV. 34.
(3) M. XII. 38; J. II. 18, P. 22; VI. 30, P. 77.
(4) M. XII. 39.

(1) Mk. VI. 45, P. 75.

baskets full of fragments took
ye up?
They say unto him, Twelve.

10. Neither the seven loaves of the four thousand, and how many baskets ye took up?

20. And when the seven among four thousand, how many baskets full of fragments took ye up?
And they said, Seven.

11. How is it that ye do not understand that I spake it not to you concerning bread, that ye should beware of the leaven of the Pharisees and of the Sadducees?
12. Then understood they how that he bade them not beware of the leaven of bread, but of the doctrine of the Pharisees and of the Sadducees.

21. And he said unto them, How is it that ye do not understand?

22. ¶ And he cometh to Bethsaida;
and they bring a blind man unto him, and besought him to touch him:
23. And he took the blind man by the hand, and led him out of the town; and when he had spit on his eyes, and put his hands upon him, he asked him if he saw aught.
24. And he looked up, and said, I see men as trees, walking.
25. After that, he put his hands again upon his eyes, and made him look up; and he was restored, and saw every man clearly.
26. And he sent him away to his house, saying, Neither go into the town: nor tell it to any in the town.

Chap. IX. from P. 75.

13. When Jesus came into the coasts of Cesarea Philippi,
he asked his disciples, saying, Whom do men say that I the Son of man am?
14. And they said, Some say that thou art John the Baptist: some, Elias: and others, Jeremias: or one of the prophets.
15. He saith unto them, But whom say ye that I am?
16. And Simon Peter answered, and said, Thou art the Christ,
the Son of the living God.
17. And Jesus answered, and said unto him, Blessed art thou

27. And Jesus went out, and his disciples, into the towns of Cesarea Philippi: and by the way, he asked his disciples, saying unto them, Whom do men say that I am?
28. And they answered, John the Baptist: But some say Elias; and others, One of the prophets.
29. And he saith unto them, But whom say ye that I am? And Peter answereth, and saith unto him, Thou art the Christ.

18. ¶ And it came to pass, as he was alone, praying, his disciples were with him: and he asked them, saying, Whom say the people that I am?
19. They answering, said, John the Baptist: but some say, Elias: and others say, That one of the old prophets is risen again.
20. He said unto them, But whom say ye that I am? Peter answering, said, The Christ of God.

See J. VI. 68, 69; P. 79.

Simon Barjona : for flesh and blood hath not revealed *it* unto thee, but my Father which is in heaven.

18. And I say also unto thee, That thou art Peter ; and upon this rock I will build my church : and the gates of hell shall not prevail against it.

19. And I will give unto thee the keys of the kingdom of heaven : and whatsoever thou shalt bind on earth shall be bound in heaven : and whatsoever thou shalt loose on earth shall be loosed in heaven. (2)

(1) See v. 23.

20. Then charged he his disciples that they should tell no man

that he was Jesus the Christ.

21. ¶ From that time forth began Jesus to show unto his disciples,

how that he must go unto Jerusalem, and suffer many things of the elders, and chief priests and scribes, and be killed, and be raised again the third day. (3)

22. Then Peter took him, and began to rebuke him,

saying, Be it far from thee, Lord : This shall not be unto thee.

23. But he turned

and said unto Peter, Get thee behind me, Satan : Thou art an offence unto me : for thou savorest not the things that be of God, but those that be of men. (4)

24. ¶ Then said Jesus unto his disciples, If any *man* will come after me, let him deny himself, and take up his cross, and follow me.

25. For whosoever will save his life, shall lose it ; and whosoever will lose his life, for my sake,

shall find it.

26. For what is a man profited if he shall gain the whole world, and lose his own soul ? or what shall a man give in exchange for his soul ?

27. For the Son of man shall come in the glory of his Father, with his angels : and then he shall reward every man according to his works.

---

30. And he charged them that they should tell no man

of him.

31. And he began to teach them that

the Son of man must suffer many things, and be rejected of the chief priests, and scribes, and be killed, and after three days rise again.

32. And he spake that saying openly. And Peter took him, and began to rebuke him.

33. But, when he had turned about and looked on his disciples, he rebuked Peter, saying, Get thee behind me, Satan : for thou savorest not the things that be of God ; but the things that be of men.

34. ¶ And when he had called the people *unto him*, with his disciples also, he said unto them ; Whosoever will come after me, let him deny himself, and take up his cross and follow me :

35. For whosoever will save his life, shall lose it : but whosoever shall lose his life for my sake, and the gospel's

the same shall save it.

36. For what shall it profit a man if he shall gain the whole world, and lose his own soul ?

37. Or what shall a man give in exchange for his soul ?

38. Whosoever therefore shall shall be ashamed of me and of my words in this adulterous and sinful generation ; of him also shall the Son of man be ashamed, when he cometh in the glory of his Father, with the holy angels.

---

21. And he straitly charged them, and commanded *them* to tell no man that thing :

22. Saying, The Son of man

must suffer many things ; and be rejected of the elders, and chief priests, and scribes ; and be slain ; and be raised the third day.

23. ¶ And he said to *them* all,

If any *man* will come after me, let him deny himself, and take up his cross daily, and follow me.

24. For whosoever will save his life shall lose it : but whosoever will lose his life for my sake,

the same shall save it.

25. For what is a man advantaged if he gain the whole world, and lose himself, or be cast away ?

26. For whosoever shall be ashamed of me, and of my words, of him shall the Son of man be ashamed, when he shall come in his own glory and *in his* Father's and of the holy angels.

(2) M. XVIII. 18 ; J. XX. 23, P. 182.
(3) M. XVII. 23. (4) *Vide* 18, 19.

28. Verily, I say unto you there be some standing here, which shall not taste of death, till they see the Son of man coming in his kingdom. (1)

CHAP. IX.

1. And he said unto them, Verily I say unto you, That there be some of them that stand here, which shall not taste of death, till they have seen the kingdom of God come with power.

Chap. IX. from P. 85.

27. But I tell you of a truth, There be some standing here, which shall not taste of death, till they see the kingdom of God.

See J. XXI. 22, 23, P. 184.

CHAP. XVII.

1. And after six days Jesus taketh Peter, James, and John his brother, and bringeth them up into an high mountain apart,

2. And was transfigured before them: and his face did shine as the sun: and his raiment was white as the light.

2. ¶ And after six days Jesus taketh *with him* Peter and James and John, and leadeth them up into an high mountain apart by themselves ; and he was transfigured before them,

28. ¶ And it came to pass, about an eight days after these sayings, he took Peter and John and James and went up into a mountain to pray.

29. And as he prayed the fashion of his countenance was altered, and his raiment *was* white *and* glistering.

3. And behold there appeared unto them Moses and Elias,

3. And his raiment became shining, exceeding white as snow : so as no fuller on earth can white them.

4. And there appeared unto them Elias with Moses :

talking with him.

and they were talking with Jesus.

30. And behold, there talked with him two men, which were Moses and Elias ;

31. Who appeared in glory, and spake of his decease which he should accomplish at Jerusalem.

32. But Peter and they that were with him were heavy with sleep : and when they were awake they saw his glory, and the two men that stood with him.

33. And it came to pass, as they departed from him, Peter said unto Jesus, Master, it is good for us to be here : and let us make three tabernacles : one for thee, one for Moses, and one for Elias : not knowing what he said.

4. Then answered Peter, and said unto Jesus, Lord, it is good for us to be here : if thou wilt let us make here three tabernacles : one for thee, and one for Moses and one for Elias.

5. And Peter answered and said to Jesus, Master, it is good for us to be here : and let us make three tabernacles ; one for thee, and one for Moses, and one for Elias.

6. For he wist not what to say ; for they were sore afraid.

5. While he yet spake, behold a bright cloud overshadowed them :
and behold, a voice out of the cloud, which said, This is my beloved Son, in whom I am well pleased :
hear ye him.

7. And there was a cloud that overshadowed them :
and a voice came out of the cloud, saying, This is my beloved Son,

34. While he thus spake, there came a cloud, and overshadowed them :
and they feared as they entered into the cloud.

35. And there came a voice out of the cloud, saying, This is my beloved Son,

hear him.

hear him.

6. And when the disciples heard *it*, they fell on their face and were sore afraid.

7. And Jesus came and touched them, and said, Arise, and be not afraid.

(1) J. XXL 22, 23, P. 184.

8. And when they had lifted up their eyes

they saw no man save Jesus only.

9. And as they came down from the mountain, Jesus charged them, saying, Tell the vision to no man until the Son of man be risen again from the dead.

8. And suddenly, when they had looked round about, they saw no man any more, save Jesus only with themselves.

9. And as they came down from the mountain, he charged them that they should tell no man what things they had seen, till the Son of man were risen from the dead.

10. And they kept that saying with themselves, questioning one with another what the rising from the dead should mean.

36. And when the voice was past

Jesus was found alone.

and they kept it close, and told no man, in those days, and of those things which they had seen.

10. And his disciples asked him, saying, Why then say the scribes that Elias must first come?

11. And Jesus answered, and said unto them, Elias truly shall first come, and restore all things.

11. ¶ And they asked him, saying, Why say the Scribes, that Elias must first come?

12. And he answered and told them, Elias verily cometh first, and restoreth all things : and how it is written of the Son of man, that he must suffer many things, and be set at naught.

12. But I say unto you, That Elias is come already, and they knew him not, and have done unto him whatsoever they listed.

Likewise also shall the Son of man suffer of them.

13. Then the disciples understood that he spake unto them of John the Baptist.

13. But I say unto you, that Elias is indeed come ;

and they have done unto him whatsoever they listed ; as it is written of him.

37. ¶ And it came to pass that on the next day, when they were come down from the hill,

14. ¶ And when they were come to the multitude,

14. ¶ And when he came to his disciples, he saw a great multitude about them, and the Scribes questioning with them.

15. And straightway all the people, when they beheld him were greatly amazed, and running to him, saluted him.

16. And he asked the Scribes, What question ye with them?

17. And one of the multitude answered, and said,

much people met him.

38. And behold, a man of the company cried out, saying,

there came to him a certain man, kneeling down to him, and saying,

15. Lord, have mercy on my son ;

for he is lunatick, and sore vexed : for oft times he falleth into the fire, and oft into the water. (1)

Master, I have brought unto thee my son

which hath a dumb spirit :

18. And wheresoever he taketh him, he teareth him, and he foameth, and gnasheth with his teeth, and pineth away :

Master, I beseech thee, look upon my son ; for he is my only child.

39. And, lo, a spirit taketh him, and he suddenly crieth out ;

and it teareth him that he foameth again, and bruising him hardly departeth from him.

ST. MATTHEW, XVII.	ST. MARK, IX.	ST. LUKE, IX., XVII.	ST. JOHN, VII.

ST. MATTHEW, XVII.

16. And I brought him to thy disciples, and they could not cure him.

17. Then Jesus answered and said,

O, faithless and perverse generation,

How long shall I be with you? How long shall I suffer you? Bring him hither to me.

(M. XVII. 15.)

18. And Jesus rebuked the devil:

and he departed out of him: and the child was cured from that very hour.

19. Then came the disciples to Jesus apart, and said, Why could not we cast him out?

20. And Jesus said unto them, Because of your unbelief; for verily I say unto you, If ye have faith as a grain of mustard seed, ye shall say unto this mountain, Remove hence to yonder place; (1)

ST. MARK, IX.

and I spake to thy disciples that they should cast him out; and they could not.

19. He answereth him and saith,

O, faithless generation,

How long shall I be with you? How long shall I suffer you? Bring him unto me.

20. And they brought him unto him: and when he saw him, straightway the spirit tare him: and he fell on the ground, and wallowed, foaming.

21. And he asked his father, How long is it ago since this came unto him?

And he said, Of a child.

22. And oft times it hath cast him into the fire, and into the waters, to destroy him: but if thou canst do anything, have compassion on us, and help us.

23. Jesus said unto him, If thou canst believe, all things *are* possible to him that believeth.

24. And straightway the father of the child cried out, and said with tears, Lord, I believe, help thou mine unbelief.

25. When Jesus saw that the people came running together, he rebuked the foul spirit,

saying unto him, *Thou* dumb and deaf spirit, I charge thee come out of him, and enter no more into him.

26. And *the spirit* cried, and rent him sore, and came out of him:

and he was as one dead: in so much that many said, He is dead.

27. But Jesus took him by the hand, and lifted him up; and he arose.

28. And when he was come into the house his disciples asked him privately,

Why could not we cast him out?

29. And he said unto them,

(Mk. XI. 23 P. 126.)

ST. LUKE, IX., XVII.

40. And I besought thy disciples to cast him out; and they could not.

41. And Jesus answering, said,

O, faithless and perverse generation,

How long shall I be with you? and suffer you? Bring thy son hither.

42. And as he was yet a coming, the devil threw him down, and tare *him.*

And Jesus rebuked the unclean spirit,

and healed the child;

and delivered him again to his father.

43. ¶ And they were all amazed at the mighty power of God.

Verse concluded P. 89.

Chap. XVII., from P. 96.

5. And the apostles said unto the Lord, Increase our faith.

6. And the Lord said,

If ye had faith as a grain of mustard seed, ye might say unto this sycamine tree, Be thou plucked up by the root, and be thou planted in the sea;

(1) M. XXI. 21.

and it shall remove : and nothing shall be impossible unto you.

21. How be it this kind goeth not out but by prayer and fasting.

22. ¶ And while they abode in Galilee,

Jesus said unto them,
The Son of man shall be betrayed into the hands of men :
23. And they shall kill him, and the third day he shall be raised again. (1)
And they were exceeding sorry.

24. ¶ And when they were come to Capernaum,
they that received tribute *money* came to Peter, and said, Doth not your master pay tribute ?
25. He saith, Yes.
And when he was come into the house, Jesus prevented him, saying, What thinkest thou, Simon? Of whom do the kings of the earth take custom, or tribute? Of their own children, or of strangers ?
26. Peter saith unto him, of strangers? Jesus saith unto him, Then are the children free.
27. Notwithstanding, lest we should offend them, go thou to the sea, and cast an hook, and take up the fish that first cometh up : and when thou hast opened his mouth thou shalt find a piece of money : That take, and give unto them for me and thee.

CHAP. XVIII.

1. At the same time came the disciples unto Jesus, saying, Who is the greatest in the kingdom of heaven ?

2. And Jesus called a little

(1 M. XVI. 21 ; XX. 18.

---

this kind can come forth by nothing, but by prayer and fasting.

30. ¶ And they departed thence, and passed through Galilee : and he would not that any man should know *it*.
31. For he taught his disciples, and said unto them,
The Son of man is delivered into the hands of men ; (1)
and they shall kill him : and after that he is killed, he shall rise the third day.
32. But they understood not that saying,

and were afraid to ask him.
33. ¶ And he came to Capernaum :

and, being in the house,

he asked them, What was it that ye disputed among yourselves, by the way ?

34. But they held their peace, for, by the way, they had disputed among themselves who *should be* the greatest.

35. And he sat down, and called the twelve, and saith unto them, If any man desire to be first, *the same* shall be last of all, and servant of all. (2)

36. And he took a child, and

(1) Mk. VIII. 31, P. 85.
(2) Mk. X. 42, 44, P. 119.

---

and it should obey you.
Continued P. 96.

Ch. IX. 43 continued from P. 88.
43. But while they wondered every one at all things which Jesus did, he said unto his disciples,

44. Let these sayings sink down into your ears :
for the Son of man shall be delivered into the hands of men.

45. But they understood not this saying, and it was hid from them, that they perceived it not : and they feared to

ask him of that saying.

46. ¶ Then there arose a reasoning among them, which of them should be greatest.

47. And Jesus, perceiving the thought of their heart,
took a child, and set him

child unto him, and set him in the midst of them ;

3. And said, Verily I say unto you, Except ye be converted, and become as little children, ye shall not enter into the kingdom of heaven.

4. Whosoever therefore shall humble himself as this little child, the same is greatest in the kingdom of heaven.

5. And whoso shall receive one such little child in my name receiveth me.

---

set him in the midst of them ; and when he had taken him in his arms he said unto them,

---

by him ;

48. And said unto them,

---

37. Whosoever shall receive one of such children in my name, receiveth me :
and whosoever shall receive me, receiveth not me, but him that sent me.

38. ¶ And John answered him, saying, Master, we saw one casting out devils in thy name ; and he followeth not us : and we forbad him, because he followeth not us.

39. But Jesus said, Forbid him not ;
for there is no man which shall do a miracle in my name, that can lightly speak evil of me.

40. For he that is not against us
is on our part.

41. (see P. 55.)
From P. 56.

Whosoever shall receive this child in my name, receiveth me: and whosoever shall receive me receiveth him that sent me : for he that is least among you all, the same shall be great.

49. ¶ And John answered and said, Master, we saw one casting out devils in thy name ;
and we forbad him, because he followeth not with us.

50. And Jesus said unto him, Forbid him not,

for he that is not against us is for us.

Continued P. 117.

---

6. But whoso shall offend one of these little ones which believe in me, it were better for him that a millstone were hanged about his neck, and that he were drowned in the depth of the sea.

7. ¶ Woe unto the world because of offences ! For it must needs be that offences come ; but woe to that man by whom the offence cometh !

---

42. And whosoever shall offend one of these little ones that believe in me, it is better for him that a millstone were hanged about his neck, and he were cast into the sea.

CHAP. XVII. from P. 95.

2. It were better for him that a millstone were hanged about his neck, and he cast into the sea, than that he should offend one of these little ones.

1. Then said he unto the disciples, It is impossible but that offences will come : but woe unto him through whom they come.

} Transposed.

Continued P. 96.

CHAP. X. (see P. 57.)

CHAP. XI. (see P. 37.)

CHAP. XII. (see P. 54.

CHAP. XIII. (see P. 60.)

CHAP. XIV. ((see P. 123.

---

8. Wherefore if thy hand or thy foot* offend thee, cut them off, and cast them from thee ;

*₊M. v. 30, Mk. IX. 45., P. 91.

---

43. And if thy hand offend thee, cut it off ;

it is better for thee to enter into life halt or maimed, rather than
having two hands, or two feet, to be cast into everlasting fire.

it is better for thee to enter into life
maimed, than
having two hands to go into hell ; into the fire that never shall be quenched.

44. Where their worm dieth not, and the fire is not quenched.

45. And if thy foot offend thee, cut it off : it is better for thee to enter halt into life, than having two feet, to be cast into hell fire; into the fire that never shall be quenched :

46. [Where their worm dieth not ; and the fire is not quenched :]†

[† Wanting in most of the ancient MSS.—Alford.]

9. And if thine eye offend thee, pluck it out, and cast it from thee : it is better for thee to enter life (1)
with one eye, rather than having two eyes to be cast into hell fire.

47. And if thine eye offend thee, pluck it out : it is better for thee to enter into the kingdom of God
with one eye, than, having two eyes, to be cast into hell fire :

48. Where their worm dieth not, and the fire is not quenched.

49. For every one shall be salted with fire ; and every sacrifice shall be salted with salt.

50. Salt is good ; but if the salt have lost his saltness, wherewith will ye season it ? (1) Have salt in yourselves, and have peace one with another.

(1) L. XIV. 34. P. 33　M. V 13.

10. Take heed that ye despise not one of these little ones : for I say unto you that in heaven their angels do always behold the face of my Father which is in heaven.

11. [For the Son of man is come to save that which was lost.]* (2)

*[Not found in our most ancient MSS.—Alford.]

For Chap. X. see P. 97.

L. XIX. 10, P. 121.

CHAP. XV. (from P. 33.)

1. Then drew near unto him all the publicans and sinners for to hear him.

2. And the Pharisees and scribes murmured, saying, This man receiveth sinners and eateth with them.

3. ¶ And he spake this parable unto them, saying,

3. What man of you having an hundred sheep, if he lose one of them, doth not leave the ninety and nine in the wilderness, and go after that which is lost, until he find it ?

12. How think ye, If a man have an hundred sheep, and one of them be gone astray ; doth he not leave the ninety and nine, and goeth into the mountains, and seeketh that which is gone astray ?

13. And if so be that he find it, verily I say unto you, He rejoiceth more of that sheep than

5. And when he hath found it, he layeth it on his shoulders, rejoicing.

(1) M. V. 29.
(2) L. XIX. 10. P. 121.

of the ninety and nine which went not astray.

14. Even so it is not the will of your Father which is in heaven that one of these little ones should perish.

Continued P. 96.

6. And when he cometh home, he calleth *his* friends and neighbours, saying unto them, Rejoice with me, for I have found my sheep which was lost.

7. I say unto you, That likewise joy shall be in heaven over one sinner that repenteth more than over ninety and nine just persons, which need no repentance.

8. ¶ Either what woman having ten pieces of silver, if she lose one piece, doth not light a candle, and sweep the house, and seek diligently till she find *it* ?

9. And when she hath found *it*, she calleth *her* friends and *her* neighbours together, saying, Rejoice with me ; for I have found the piece which I had lost.

10. Likewise I say unto you, There is joy in the presence of the angels of God, over one sinner that repenteth.

11. ¶ And he said, A certain man had two sons :

12. And the younger said to *his* father, Father give me the portion of goods that falleth *to me.* And he divided unto them his living.

13. And not many days after, the younger son gathered all together, and took his journey into a far country, and there wasted his substance with riotous living.

14. And when he had spent all, there arose a mighty famine in that land . and he began to be in want.

15. And he went and joined himself to a citizen in that country ; and he sent him into his field to feed swine.

16. And he would fain have filled his belly with the husks that the swine did eat : and no man gave unto him.

17. And when he came to himself he said, How many hired servants of my father's have bread enough, and to spare ; and I perish with hunger !

18. I will arise and go to my father, and will say unto him, Father, I have sinned against heaven, and before thee,

19. And am no more worthy to be called thy son : make me as one of thy hired servants.

20. And he arose and came to his father. But when he was a great way off, his father saw him, and had compassion,

93

and ran ; and fell on his neck ; and kissed him.

21. And the son said unto him, Father, I have sinned against heaven, and in thy sight, and am no more worthy to be called thy son.

22. But the Father said to his servants, Bring forth the best robe, and put *it* on him ; and put a ring on his hand, and shoes on *his* feet :

23. And bring hither the fatted calf, and kill *it ;* and let us eat, and be merry :

24. For this my son was dead, and is alive again ; he was lost, and is found. And they began to be merry :

25. Now his elder son was in the field : and as he came, and drew nigh to the house, he heard music and dancing.

26. And he called one of the servants and asked what these things meant.

27. And he said unto him, Thy brother is come ; and thy father hath killed the fatted calf ; because he hath received him safe and sound.

28. And he was angry ; and would not go in : therefore came his father out, and entreated him.

29. And he answering said to *his* father, Lo ! these many years do I serve thee, neither transgressed I at any time thy commandment ; and yet thou never gavest me a kid ; that I might make merry with my friends :

30. But as soon as this thy son was come, which hath devoured thy living with harlots ; thou hast killed for him the fatted calf.

31. And he said unto him, Son, thou art ever with me ; and all that I have is thine.

32. It was meet that we should make merry, and be glad : for this thy brother was dead, and is alive again : he was lost, and is found.

Chap. XVI.

1. And he said also unto his disciples, There was a certain rich man which had a steward ; and the same was accused unto him that he had wasted his goods.

2. And he called him, and

said unto him, How is it that I hear this of thee? give an account of thy stewardship; for thou mayest be no longer steward.

3. Then the steward said within himself, What shall I do? for my Lord taketh away from me the stewardship. I cannot dig; to beg I am ashamed.

4. I am resolved what to do: that when I am put out of the stewardship, they may receive me into their houses.

5. So he called every one of his Lord's debtors *unto him;* and said unto the first, How much owest thou unto my Lord?

6. And he said, an hundred measures of oil. And he said unto him, Take thy bill and sit down quickly, and write fifty.

7. Then said he to another, And how much owest thou? And he said, An hundred measures of wheat. And he said unto him, Take thy bill, and write fourscore.

8. And the Lord commended the unjust steward, because he had done wisely: for the children of this world are in their generation wiser than the children of light.

9. And I say unto you, Make to yourselves friends of the mammon of unrighteousness that, when ye fail, they may receive you into everlasting habitations.

10. He that is faithful in that which is least, is faithful also in much: and he that is unjust in the least, is unjust also in much.

11. If therefore ye have not been faithful in the unrighteous mammon, who will commit to your trust the true *riches?*

12. And if ye have not been faithful in that which is another man's, who shall give you that which is your own?

13   *(see P. 38.)*

14. And the Pharisees also, who were covetous, heard all these things, and they derided him.

15. And he said unto them, Ye are they which justify yourselves before men: but God knoweth your hearts: for that which is highly esteemed among men is abominable in the sight of God.

16. The law and the prophets *were* until John. Since that time the kingdom of God is preached, and every man presseth into it.   M. XI. 12, 13.

17. And it is easier for heaven and earth to pass, than one title of the law to fail. M. V. 18.

18. *See P. 110.*

19. ¶ There was a certain rich man which was clothed in purple and fine linen, and fared sumptuously every day.

20. And there was a certain beggar named Lazarus, which was laid at his gate, full of sores,

21. And desiring to be fed with the crumbs which fell from the rich man's table. Moreover the dogs came and licked his sores.

22. And it came to pass that the beggar died ; and was carried by the angels into Abraham's bosom. The rich man also died ; and was buried.

23. And in hell he left up his eyes, being in torments : and seeth Abraham afar off : and Lazarus in his bosom.

24. And he cried and said, Father Abraham, have mercy on me ; and send Lazarus ; that he may dip the tip of his finger in water ; and cool my tongue : for I am tormented in this flame.

25. But Abraham said ; Son, remember that thou in thy lifetime receivedst thy good things ; and likewise Lazarus evil things : but now he is comforted ; and thou art tormented :

26. And beside all this ; between us and you there is a great gulph fixed : so that they which would pass from hence to you, cannot : neither can they pass to us, that *would come* from thence.

27. Then he said ; I pray thee, therefore, Father, that thou wouldest send him to my father's house ;

28. For I have five brethren : that he may testify unto them : lest they also come into this place of torment.

29. Abraham saith unto him ; They have Moses and the prophets : let them hear them.

30. And he said : Nay, Father Abraham ; but if one went unto them from the dead, they will repent.

31. And he said unto him : If they hear not Moses and the prophets ; neither will they be persuaded, though one rose from the dead.

ST. MATTHEW, XVIII.

ST. MARK, X.

ST. LUKE, XVII.

CHAP. XVII.

1. } see P. 90.
2.

15. ¶ Moreover if thy brother shall trespass against thee, go and tell him his fault between thee and him alone : if he shall hear thee thou hast gained thy brother.

16. But if he will not hear thee, then take with thee one or two more, that in the mouth of two or three witnesses every word may be established.

17. And if he shall neglect to hear them, tell it unto the church; but if ye neglect to hear the church let him be unto thee as an heathen and a publican.

18. Verily, I say unto you, Whatsoever ye shall bind on earth shall be bound in heaven : and whatsoever ye shall loose on earth shall be loosed in heaven.

M. XVI. 19.

19. Again I say unto you, That if two of you shall agree on earth as touching anything that they shall ask, it shall be done for them of my Father which is in heaven.

20. For where two or three are gathered together in my name, there am I in the midst of them.

21. ¶ Then came Peter to him, and said, Lord, how oft shall my brother sin against me, and I forgive him? Till seven times?

22. Jesus saith unto him, I say not unto thee, until seven times : but, Until seventy times seven.

3. ¶ Take heed to yourselves : If thy brother trespass against thee, rebuke him : and if he repent forgive him.

4. And if he trespass against thee seven times in a day, and seven times in a day turn again to thee, saying, I repent, thou shalt forgive him.

5. } continued P. 88.
6.

7. But which of you having a servant ploughing or feeding cattle, will say unto him by and by, when he is come from the field, Go and sit down to meat?

8. And will not rather say unto him, Make ready wherewith I may sup; and gird thyself, and serve me, till I have eaten and drunken : and afterward thou shalt eat and drink?

9. Doth he thank that servant because he did those things which were commanded him? I trow not.

10. So likewise ye, when ye shall have done all things which are commanded you, say, We are unprofitable servants; we have done that which was our duty to do.

Continued P. 119.

St. MATTHEW, XIX.   St. MARK, X.   St. LUKE, XVII.   St. JOHN, VII.

23. ¶ Therefore is the kingdom of heaven likened unto a certain king, which would take account of his servants.

24. And when he had begun to reckon, one was brought unto him which owed him ten thousand talents.

25. But forasmuch as he had not to pay, his lord commanded him to be sold, and his wife, and children, and all that he had; and payment to be made.

26. The servant therefore fell down and worshipped him, saying, Lord, have patience with me, and I will pay thee all.

27. Then the lord of that servant was moved with compassion, and loosed him, and forgave him the debt.

28. But the same servant went out and found one of his fellowservants which owed him an hundred pence; and he laid hands on him, and took *him* by the throat, saying, Pay me that thou owest.

29. And his fellowservant fell down at his feet, and besought him, saying, Have patience with me, and I will pay thee all.

30. And he would not: but went and cast him into prison, till he should pay the debt.

31. So when his fellowservants saw what was done, they were very sorry; and came and told unto their lord all that was done.

32. Then his lord, after that he had called him, said unto him, O thou wicked servant, I forgave thee all that debt, because thou desiredst me:

33. Shouldst not thou also have had compassion on thy fellowservant, even as I had pity on thee?

34. And his lord was wroth; and delivered him to the tormentors till he should pay all that was due unto him.

35. So also shall my heavenly Father do unto you, if ye from your hearts forgive not everyone his brother their trespasses.

CHAP. XIX.

1. And it came to pass, *that* when

CHAP. X]

1. And he arose from thence
Continued P. 109.

From P. 81.
2. Now the Jews' feast of tabernacles was at hand.

3. His brethren therefore said

ST. MATTHEW, XIX.	ST. MARK, X.	ST. LUKE, XVII.	ST. JOHN, VII.

Jesus had finished these sayings he departed from Galilee.

Continued P. 109.

(Third Visit.)

unto him, depart hence, and go into Judea, that thy disciples also may see the works that thou doest.

4. For *there is* no man *that* doeth anything in secret, and he himself seeketh to be known openly. If thou do these things shew thyself to the world.

5. For neither did his brethren believe in him.

6. Then Jesus said unto them, My time is not yet come: but your time is alway ready.

7. The world cannot hate you: but me it hateth; because I testify of it, that the works thereof are evil.

8. Go ye up unto this feast: I go not up yet unto this feast: for my time is not yet full come.

9. When he had said these words unto them, he abode *still* in Galilee.

10. ¶ But when his brethren were gone up, then went he also up unto the feast, not openly, but as it were in secret.

11. Then the Jews sought him at the feast, and said, Where is he?

12. And there was much murmuring among the people concerning him: for some said, He is a good man: others said, Nay, but he deceiveth the people.

13. Howbeit no man spake openly of him for fear of the Jews.

14. ¶ Now about the midst of the feast Jesus went up into the temple, and taught.

15. And the Jews marvelled, saying, How knoweth this man letters, having never learned?

16. Jesus answered them, and said, My doctrine is not mine, but his that sent me.

17. If any man will do his will, he shall know of the doctrine, whether it be of God, or *whether* I speak of myself.

18. He that speaketh of himself seeketh his own glory: but he that seeketh his glory that sent him, the same is true, and no unrighteousness is in him.

19. Did not Moses give you the law, and *yet* none of you keepeth the law? Why go ye about to kill me?

20. The people answered, and said, Thou hast a devil: Who goeth about to kill thee?

21. Jesus answered, and said unto them, I have done one work, and ye all marvel.

22. Moses therefore gave unto you circumcision ; (not because it is of Moses, but of the fathers ;) and ye on the sabbath day circumcise a man.

23. If a man on the sabbath day receive circumcision, that the law of Moses should not be broken ; are ye angry at me, because I have made a man every whit whole on the sabbath day ?

M. XII. 10.

24. Judge not according to the appearance, but judge righteous judgment.

25. Then said one of them of Jerusalem, Is not this he whom they seek to kill?

26. But, lo ! he speaketh boldly, and they say nothing unto him. Do the rulers know indeed that this is the very Christ?

27. Howbeit we know this man, whence he is : but when Christ cometh, no man knoweth whence he is.

28. Then cried Jesus in the temple, as he taught, saying, Ye both know me, and ye know whence I am : and I am not come of myself : but he that sent me is true, whom ye know not.

29. But I know him : for I am from him, and he hath sent me.

30. Then they sought to take him : but no man laid hands on him ; because his hour was not yet come.

31. And many of the people believed on him, and said, When Christ cometh, will he do more miracles than these which this *man* hath done ?

32. ¶ The Pharisees heard that the people murmured such things concerning him ; and the Pharisees and the chief priests sent officers to take him.

33. Then said Jesus unto them, Yet a little while am I with you ; and *then* I go unto him that sent me.

34. Ye shall seek me, and shall not find *me:* and where I am *thither* ye cannot come.

35. Then said the Jews among themselves, Whither will he go, that we shall not find him ? Will he go unto the dispersed among the Gentiles ?

36. What *manner of* saying is this that he said, Ye shall seek me, and shall not find *me:* and where I am, *thither* ye cannot come ?

37. In the last day, that great *day* of the feast, Jesus stood, and cried, saying, If any man thirst,

let him come unto me and drink.

38. He that believeth on me, as the scripture hath said, out of his belly shall flow rivers of living water.

39. (But this spake he of the spirit, which they that believe on him should receive : for the Holy Ghost was not yet *given:* because that Jesus was not yet glorified.)

40. ¶ Many of the people therefore, when they heard this saying, said, Of a truth this is the Prophet.

41. Others said, This is the Christ. But others said, Shall Christ come out of Galilee?

M. II, 1.   42. Hath not the scripture said that Christ cometh of the seed of David, and out of the town of Bethlehem, where David was?

43. So there was a division among the people because of him.

44. And some of them would have taken him ; but no man laid hands on him.

45. ¶ Then came the officers to the chief priests and Pharisees; and they said unto them, Why have ye not brought him?

46. The officers answered, Never man spake like this man.

47. Then answered them the Pharisees, Are ye also deceived?

48. Have any of the rulers, or of the Pharisees believed on him?

49. But this people who knoweth not the law are cursed.

50. Nicodemus saith unto them, (he that came to Jesus by night, being one of them,)

51. Doth our law judge *any* man before it hear him, and know what he doeth?

52. They answered and said unto him, Art thou also of Galilee? Search, and look : for out of Galilee ariseth no prophet.

53. And every man went unto his own house.

CHAP. VIII.

See note next page.

1. Jesus went unto the mount of Olives.

2. And early in the morning he came again into the temple : and all the people came unto him : and he sat down and taught them.

3. And the scribes and Pharisees brought unto him a woman taken in adultery : and when they had set her in the midst,

101

ST. MATTHEW, XIX.   ST. MARK, X.   ST. LUKE, XVII.   ST. JOHN, VIII.

4. They say unto him, Master, this woman was taken in adultery, in the very act.

5. Now Moses in the law commanded us that such should be stoned : but what sayest thou ?

6. This they said tempting him, that they might have to accuse him. But Jesus stooped down, and with *his* finger wrote on the ground : *as tho' he heard them not.*

7. So when they continued asking him, he lifted up himself, and said unto them, He that is without sin among you, let him first cast a stone at her.

8. And again he stooped down, and wrote on the ground.

9. And they which heard *it*, being convinced by *their own* conscience, went out one by one, beginning at the eldest, *even* unto the last : and Jesus was left alone, and the woman standing in the midst.

10. When Jesus had lifted up himself, and saw none but the woman, he said unto her, Woman, where are those thine accusers ? Hath no man condemned thee ?

11. She said, No man, Lord. And Jesus said unto her, Neither do I condemn thee : Go ; and sin no more.

12. ¶ Then spake Jesus again unto them, saying, I am the light of the world : he that followeth me shall not walk in darkness, but shall have the light of life.

13. The Pharisees therefore said unto him, Thou bearest record of thyself ; thy record is not true.

14. Jesus answered and said unto them, Though I bear record of myself, *yet* my record is true : for I know whence I came, and whither I go. But ye cannot tell whence I come, and whither I go.

15. Ye judge after the flesh. I judge no man.

16. And yet if I judge, my judgment is true : for I am not alone ; but I and the Father that sent me.

17. It is also written in your law, that the testimony of two men is true.

18. I am one that bear witness of myself, and the Father that sent me beareth witness of me.

19. Then said they unto him, Where is thy Father ? Jesus

[Wanting in the best ancient MSS. The Cambridge is the only one which contains it. —Alford.]

St. MATTHEW, XIX.   St. MARK, X.   St. LUKE, XVII.   St. JOHN, VIII.

answered, Ye neither know me nor my Father: If ye had known me, ye should have known my Father also.

20. These words spake Jesus in the treasury, as he taught in the temple: and no man laid hands on him; for his hour was not yet come.

21. Then said Jesus again unto them, I go my way, and ye shall seek me, and shall die in your sins: whither I go, ye cannot come?

22. Then said the Jews, Will he kill himself? Because he saith, Whither I go, ye cannot come?

23. And he said unto them, Ye are from beneath: I am from above. Ye are of this world: I am not of this world.

24. I said therefore unto you, that ye shall die in your sins: for if ye believe not that I am *he*, ye shall die in your sins.

25. Then said they unto him, Who art thou? And Jesus said unto them, [Even *the same* that I said unto you from the beginning.]

["*In every deed that same that I also speak unto you*"—*Alford.*]

26. I have many things to say, and to judge of you: but he that sent me is true; and I speak to the world those things which I have heard of him.

27. They understood not that he spake to them of the Father.

28. Then said Jesus unto them, When ye have lifted up the Son of man, then shall ye know that I am *he* and *that* I do nothing of myself: but as my Father hath taught me, I speak these things.

29. And he that sent me is with me. The Father hath not left me alone; for I do always those things that please him.

30. As he spake these words many believed on him.

31. Then said Jesus to those Jews which believed on him, If ye continue in my word, *then* are ye my disciples indeed:

32. And ye shall know the truth, and the truth shall make you free.

33. ¶ They answered him, We be Abraham's seed, and were never in bondage to any man: How sayest thou, Ye shall be made free?

34. Jesus answered them, Verily

verily, I say unto you, Whosoever committeth sin is the servant of sin.

35. And the servant abideth not in the house for ever : *but* the Son abideth ever.

36. If the Son therefore shall make you free, ye shall be free indeed.

37. I know that ye are Abraham's seed : but ye seek to kill me because my word hath no place in you.

38. I speak that which I have seen with my Father : and ye do that which ye have seen with your father.

39. They answered, and said unto him, Abraham is our father. Jesus saith unto them, If ye were Abraham's children, ye would do the works of Abraham.

40. But now ye seek to kill me, a man that hath told you the truth, which I have heard of God : this did not Abraham.

41. Ye do the deeds of your father. Then said they to him, We be not born of fornication. We have one father, *even* God.

42. Jesus said unto them, If God were your father, ye would love me : for I proceeded forth from God : neither came I of myself ; but he sent me.

43. Why do ye not understand my speech? *Even* because ye cannot hear my word.

44. Ye are of *your* father the devil ; and the lusts of your father ye will do. He was a murderer from the beginning, and abode not in the truth, because there is no truth in him. When he speaketh a lie, he speaketh of his own : for he is a liar, and the father of it.

45. And because I tell *you* the truth ye believe me not.

46. Which of you convinceth me of sin? And if I say the truth, why do ye not believe me?

47. He that is of God heareth God's words ; Ye therefore hear *them* not, because ye are not of God.

48. Then answered the Jews, and said unto him, Say we not well that thou art a Samaritan, and hast a devil?

49. Jesus answered, I have not a devil, but I honour my Father,

and ye do dishonour me.

50. And I seek not mine own glory; there is one that seeketh and judgeth.

51. Verily, verily, I say unto you, If a man keep my saying, he shall never see death.

52. Then said the Jews unto him, Now we know that thou hast a devil. Abraham is dead, and the prophets; and thou sayest, If a man keep my saying, he shall never taste of death.

53. Art thou greater than our father Abraham, which is dead? And the prophets are dead: whom makest thou thyself?

54. Jesus answered, If I honour myself, my honour is nothing. It is my Father that honoureth me; of whom ye say that he is your God:

55. Yet ye have not known him: and if I should say, I know him not, I shall be a liar like unto you: but I know him, and keep his saying.

56. Your father Abraham rejoiced to see my day; and he saw it, and was glad.

L. III. 23. P. 16.

57. Then said the Jews unto him, Thou art not yet fifty years old, and hast thou seen Abraham?

58. Jesus said unto them, Verily, verily, I say unto you, Before Abraham was, I am.

59. Then took they up stones to cast at him: but Jesus hid himself, and went out of the temple; going through the midst of them: and so passed by.

CHAP. IX.

1. And as Jesus passed by, he saw a man which was blind from his birth.

2. And his disciples asked him, saying, Master, who did sin, this man or his parents, that he was born blind?

3. Jesus answered, Neither hath this man sinned, nor his parents: but that the works of God should be made manifest in him.

4. I must work the works of him that sent me while it is day. The night cometh, when no man can work.

5. As long as I am in the world, I am the light of the world.

6. When he had thus spoken he spat on the ground, and made clay of the spittle; and he anointed the eyes of the blind man with the clay:

7. And said unto him, Go, wash in the pool of Siloam, (which is by interpretation, Sent.) He went his way therefore and washed; and came seeing.

8. ¶ The neighbours therefore, and they which before had seen him that he was blind, said, Is not this he that sat and begged?

9. Some said, This is he. Others said, He is like him. But he said, I am he.

10. Therefore said they unto him, How were thine eyes opened?

11. He answered, and said, A man that is called Jesus made clay and anointed mine eyes, and said unto me, Go to the pool of Siloam, and wash. And I went, and washed; and I received sight.

12. Then said they unto him, Where is he? He said, I know not.

13. ¶ They brought to the Pharisees him that aforetime was blind.

14. And it was the sabbath day when Jesus made the clay, and opened his eyes.

15. Then again the Pharisees also asked him, how he had received his sight. He said unto them, He put clay upon mine eyes: and I washed, and do see.

16. Therefore, said some of the Pharisees, this man is not of God, because he keepeth not the sabbath day. Others said, How can a man that is a sinner do such miracles? And there was a division among them.

17. They say unto the blind man again, What sayest thou of him, That he hath opened thine eyes? He said, He is a Prophet.

18. But the Jews did not believe concerning him, that he had been blind and received his sight, until they called the parents of him that had received his sight.

19. And they asked them, saying, Is this your son, who ye say was born blind? How then doth he now see?

20. His parents answered them, and said, We know that this is our son, and that he was born blind:

21. But by what means he now

seeth, we know not; or who hath opened his eyes we know not. He is of age: ask him: he shall speak for himself.

22. These *words* spake his parents, because they feared the Jews. For the Jews had agreed already, that if any man did confess that he was Christ he should be put out of the synagogue.

23. Therefore said his parents, he is of age, ask him.

24. Then again called they the man that was blind, and said unto him, Give God the praise: we know that this man is a sinner.

25. He answered and said, Whether he be a sinner *or no*, I know not. One thing I know, that whereas I was blind, now I see.

26. Then said they unto him again, What did he to thee? How opened he thine eyes?

27. He answered them, I have told you already, and ye did not hear. Wherefore would ye hear *it* again? Will ye also be his disciples?

28. Then they reviled him, and said, Thou art his disciple; but we are Moses' disciples.

29. We know that God spake unto Moses: *as for* this *fellow*, we know not from whence he is.

30. The man answered and said unto them, Why herein is a marvellous thing, that ye know not from whence he is, and *yet* he hath opened mine eyes.

31. Now we know that God heareth not sinners: but if any man be a worshipper of God, and doeth his will, him he heareth.

32. Since the world began was it not heard that any one opened the eyes of one that was born blind?

33. If this man were not of God, he could do nothing.

34. They answered and said unto him, Thou wast altogether born in sins, and dost thou teach us? And they cast him out.

35. Jesus heard that they had cast him out: and when he had found him, said unto him, Dost thou believe on the Son of God?

36. He answered and said, Who is he, Lord, that I might believe on him?

37. And Jesus said unto him, Thou hast both seen him, and it is he that talketh with thee.

38. And he said, Lord, I believe, and he worshipped him.

39. ¶ And Jesus said, For judgment I am come into this world, that they which see not might see : and that they which see might be made blind.

40. And *some* of the Pharisees which were with him heard these words, and said unto him, Are we blind also ?

41. Jesus said unto them, If ye were blind, ye should have no sin ; but now ye say, We see : therefore your sin remaineth.

Chap. X.

1. Verily, verily, I say unto you, He that entereth not by the door, into the sheepfold, but climbeth up some other way, the same is a thief and a robber.

2. But he that entereth in by the door is the shepherd of the sheep.

3. To him the porter openeth, and the sheep hear his voice : and he calleth his own sheep by name, and leadeth them out.

4. And when he putteth forth his own sheep he goeth before them, and the sheep follow him, for they know his voice.

5. And a stranger will they not follow ; but will flee from him : for they know not the voice of strangers.

6. This parable spake Jesus unto them : but they understood not what things they were which he spake unto them.

7. Then said Jesus unto them again, Verily, verily, I say unto you, I am the door of the sheep.

8. All that ever came before me are thieves and robbers : but the sheep did not hear them.

9. I am the door : by me if any man enter in, he shall be saved : and shall go in and out, and find pasture.

10. The thief cometh not but for to steal, and to kill, and to destroy. I am come that they might have life, and that they might have *it* more abundantly.

11. I am the good shepherd. The good shepherd giveth his life for the sheep.

12. But he that is an hireling, and not the shepherd, whose

own the sheep are not, seeth the wolf coming, and leaveth the sheep, and fleeth; and the wolf catcheth them; and scattereth the sheep.

13. The hireling fleeth because he is an hireling, and careth not for the sheep.

14. I am the good shepherd, and know my *sheep;* and am known of mine.

15. As the Father knoweth me, even so know I the Father: and I lay down my life for the sheep.

16. And other sheep I have, but not of this fold: them also I must bring, and they shall hear my voice: and there shall be one fold, *and* one shepherd.

17. Therefore doth my Father love me; because I lay down my life; that I might take it again.

18. No man taketh it from me; but I lay it down of myself. I have power to lay it down: and I have power to take it again. This commandment have I received of my Father.

19. ¶ There was a division therefore again among the Jews for these sayings.

20. And many of them said, He hath a devil and is mad. Why hear ye him?

21. Others said, These are not the words of him that hath a devil. Can a devil open the eyes of the blind?

J. X. 40. 22. ¶ And it was at Jerusalem the feast of dedication; and it was winter.

M. XIX. 1. 23. And Jesus walked in the temple in Solomon's porch.

24. Then came the Jews round about him, and said unto him, How long dost thou make us to doubt? If thou be the Christ tell us plainly.

25. Jesus answered them; I told you and ye believed not. The works that I do in my Father's name, they bear witness of me.

26. But ye believe not; because ye are not of my sheep; as I said unto you.

27. My sheep hear my voice; and I know them, and they fellow me.

28. And I give unto them eternal life: and they shall never perish, neither shall any *man* pluck them out of my hand.

29. My father, which gave *them* me, is greater than all: and no *man* is able to pluck *them* out of my Father's hand.

30. I and *my* Father are one.

31. Then the Jews took up stones again to stone him.

32. Jesus answered them, Many good works have I showed you from my Father: for which of those works do ye stone me?

33. The Jews answered him, saying, For a good work we stone thee not: but for blasphemy; and because that thou, being a man, makest thyself God.

34. Jesus answered them, Is it not written in your law, I said, Ye are gods?

35. If he called them gods, unto whom the word of God came; and the scripture cannot be broken;

36. Say ye of him whom the Father hath sanctified, and sent into the world, Thou blasphemest, because I said, I am the Son of God?

37. If I do not the works of my Father, believe me not.

38. But if I do; though ye believe not me; believe the works: that ye may know and believe that the Father is in me, and I in him.

39. Therefore they sought again to take him: but he escaped out of their hand.

40. And went away again beyond Jordan, unto the place where John at first baptized: and there he abode.

41. And many resorted unto him,

and said, John did no miracle; but all things that John spake of this man were true.

42. And many believed on him there.

For Chap. XI. see P. 111.

Continued from P. 93.

and came into the coasts of Judea beyond Jordan.

2. And great multitudes followed him; and he healed them there.

From P. 97.

and cometh into the coasts of Judea, by the farther side of Jordan.

and the people resort unto him again: and, as he was wont, he taught them again.

J. X. 23, P. 108.
M. XIX. 1.

3. ¶ The Pharisees also came unto him, tempting him, and saying unto him, Is it lawful for a man to put away his wife   for every cause?

4. And he answered and said unto them;

2. ¶ And the Pharisees came to him, and asked him, Is it lawful for a man to put away *his* wife? tempting him.

3. And he answered, and said unto them, What did Moses command you?

4. And they said, Moses suffered to write a bill of divorcement, and to put *her* away.

5. And Jesus answered, and said unto them, For the hardness of your heart he wrote

M XIX. 7, 8.

St. MATTHEW, XIX.　　St. MARK, X.　　St. LUKE, XVI., XVIII.　　St. JOHN, XI.

Have ye not read
that he which made *them* at the beginning made them male and female,

5. And said, For this cause shall a man leave father and mother, and shall cleave to his wife : and they twain shall be one flesh ?

6. Wherefore they are no more twain, but one flesh.
What therefore God hath joined together let no man put asunder.

you this precept.

6. But from the beginning of the creation God made them male and female.

7. For this cause shall a man leave his father and mother, and cleave to his wife ;

8. And they twain shall be one flesh :
so then they are no more twain but one flesh.

9. What therefore God hath joined together let not man put asunder.

10. And in the house his disciples asked him again of the same *matter.* (1)

7. They say unto him, Why did Moses then command to give a writing of divorcement, and to put her away ?

8. He saith unto them, Moses, because of the hardness of your hearts, suffered you to put away your wives : but from the beginning it was not so.

Mk. X. 4, 5. P. 109.

9. And I say unto you, Whosoever shall put away his wife, except *it be* for fornication, and shall marry another committeth adultery :
and whoso marrieth her which is put away
doth commit adultery.

11. And he saith unto them, Whosoever shall put away his wife
and marry another, committeth adultery against her.

12. And if a woman put away her husband, and be married to another, she committeth adultery.

Chap. XVI. from P. 95.
18. Whosoever putteth away his wife, and marrieth another, committeth adultery.

And whosoever marrieth her that is put away from *her* husband committeth adultery.
Continued P. 95.

10. ¶ His disciples say unto him, If the case of the man be so with *his* wife, it is not good to marry.

11. But he said unto them, All *men* cannot receive this saying, save *they* to whom it is given.

12. For there are some eunuchs, which were so born from their mother's womb : and there are some eunuchs which were made eunuchs of men : and there be eunuchs which have made themselves eunuchs for the kingdom of heaven's sake. He that is able to receive *it*, let him receive *it*.

Mk. X. 10.

CHAP. XVIII. *From P. 143.*

1. And he spake a parable unto them *to this end* that men ought always *to* pray and not to faint ;

2. Saying, There was in a city a judge, which feared not God, neither regarded man.

3. And there was a widow in that city, and she came unto him, saying, Avenge me of mine adversary.

4. And he would not for a while : but afterwards he said within himself, Though I fear not God, nor regard man ;

(1) M. XIX. 10.

5. Yet, because this widow troubleth me, I will avenge her, lest by her continual coming she weary me.

6. And the Lord said, Hear what the unjust judge saith.

7. And shall not God avenge his own elect, which cry day and night unto him, though he bear long with them?

8. I tell you that he will avenge them speedily. Nevertheless when the Son of man cometh, shall he find faith on the earth?

9. And he spake this parable unto certain which trusted in themselves that they were righteous, and despised others.

10. Two men went up into the temple to pray: the one a Pharisee, and the other a publican.

11. The Pharisee stood and prayed thus with himself: God, I thank thee that I am not as other men *are;* extortioners, unjust, adulterers, or even as this publican.

12. I fast twice in the week: I give tithes of all I possess.

13. And the publican, standing afar off, would not lift up so much as *his* eyes unto heaven; but smote upon his breast, saying, God, be merciful to me a sinner.

14. I tell you, This man went down to his house justified *rather* than the other. For everyone that exalteth . himself shall be abased : and he that humbleth himself shall be exalted.

13. ¶Then were there brought unto him little children, that he should put *his* hands on them   and pray :

and the disciples rebuked them.

14. But Jesus said,

suffer little children, and forbid them not to come unto me : for of such is the kingdom of heaven. (1)

13. ¶ And they brought young children to him, that he should touch them : and *his* disciples rebuked those that brought *them.*

14. But when Jesus saw *it,*

he was much displeased, and said unto them, Suffer the little children to come unto me, and forbid them not : for of such is the kingdom of God.

15. Verily I say unto you, Whosoever shall not receive the kingdom of God as a little child, he shall not enter therein.

16. And he took them up his arms, put *his* hands upon them, and blessed them.

17. ¶ And when he was gone forth into the way,

15. And they brought unto him also infants, that he would touch them. But when *his* disciples saw *it,* they rebuked them.

16. But Jesus called them *unto him,*

and said, Suffer little children to come unto me, and forbid them not : for of such is the kingdom of God.

17. Verily I say unto you, Whosoever shall not receive the kingdom of God as a little child shall in no wise enter therein.

Continued P. 115.

15. And he laid *his* hands on them, and departed thence.

Continued P. 115.

CHAP. XI. *(from P. 109).*

1. Now a certain *man* was sick, *named* Lazarus, of Bethany, the town of Mary and her sister Martha.

(1) M. XVIII. 10.

2. (It was *that* Mary which anointed the Lord with ointment, and wiped his feet with her hair, whose brother Lazarus was sick.)

3. Therefore his sisters sent unto him, saying, Lord, behold, he whom thou lovest is sick.

4. When Jesus heard *that*, he said, This sickness is not unto death, but for the glory of God, that the Son of God might be glorified thereby.

5. Now Jesus loved Martha, and her sister, and Lazarus.

6. When he had heard therefore that he was sick, he abode two days still in the place where he was.

7. Then after that, saith he to *his* disciples, Let us go into Judea again.＊

＊ M. XIX. 1. J. X. 40, 31, 39. P. 109.

8. *His* disciples say unto him, Master, the Jews of late sought to stone thee ; and goest thou thither again ?

9. Jesus answered, Are there not twelve hours in the day ? If a man walk in the day, he stumbleth not, because he seeth the light of this world.

10. But if a man walk in the night he stumbleth, because there is no light in him.

11. These things said he, and after that, he saith unto them, Our friend Lazarus sleepeth : but I go that I may awake him out of sleep.

12. Then said his disciples, Lord, if he sleep, he shall do well.

13. Howbeit Jesus spake of his death : but they thought that he had spoken of taking of rest in sleep.

14. Then said Jesus unto them plainly, Lazarus is dead.

15. And I am glad for your sakes that I was not there ; to the intent ye may believe : nevertheless let us go unto him.

16. Then said Thomas, which is called Didymus, unto his fellow disciples, Let us also go, that we may die with him.

17. Then when Jesus came, he found that he had *lain* in the grave four days already.

18. Now Bethany was nigh unto Jerusalem ; about fifteen furlongs off.

(Fourth visit.)

19. And many of the Jews came to Martha and Mary to comfort them concerning their brother.

20. Then Martha, as soon as she heard that Jesus was coming, went and met him : but Mary sat *still* in the house.

St. MATTHEW, XIX.　　　St. MARK, X.　　　St. LUKE, XVIII.　　　St. JOHN, XI.

21. Then said Martha unto Jesus, Lord, If thou hadst been here my brother had not died.

22. But I know that even now, whatsoever thou wilt ask of God, God will give *it* thee.

23. Jesus said unto her, Thy brother shall rise again.

24. Martha saith unto him, I know that he shall rise again in the resurrection at the last day.

25. Jesus said unto her, I am the resurrection and the life : he that believeth in me, though he were dead, yet shall he live :

26. And whosoever liveth and believeth in me shall never die. Believest thou this ?

27. She saith unto him, yea, Lord ; I believe that thou art the Christ, the Son of God, which should come into the world.

28. And when she had so said, she went her way, and called Mary her sister secretly ; saying, The Master is come and calleth for thee.

29. As soon as she heard *that*, she arose quickly and came unto him.

30. Now Jesus was not yet come into the town ; but was in that place where Martha met him.

31. The Jews then which were with her in the house, and comforted her, when they saw Mary that she rose up hastily and went out, followed her; saying, She goeth unto the grave to weep there.

32. Then when Mary was come where Jesus was, and saw him, she fell down at his feet, saying unto him, Lord, if thou hadst been here, my brother had not died.

33. When Jesus therefore saw her weeping, and the Jews also weeping which came with her, he groaned in the spirit, and was troubled :

34. And said, Where have ye laid him? They said unto him, Lord, Come and see.

35. Jesus wept.

36. Then said the Jews, Behold how he loved him !

37. And some of them said, Could not this man, which opened the eyes of the blind, have caused that even this man should not have died ?

38. Jesus therefore, again groaning in himself, cometh to the grave. It was a cave, and a stone lay upon it.

39. Jesus said, Take ye away

the stone. Martha, the sister of him that was dead, saith unto him, Lord, by this time he stinketh, for he hath been *dead* four days.

40. Jesus saith unto her, Said I not unto thee that, if thou wouldest believe, thou shouldest see the glory of God?

41. Then they took away the stone *from the place* where the dead was laid; and Jesus lifted up *his* eyes, and said, Father, I thank thee that thou hast heard me:

42. And I know that thou hearest me always; but because of the people which stand by I said *it;* that they may believe that thou hast sent me.

43. And when he had thus spoken, he cried with a loud voice, Lazarus, come forth.

44. And he that was dead came forth, bound hand and foot with grave clothes: and his face was bound about with a napkin. Jesus saith unto them, Loose him, and let him go.

45. Then many of the Jews which came to Mary, and had seen the things which Jesus did, believed on him.

46. But some of them went their ways to the Pharisees, and told them what things Jesus had done.

47. ¶ Then gathered the chief priests and the Pharisees a council; and said, What do we? for this man doeth many miracles.

48. If we let him thus alone, all *men* will believe on him: and the Romans shall come and take away both our place and nation.

49. And one of them named Caiaphas, being the high priest that same year,* said unto them, Ye know nothing at all;

* M. XXVI. 57.; L. III. 2, P. 13.

50. Nor consider that it is expedient for us, that one man should die for the people; and that the whole nation perish not.

51. And this spake he not of himself: but, being high priest that year, he prophesied that Jesus should die for that nation:

52. And not for that nation only, but that also he should gather together in one the children of God that were scattered abroad.

53. Then from that day forth they took counsel together for to put him to death.

54. Jesus therefore walked no more openly among the Jews;

but went thence into a country near to the wilderness; into a city called Ephraim; and there continued with his disciples.

Continued P. 117.

Sᴛ. MATTHEW, XIX.

16. ¶ And behold, one came,

and said unto him, Good Master, what good thing shall I do, that I may have eternal life?

17. And he said unto him, Why callest thou me good? *There is* none good but one, *that is*, God: but if thou wilt enter into life, keep the commandments.

18. He saith unto him, Which? Jesus said, Thou shalt do no murder; thou shalt not commit adultery; thou shalt not steal; thou shalt not bear false witness;

19. Honour thy father, and *thy* mother: and thou shalt love thy neighbour as thyself.

20. The young man saith unto him, All these things have I kept from my youth up: What lack I yet?

21. Jesus said unto him, If thou wilt be perfect, Go, *and* sell that thou hast, and give to the poor: and thou shalt have treasure in heaven: and come *and* follow me.

22. But when the young man heard that saying, he went away sorrowful: for he had great possessions.

23. ¶ Then said Jesus unto his disciples, Verily, I say unto you, That a rich man shall hardly enter into the kingdom of heaven.

24. And again I say unto you, It is easier for a camel to go through the eye of a needle, than for a rich man to enter into the kingdom of God.

25. When his disciples heard *it*, they were exceedingly amazed; saying, Who then can be saved?

26. But Jesus beheld *them*, and said unto them, With men, this is impossible, but with God, all things are possible.

Sᴛ. MARK, X.

From P. 111.

there came one running and kneeled to him, and asked him, Good Master, What shall I do that I may inherit eternal life?

18. And Jesus said unto him, Why callest thou me good? *There is* none good but one, *that is* God.

19. Thou knowest the commandments,

do not commit adultery; do not kill; do not steal; do not bear false witness; defraud not; honour thy father and mother.

20. And he answered and said unto him, Master, all these have I observed from my youth:

21. Then Jesus, beholding him, loved him; and said unto him, One thing thou lackest; go thy way, sell whatsoever thou hast, and give to the poor; and thou shalt have treasure in heaven: and come, take up thy cross, and follow me.

22. And he was sad at that saying, and went away grieved: for he had great possessions.

23. ¶ And Jesus looked round about, and saith unto his disciples, How hardly shall they that have riches enter into the kingdom of God.

24. And the disciples were astonished at his words. But Jesus answereth again, and saith unto them, Children, how hard is it for them that trust in riches to enter into the kingdom of God!

25. It is easier for a camel to go through the eye of a needle, than for a rich man to enter into the kingdom of God.

26. And they were astonished out of measure, saying among themselves, Who then can be saved?

27. And Jesus, looking upon them, saith, With men *it is* impossible; but not with God; for with God all things are possible.

Sᴛ. LUKE, XVIII.

Cʜᴀᴘ. XVIII. *from P. 111.*

18. And a certain ruler

asked him saying, Good Master, what shall I do to inherit eternal life?

19. And Jesus said unto him, Why callest thou me good? None is good save one; *that is* God.

20. Thou knowest the commandments,

do not commit adultery; do not kill; do not steal; do not bear false witness;

honour thy father and thy mother;

21. And he said, All these have I kept from my youth up.

22. Now when Jesus heard these things, he said unto him, Yet lackest thou one thing: sell all that thou hast and distribute unto the poor; and thou shalt have treasure in heaven: and come, follow me.

23. And when he heard this, he was very sorrowful, for he was very rich.

24. And when Jesus saw that he was very sorrowful, he said, How hardly shall they that have riches enter into the kingdom of God!

25. For it is easier for a camel to go through a needle's eye, than for a rich man to enter into the kingdom of God.

26. And they that heard *it* said, Who then can be saved?

27. And he said,

The things which are impossible with men are possible with God,

St. MATTHEW, XX.

27. ¶ Then answered Peter, and said unto him, Behold, we have forsaken all, and followed thee :
What shall we have therefore?
28. And Jesus said unto them, Verily, I say unto you,
That ye which have followed me in the regeneration, when the Son of man shall sit in the throne of his glory,

ye also shall sit upon twelve thronee judging the twelve tribes of Israel.

29. And every one that hath forsaken houses, or brethren, or sisters, or father, or mother, or wife, or children, or lands, for my name's sake,
shall receive [an hundred]* fold,

and shall inherit everlasting life.

30. But many *that are* first shall be last ; and the last *shall be* first. (1)

St. MARK, X.

28. ¶ Then Peter began to say unto him, Lo ! we have left all, and have followed thee.

29. And Jesus answered and said, Verily I say unto you,
There is no man that hath left house, or brethren, or sisters, or father, or mother, or wife, or children, or lands, for my sake and the gospel's,
30. But he shall receive an hundred fold now in this time, houses, and brethren, and sisters, and mothers, and children, and lands, with persecutions ;
and in the world to come eternal life.
31. But many *that are* first shall be last, and the last first.

St. LUKE, XVIII., XXII.

28. Then Peter said, Lo ! We have left all, and followed thee.

Continued below.

Chap. XXII. from P. 119.

28. Ye are they which have continued with me in my temptations.
29. And I appoint unto you a kingdom, as my Father hath appointed unto me ;
30. That ye may eat and drink at my table in my kingdom, and sit on thrones judging the twelve tribes of Israel.
Continued P. 154.

Chap. XVIII.
29. And he said unto them, Verily I say unto you,
there is no man that hath left house, or parents, or brethren, or wife, or children,
for the kingdom of God's sake,
30. Who shall not receive many fold more in this present time,

and in the world to come, life everlasting.
Continued P. 118.
L. XIII., 30, P. 42.

St. JOHN, XI.

CHAP. XX.

1. For the kingdom of heaven is like unto a man *that is* an householder, which went out early in the morning to hire labourers into his vineyard.
2. And when he had agreed with the labourers for a penny a day, he sent them into his vineyard.
3. And he went out about the third hour, and saw others standing idle in the market-place ;
4. And said unto them, Go ye also into the vineyard, and whatsoever is right I will give you. And they went their way.
5. Again he went out about the sixth and ninth hour, and did likewise.
6. And about the eleventh hour he went out, and found others standing idle, and saith unto them, Why stand ye here all the day idle ?

[" *Shall receive many fold.*"—*Alford*]
1) M. XX. 16.

ST. MATTHEW, XX.   ST. MARK, X.   ST. LUKE, IX.   ST. JOHN, XI.

St. Matthew, XX.

7. They say unto him, Because no man hath hired us. He saith unto them, Go ye also into the vineyard; and whatsoever is right, *that* shall ye receive.

8. So when even was come, the lord of the vineyard saith unto his steward, Call the laborers, and give them *their* hire, beginning from the last unto the first.

9. And when they came that *were hired* about the eleventh hour, they received every man a penny.

10. But when the first came, they supposed that they should have received more; and they likewise received every man a penny.

11. And when they received *it*, they murmured against the good man of the house;

12. Saying, These last have wrought *but* one hour, and thou hast made them equal unto us, which have borne the burden and heat of the day.

13. But he answered one of them, and said, Friend, I do thee no wrong. Didst not thou agree with me for a penny?

14. Take *that* thine *is*, and go thy way: I will give unto this last even as unto thee.

15. Is it not lawful for me to do what I will with mine own? Is thine eye evil, because I am good?

16. So the last shall be first, and the first last. [For many be called, but few chosen.]*

¶ 17. And Jesus, going up to Jerusalem,

St. Mark, X.

[*Not in our ancient MSS.—Alford*]

32. ¶ And they were in the way going up to Jerusalem;

and Jesus went before them, and they were amazed; and as they followed, they were afraid.

St. Luke, IX.

Chap. IX., from P. 90.

51. ¶ And it came to pass, when the time was come that he should be received up, he steadfastly set his face to go to Jerusalem.

52. And sent messengers before his face: and they went and entered into a village of the Samaritans, to make ready for him.

53. And they did not receive him, because his face was as though he would go to Jerusalem.

54. And when his disciples, James and John saw *this*, they said, Lord, Wilt thou that we

St. John, XI.

55. ¶ And the Jews' passover was nigh at hand, and many went out of the country up to Jerusalem,* before the passover, to purify themselves.

56. Then sought they for Jesus, and spake amongst themselves, as they stood in the temple, What think ye, That he will not come to the feast?

57. Now both the chief priests and the Pharisees had given a commandment, that if any man knew where he were, he should show *it*, that they might take him.

For Chap. XII., see P. 148.

* M. XIX. 30; XX. 16.   *J. II. 13–16. P. 22. M. XXI. 12, 13.

St. MATTHEW, XX.

St. MARK, X.

St. LUKE, IX., XVIII., XXII.

St. JOHN, XII.

command fire to come down from heaven, and consume them, even as Elias did?

55. [But he turned and rebuked them, and said, Ye know not what manner of spirit ye are of.]

[Verse 55 not found in the oldest MSS.—A.]

56. [For the Son of man is not come to destroy men's lives, but to save them. And they went to another village.]

[Verse 56 is wanting in 6 oldest MSS.—A.]

Continued P. 45.

Jerusalem took the twelve disciples apart in the way, and said unto them,

18. Behold, we go up to Jerusalem ; and the Son of man shall be betrayed unto the chief Priests, and unto the Scribes ; and they shall condemn him to death ;

19. And deliver him to the Gentiles to mock ; and to scourge ;

and to crucify *him*,

And the third day he shall rise again.

And he took again the twelve, and began to tell them what things should happen unto him ;

33. *Saying*, Behold, we go up to Jerusalem ; and the Son of man shall be delivered unto the chief Priests, and unto the Scribes; and they shall condemn him to death : and shall deliver him to the Gentiles

34. And they shall mock him ; and shall scourge him ;

and shall spit upon him ; and shall kill him ;

And the third day he shall rise again.

Chap. XVIII. from P. 116.

31. ¶ Then he took *unto him* the twelve, and said unto them, Behold, we go up to Jerusalem ; and all things that are written by the Prophets concerning the Son of man shall be accomplished.

32. For he shall be delivered unto the Gentiles and mocked ; and spitefully entreated ; and spitted on ;

33. And they shall scourge *him ;*

and put him to death ;

and the third day he shall rise again.

34. And they understood none of these things : and this saying was hid from them : neither knew they the things which were spoken.

Continued P. 119.

---

20. ¶ Then came to him the mother of Zebedee's children with her sons, worshipping *him*, and desiring a certain thing of him.

21. And he said unto her, What wilt thou ?

She saith unto him, Grant that these my two sons may sit the one on thy right hand and the other on the left, in thy kingdom.

22. But Jesus answered, and said, Ye know not what ye ask : Are ye able to drink of the cup that I shall drink of, [and to be baptized with the baptism that I am baptized with ?]* They say unto him, We are able.

23. And he saith unto them, Ye shall drink indeed of my cup, [and be baptized with the baptism that I am baptized with :]†

but to sit on my right hand, and on my left, is not mine to give : but *it shall be given to them* for whom it is prepared of my Father.

24. And when the ten heard it,

35. ¶ And James and John, the sons of Zebedee, come unto him saying, Master, We would that thou shouldest do for us whatsoever we shall desire.

36. And he said unto them, What would ye that I should do for you ?

37. They said unto him, Grant unto us that we may sit, one on thy right hand, and the other on thy left hand, in thy glory.

38. But Jesus said unto them, Ye know not what ye ask : Can ye drink of the cup that I drink of ? And be baptized with the baptism that I am baptized with ?

39. And they say unto him, We can.

And Jesus said unto them, Ye shall indeed drink of the cup that I drink of, and with the baptism that I am baptized withal, shall ye be baptized :

40. But to sit on my right hand and on my left hand, is not mine to give ; but *it shall be given to them* for whom it is prepared.

41. And when the ten heard *it*,

Chap. XXII., from P. 153.

24. ¶ And there was also a strife among them, which of them should be accounted the greatest.

they were moved with indignation against the two brethren.

25. But Jesus called them *unto him*, and said,
Ye know that the princes of the Gentiles exercise dominion over them ; and they that are great exercise authority upon them.

26. But it shall not be so among you : but whosoever will be great among you, let him be your minister :
27. And whosoever will be chief among you, let him be your servant.
28. Even as the Son of man came not to be ministered unto, but to minister,

and to give his life a ransom for many.

they began to be much displeased with James and John.

42. But Jesus called them *to him*, and saith unto them,
Ye know that they which are accounted to rule over the Gentiles exercise lordship over them ; and their great ones exercise authority upon them.

43. But so shall it not be among you ; but whosoever will be great among you shall be your minister :
44. And whosoever of you will be the chiefest, shall be the servant of all.
45. For even the Son of man came not to be ministered unto, but to minister,

and to give his life a ransom for many.

25. And he said unto them,

The kings of the Gentiles exercise lordship over them : and they that exercise authority upon them, are called benefactors.
26. But ye *shall* not *be* so : but he that is greatest among you, let him be as the younger ;

and he that is chief, as he that doth serve.
27. For whether *is* greater, he that sitteth at meat ; or he that serveth.
Is not he that sitteth at meat ? But I am among you as he that serveth.
Continued P. 116.

Chap. XVII. from P. 96.
11. ¶ And It came to pass, as he went to Jerusalem, that he passed through the midst of Samaria and Galilee.
12. And as he entered into a certain village, there met him ten men that were lepers, which stood afar off.
13. And they lifted up *their* voices, and said, Jesus, Master, have mercy on us.
14. And when he saw *them*, he said unto them, Go, shew yourselves unto the priests. And it came to pass that, as they went, they were cleansed.
15. And one of them, when he saw that he was healed, turned back, and with a loud voice glorified God.
16. And fell down on *his* face, at his feet, giving him thanks. And he was a Samaritan.
17. And Jesus answering said, Were there not ten cleansed ? But where *are* the nine ?
18. There are not found' that returned to give glory to God, save this stranger.
19. And he said unto him, Arise, go thy way : thy faith hath made the whole.
Continued P. 140.

Chap. XVIII. from P. 118.
35. ¶ And it came to pass, that as he was come nigh unto Jericho,

46. ¶ And they came to Jericho;

L. XIX 1. P. 120.

St. MATTHEW, XX.

29. And as they departed from Jericho, a great multitude followed him. (1)

30. ¶ And behold two blind men, sitting by the way side,

when they heard Jesus passed by,

cried out, saying, Have mercy on us, O Lord, *thou* Son of David.(2)

31. And the multitude rebuked them, because they should hold their peace : but they cried the more, saying, Have mercy on us, O Lord, *thou* Son of David.

32. And Jesus stood still, and called them,

and said, What will ye that I should do unto you ?

33. They say unto him, Lord, that our eyes may be opened.

34. So Jesus had compassion on *them*,

and touched their eyes : and immediately their eyes received sight ; and they followed him.

St. MARK, X.

and as he went out of Jericho, with his disciples, and a great number of people,

blind Bartimæus, the son of Timeus, sat by the highway side, begging.

47. And when he heard that it was Jesus of Nazareth,

he began to cry out, and say, Jesus, *thou* Son of David, have mercy on me.

48. And many charged him that he should hold his peace : but he cried the more a great deal, Thou Son of David, have mercy on me.

49. And Jesus stood still, and commanded him to be called. And they called the blind man, saying unto him, Be of good comfort ; rise, he calleth thee.

50. And he, casting away his garments, rose and came to Jesus.

51. And Jesus answered, and said unto him, What wilt thou that I should do unto thee? The blind man said unto him, Lord, that I might receive my sight.

52. And Jesus said unto him, Go thy way : thy faith hath made thee whole. And immediately he received his sight, and followed Jesus in the way.

St. LUKE, XVIII., XIX.

a certain blind man sat by the way side begging.

36. And hearing the multitude pass by he asked what it meant.

37. And they told him that Jesus of Nazareth passeth by.

38. And he cried, saying, Jesus, *thou* Son of David, have mercy on me.

39. And they which went before, rebuked him, that he should hold his peace : but he cried so much the more, *Thou* Son of David have mercy on me.

40. And Jesus stood, and commanded him to be brought unto him.

And when he was come near, he asked him.

41. Saying, What wilt thou that I shall do unto thee? And he said, Lord, that I may receive my sight.

42. And Jesus said unto him, Receive thy sight : thy faith hath saved thee.

43. And immediately he received his sight ; and followed him,

glorifying God.

And all the people when they saw *it* gave praise unto God.

M. XX. 29.

Chap. XIX.

1. And *Jesus* entered and passed through Jericho :

2. And behold *there was* a man named Zaccheus, which was the chief among the publicans : and he was rich.

3. And he sought to see Jesus, who he was ; and could not for the press, because he was little of stature.

4. And he ran before, and climbed up into a sycamore tree to see him ; for he was to pass that *way*.

5. And when Jesus came to the place, he looked up, and saw him, and said unto him, Zaccheus, make haste, and come down, for to-day I must abide at thy house.

6. And he made haste, and came down and received him joyfully.

(1) L. XIX. 1. P. 120.
(2) M. IX. 27.

7. And when they saw it, they all murmured, saying, That he was gone to be guest with a man that is a sinner.

8. And Zaccheus stood, and said unto the Lord, Behold, Lord, the half of my goods I give to the poor : and if I have taken anything from any man by false accusation, I restore him four fold.

9. And Jesus said unto him, This day is salvation come to this house, for so much as he also is a son of Abraham.

M. XVIII. 11.

10. For the Son of man is come to seek and to save that which was lost.

Continued P. 145.

CHAP. XXI.

1. And when they drew nigh unto Jerusalem ; and were come to Bethphage
unto the mount of Olives ; then sent Jesus two disciples,

2. Saying unto them, Go into the village over against you, and straightway ye shall find an ass tied and a colt with her. Loose them and bring them unto me.

3. And if any man say aught unto you, ye shall say, The Lord hath need of them : and straightway he will send them.

4. All this was done that it might be fulfilled which was spoken by the prophet saying,

5. Tell ye the daughter of Sion, Behold thy king cometh unto thee, meek and sitting upon an ass, and a colt the foal of an ass.

CHAP. XI.

1. And when they came nigh to Jerusalem, unto Bethphage and Bethany, at the mount of Olives, he sendeth forth two of his disciples :

2. And saith unto them, Go your way into the village over against you ; and as soon as ye be entered into it, ye shall find a colt tied, whereon never man sat : loose him and bring him.

3. And if any man say unto you, Why do ye this? say ye, that the Lord hath need of him ;
and straightway he will send him hither.

Chap. XIX., from P. 147.
29. And it came to pass, when he was come nigh to Bethphage and Bethany, at the mount called the mount of Olives, he sent two of his disciples,

30. Saying, Go ye into the village over against you, in the which at your entering ye shall find a colt tied, whereon yet never man sat : loose him, and bring him hither.

31. And if any man ask you, Why do ye loose him, Thus shall ye say unto him, Because the Lord hath need of him.

Chap. XII., from P. 122.
14. And Jesus, when he had found a young ass, sat thereon ;

as it is written,

15. Fear not, daughter of Sion ; Behold thy king cometh, sitting on an ass's colt.

16. These things understood not his disciples at the first : but when Jesus was glorified, then remembered they that these things were written of him : and that they had done these things unto him.

Continued P. 122.

6. And the disciples went, and did as Jesus commanded them.

4. And they went their way, and found the colt tied by the door without, in a place where two ways met ; and they loose him.

5. And certain of them that stood there said unto them, What do ye loosing the colt ?

6. And they said unto them even as Jesus had commanded : and they let them go.

32. And they that were sent went their way, and found even as he had said unto them.

33. And as they were loosing the colt the owners thereof said unto them, Why loose ye the colt ?

34. And they said, The Lord hath need of him.

35. And they brought him to Jesus :

7. And brought the ass and the colt, and put on them their clothes ;
and they set him thereon.

7. And they brought the colt to Jesus ; and cast their garments on him ;
and he sat upon him.

and they cast their garments upon the colt ; and they set Jesus thereon.

St. MATTHEW, XXI.	St. MARK, XI.	St. LUKE, XIX.	St. JOHN, XII.
8. And a very great multitude spread their garments in the way :	8. And many spread their garments in the way :	36. And as they went, they spread their clothes in the way.	*From P. 151.* 12. ¶ On the next day much people that were come to the feast, when they heard that Jesus was coming to Jerusalem, (1)
others cut down branches from the trees, and strawed *them* in the way.	and others cut down branches off the trees, and strawed *them* in the way.		13. Took branches of palm trees, and went forth to meet him.
9. And the multitudes that went before, and that followed, cried,	9. And they that went before, and they that followed, cried,	37. And when he was come nigh, even now at the descent of the mount of Olives, the whole multitude of the disciples began to rejoice and praise God with a loud voice for all the mighty works that they had seen ;	
saying, Hosanna to the Son of David : Blessed is he that cometh in the name of the Lord.	saying, Hosanna : blessed *is* he that cometh in the name of the Lord : 10. Blessed be the kingdom of our Father David, that cometh in the name of the Lord : Hosanna in the highest.	38. Saying, Blessed *be* the King* that cometh in the name of the Lord : peace in heaven and glory in the highest.	and cried, Hosanna : Blessed *is* the King of Israel, that cometh in the name of the Lord. (2) *Continued P. 121.* *From P. 121.*
Hosanna in the highest.			17. The people therefore that was with him when he called Lazarus out of his grave and raised him from the dead, bare record.
Continued P. 124.			18. For this cause the people also met him, for that they heard that he had done this miracle.
		39. And some of the Pharisees from among the multitude said unto him, Master, rebuke thy disciples. 40. And he answered, and said unto them, I tell you that, if these should hold their peace, the stones would immediately cry out. *Continued P. 124.*	19. The Pharisees therefore said among themselves, Perceive ye how ye prevail nothing ? Behold the world is gone after him.
			20. ¶ And there were certain Greeks among them that came up to worship at the feast : 21. The same came therefore to Philip which was of Bethsaida of Galilee, and desired him, saying, Sir, We would see Jesus. 22. Philip cometh and telleth Andrew : and again Andrew and Philip tell Jesus. 23. And Jesus answered them, saying, The hour is come that the Son of man should be glorified. 24. Verily, verily, I say unto you, Except a corn of wheat fall into the ground, and die, it abideth alone : but if it die, it bringeth forth much fruit. 25. He that loveth his life shall lose it ; and he that hateth his life in this world, shall keep it unto life eternal. (3) 26. If any man serve me,

* *See notes J. VI. 15. P. 75.*

(1) J. II. 13 ; V. 1; VII. 10. }5 *visits*
X. 22. ; XI. 13. ; XII. 12.
(2) See notes J. VI. 15. P. 75.
(3) M. X. 39. ; XIV. 25.

let him follow me ; and where I am, there shall also my servant be. If any man serve me, him will *my* Father honour.

27. Now is my soul troubled : and what shall I say ? Father, save me from this hour : but for this cause came I unto this hour.

M. XXVI. 38. 39.

28. Father, glorify thy name. Then came there a voice from heaven, *saying*, I have both glorified *it*, and will glorify *it* again.

L. XXII. 43. P. 162.

29. The people therefore, that stood by and heard *it*, said, that it thundered : others said, An angel spake to him.

30. Jesus answered, and said, This voice came not because of me, but for your sakes.

31. Now is the judgment of this world ; now shall the prince of this world be cast out.

32. And I, if I be lifted up, will draw all *men* unto me.

33. This he said, signifying what death he should die.

34. The people answered him, We have heard out of the law, that Christ abideth for ever : and how sayest thou, The Son of man must be lifted up ? Who is this Son of man ?

35. Then Jesus said unto them, Yet a little while is the light with you. Walk while ye have the light ; lest darkness come upon you : for he that walketh in darkness knoweth not whither he goeth.

36. While ye have light, believe in the light ; that ye may be the children of light. These things spake Jesus, and departed, and did hide himself from them.

37. ¶ But though he had done so many miracles before them, yet they believed not on him :

38. That the saying of Esaias the prophet might be fulfilled, which he spake, Who hath believed our report ? and, To whom hath the arm of the Lord been revealed ?

39. Therefore they could not believe, because that Esaias said again,

40. He hath blinded their eyes, and hardened their heart : that they should not see with *their* eyes, nor understand with *their* heart, and be converted ; and I should heal them.

41. These things said Esaias

St. MATTHEW, XXI.   St. MARK, XI.   St. LUKE, XIX.   St. JOHN, XII.

when he saw his glory, and spake of him.

42. ¶ Nevertheless among the chief rulers also many believed on him : but because of the Pharisees they did not confess *him*, lest they should be put out of the synagogue.

43. For they loved the praise of men more than the praise of God.

44. ¶ Jesus cried and said, He that believeth on me, believeth not on me, but on him that sent me.

46. I am come a light into the world, that whosoever believeth on me should not abide in darkness.

47. And if any man hear my words, and believe not, I judge him not, for I came not to judge the world, but to save the world.

48. He that rejecteth me, and receiveth not my words, hath one that judgeth him : the word that I have spoken, the same shall judge him at the last day.

49. For I have not spoken of myself ; but the Father which sent me, he gave me a commandment, what I should say, and what I should speak.

50. And I know that his commandment is life everlasting. Whatsoever I speak therefore, even as the Father said unto me, so I speak.

From P. 122.

41. ¶ And when he was come near, he beheld the city, and wept over it,

42. Saying, if thou hadst known, even thou, at least in this thy day, the things, *which belong* unto thy peace ! But now they are hid from thine eyes.

43. For the days shall come upon thee, that thine enemies shall cast a trench about thee, and compass thee round, and keep thee in on every side ;

44. And they shall lay thee even with the ground ; and thy children within thee : and they shall not leave in thee one stone upon another : because thou knewest not the time of thy visitation.

L. XXI. 20. P. 139.

L. XXI. 6. P. 138.

For Chap. XIII., see P. 151.

10. And when he was come into Jerusalem, all the city was moved, saying, Who is this ?

11. And the multitude said, This is Jesus the prophet, of Nazareth, of Galilee.

11. And Jesus entered into Jerusalem, and into the temple :

And when he had looked round about upon all (1)

(1) *See v 15.*

St. MATTHEW, XXI.	St. MARK, XI.	St. LUKE, XIX., X.	St. JOHN, XIII.

things, and now the eventide was come, he went out unto Bethany, with the twelve.
Continued P. 126.
From P. 126.

15. ¶ And they come to Jerusalem.

12. ¶ And Jesus went into the temple of God and cast out all them that sold and bought in the temple; and overthrew the tables of the money changers; and the seats of them that sold doves : (1)

And Jesus went into the temple, and began to cast out them that sold and bought in the temple; and overthrew the tables of the money changers; and the seats of them that sold doves;

45. And he went into the temple, and began to cast out them that sold therein, and them that bought,

See J. II., 14, 15, 16, P. 22.

16. And would not suffer that any man should carry *any* vessel through the temple.

13. And said unto them, It is written, My house shall be called the house of prayer, but ye have made it a den of thieves.

17. And he taught, saying unto them, Is it not written, My house shall be called of all nations, the house of prayer? But ye have made it a den of thieves.

46. Saying unto them, It is written, My house is the house of prayer, but ye have made it a den of thieves.

14. And the blind and the lame came to him in the temple : and he healed them.
15. And when the chief priests and scribes saw the wonderful things that he did, and the children crying in the temple : and saying, Hosanna to the Son of David; they were sore displeased;
16. And said unto him, Hearest thou what these say? And Jesus saith unto them, Yea : have ye never read, Out of the mouth of babes and sucklings thou hast perfected praise?
17. ¶ And he left them, and went out of the city, into Bethany ; and he lodged there (2)

18. And the Scribes and chief priests heard *it*, and sought how they might destroy him ; for they feared him because all the people was astonished at his doctrine.

47. And he taught daily in the temple. But the chief priests and the Scribes, and the chief of the people sought to destroy him :

J. XI., 57, P. 117.

48. And could not find what they might do : for all the people were very attentive to hear him.

For Chap. XX., see P. 126.

19. And when even was come he went out of the city.
Continued P. 126.

Chap. X., from P. 134.
38. ¶ Now it came to pass as they went, that he entered into a certain village : and a certain woman named Martha received him into her house.

J. XII. 1, 2, 3. P. 148. 149.
M. XXI. 17.
Mk. XI. 11, 19. P. 125.

39. And she had a sister called Mary, which also sat at Jesus' feet, and heard his word.
40. But Martha was cumbered about much serving ; and came to him and said, Lord, Dost thou not care that my sister hath left me to serve alone? Bid her therefore that she help me.
41. And Jesus answered, and said unto her, Martha, Martha, thou art careful and troubled about many things :
42. But one thing is needful : and Mary hath chosen that good part, which shall not be taken away from her.

(1) See J. II. 14, 15, 16. P. 22.
L. X. 38. P. 125—XXI. 37. P. 144.
2 { Mk. XI. 11. P. 125.
{ J. XII. 1. P. 149.

For Chap. XI., see Page 37.

18. Now in the morning, as he returned into the city, he hungred.

19. And when he saw a fig tree in the way, he came to it

and found nothing thereon but leaves only; and said unto it, Let no fruit grow on thee henceforward for ever.

And presently the fig tree withered away.

20. And when the disciples saw it, they marvelled, saying, How soon is the fig tree withered away!

21. Jesus answered, and said unto them, Verily I say unto you, If ye have faith, and doubt not, Ye shall not only do this *which is done* to the fig tree, but also if ye shall say unto this mountain, Be thou removed, and be thou cast into the sea; (1)

it shall be done.

22. And all things, whatsoever ye shall ask in prayer, believing,

ye shall receive.

23. ¶ And when he was come into the temple,

the chief Priests and the Elders of the people came unto him as he was teaching, and said, By what authority doest thou these things? and Who gave thee this authority?

24. And Jesus answered, and said unto them, I also will ask you one thing, which if ye tell me, I in the like wise will tell you by what authority I do these things.

25. The baptism of John, whence was it? From heaven, or of men? And they reasoned with themselves, saying, If we shall say, from heaven, he will say unto us, Why did ye not then believe him?

26. But if we shall say, of men?

(1) M, XVII. 20.

Chap. XI. from P. 125.

12. ¶ And on the morrow, when they were come from Bethany, he was hungry:

13. And seeing a fig tree afar off, having leaves; he came, if haply he might find anything thereon: and when he came to it, he found nothing but leaves; for the time of figs was not *yet.*

14. And Jesus answered, and said unto it, No man eat fruit of thee hereafter for ever. And his disciples heard *it.*
Continued P. 125.

20. ¶ And in the morning, as they passed by, they saw the fig tree dried up from the roots.

21. And Peter calling to remembrance, saith unto him, Master, Behold the fig tree which thou cursedst is withered away.

22. And Jesus answering, saith unto them, Have faith in God.

23. For verily I say unto you that whosoever shall say unto this mountain, Be thou removed, and be thou cast into the sea; and shall not doubt in his heart, but shall believe that those things which he saith shall come to pass, he shall have whatsoever he saith.

24. Therefore I say unto you, What things soever ye desire, when ye pray, believe that ye receive *them;* and ye shall have *them.*

25. } See P. 37.
26. }

27. ¶ And they come again to Jerusalem.
And as he was walking in the temple, there come to him the chief Priests, and the Scribes, and the Elders,

28. And say unto him, By what authority doest thou these things? and who gave thee this authority to do these things?

29. And Jesus answered and said unto them, I will also ask of you one question; and answer me, and I will tell you by what authority I do these things.

30. The baptism of John; Was it from heaven, or of men? Answer me.

31. And they reasoned with themselves, saying, If we shall say, from heaven, he will say, Why then did ye not believe him?

32. But if we shall say, of men,

L. XVII. 6. P. 88.

CHAP. XX. from P. 125.

1. And it came to pass *that* on one of those days, as he taught the people in the temple, and preached the gospel, the chief priests and the scribes came upon *him,* with the elders,

2. And spake unto him, saying, Tell us by what authority doest thou these things? Or, who is he that gave thee this authority?

3. And he answered and said unto them, I will also ask you one thing;
and answer me:

4. The baptism of John, was it from heaven, or of men?

5. And they reasoned with themselves, saying, If we shall say, From heaven, he will say, Why then believed ye him not?

6. But and if we say, Of men, all the

we fear the people : for all hold John as a prophet.

27. And they answered Jesus, and said, We cannot tell. And he said unto them, Neither tell I you by what authority I do these things.

28. ¶ But what think ye? A *certain* man had two sons : and he came to the first, and said, Son, go work to-day in my vineyard.

29. He answered and said, I will not : but afterwards he repented, and went.

30. And he came to the second, and said likewise. And he answered and said, I *go*, Sir. And went not.

31. Whether of them twain did the will of *his* father? They say unto him, The first. Jesus saith unto them, Verily I say unto you, that the publicans and the harlots go into the kingdom of God before you.

32. For John came unto you in the way of righteousness, and ye believed him not. But the publicans and the harlots believed him. And ye, when ye had seen *it*, repented not afterward, that ye might believe him.

33. ¶ Hear another parable : There was a certain householder which planted a vineyard ; and hedged it round about ; and digged a winepress in it ; and built a tower ; and let it out to husbandmen ; and went to a far country.

34. And when the time of the fruit drew near, he sent his servants to the husbandmen, that they might receive the fruits of it.

35. And the husbandmen took his servants, and beat one ; and killed another ; and stoned another.

36. Again he sent other servants more than the first ;

and they did unto them likewise.

37. But last of all he sent unto them his son ;
saying, They will reverence my son.

---

they feared the people : for all *men* counted John that he was a prophet indeed.

33. And they answered and said unto Jesus, We cannot tell.

And Jesus, answering, saith unto them, Neither do I tell you by what authority I do these things.

CHAP. XII.

1. And he began to speak unto them by parables. A *certain* man planted a vineyard ; and set an hedge about *it ;* and digged *a place for* the winefat ; and built a tower ; and let it out to husbandmen ; and went into a far country.

2. And at the season he sent to the husbandmen a servant, that he might receive from the husbandmen of the fruit of the vineyard.

3. And they caught *him* and beat *him*, and sent *him* away empty.

4. And again he sent unto them another servant ; and at him they cast stones ; and wounded *him* in the head ; and sent *him* away shamefully handled.

5. And again he sent another : and him they killed : and many others ; beating some ; and killing some.

6. Having yet therefore one son, his well-beloved, he sent him also last unto them ; saying, They will reverence my son.

---

people will stone us : for they be persuaded that John was a prophet.

7. And they answered, That they could not tell whence *it was.*

8. And Jesus said unto them, Neither tell I you by what authority I do these things.

9. Then began he to speak to the people this parable :

A certain man planted a vineyard,

and let it forth to husbandmen ; and went into a far country, for a long time.

10. And, at the season, he sent a servant to the husbandmen, that they should give him of the fruit of the vineyard.

But the husbandmen beat him, and sent *him* away empty.

11. And again he sent another servant ; and they beat him also, and entreated *him* shamefully ; and sent *him* away empty.

12. And again he sent a third. And they wounded him also, and cast *him* out.

13. Then said the lord of the vineyard, What shall I do? I will send my beloved son. It may be they will reverence *him* when they see him.

ST. MATTHEW, XXI.

38. But when the husbandmen saw the son, they said among themselves, This is the heir; come let us kill him, and let us seize on his inheritance.

39. And they caught him, and cast *him* out of the vineyard, and slew *him*.

40. When the lord therefore of the vineyard cometh, what will he do unto those husbandmen?

41. They say unto him, He will miserably destroy those wicked men; and will let out *his* vineyard unto other husbandmen, which shall render him the fruits in their seasons.

42. Jesus saith unto them, Did ye never read in the scriptures, The stone which the builders rejected, the same is become the head of the corner: This is the Lord's doing, and it is marvellous in our eyes?

43. Therefore say I unto you, the kingdom of God shall be taken from you, and given to a nation bringing forth the fruits thereof.

44. And whosoever shall fall on this stone shall be broken: but on whomsoever it shall fall, it will grind him to powder.

45. And when the chief Priests and Pharisees had heard his parables, they perceived that he spake of them.

46. But when they sought to lay hands on him, they feared the multitude, because they took him for a Prophet.

ST. MARK, XII.

7. But those husbandmen said among themselves, This is the heir; come let us kill him, and the inheritance shall be ours.

8. And they took him, and killed *him*, and cast *him* out of the vineyard.

9. What shall therefore the lord of the vineyard do?

He will come and destroy the husbandmen, and will give the vineyard unto others.

10. And have ye not read this scripture, The stone which the builders rejected is become the head of the corner;

11. This was the Lord's doing, and it is marvellous in our eyes?

12. And they sought to lay hold on him, but feared the people: for they knew that he had spoken the parable against them: and they left him, and went their way.

ST. LUKE, XX., XIV.

14. But when the husbandmen saw him, they reasoned among themselves, saying, This is the heir; come, let us kill him, that the inheritance may be ours.

15. So they cast him out of the vineyard and killed *him*.

What therefore shall the lord of the vineyard do unto them?

16. He shall come and destroy these husbandmen; and shall give the vineyard to others.

And when they heard *it*, they said, God forbid.

17. And he beheld them, and said, What is this then that is written,
The stone which the builders rejected, the same is become the head of the corner?

18. Whosoever shall fall upon that stone shall be broken: but on whomsoever it shall fall, it will grind him to powder.

19. ¶ And the chief Priests and the scribes the same hour sought to lay hands on him; and they feared the people: for they perceived that he had spoken this parable against them.
Continued P. 131.

ST. JOHN, XIII.

CHAP. XIV. *(from P. 137.)*

1. And it came to pass, as he went into the house of one of the chief Pharisees, to eat bread on the sabbath day, that they watched him.

2. And behold there was a certain man before him, which had the dropsy.

3. And Jesus answering, spake unto the lawyers and Pharisees, saying, Is it lawful to heal on the sabbath day?

M. XII. 9, 11; L. VI. 7; P. 62.

4. And they held their peace. And he took *him* and healed him; and let him go :

5. And answered them, saying, Which of you shall have an ass or an ox fallen into a pit, and will not straightway pull him out on the sabbath day ? M. XII. 11.

6. And they could not answer him again to these things.

7. ¶ And he put forth a parable to those which were bidden ; when he marked how they chose out the chief rooms : saying unto them,

8. When thou art bidden of any man to a wedding, sit not down in the highest room : lest a more honourable man than thou be bidden of him ;

9. And he that bade thee and him come, and say to thee, Give this man place ; and thou begin, with shame, to take the lowest room.

10. But when thou art bidden, go and sit down in the lowest room ; that when he that bade thee cometh, he may say unto thee, Friend, go up higher : then shalt thou have worship in the presence of them that sit at meat with thee.

11. For whosoever exalteth M. XXIII. 12. himself shall be abased : and he that humbleth himself shall be exalted.

12. ¶ Then said he also to him that bade him, When thou makest a dinner or a supper ; call not thy friends, nor thy brethren, neither thy kinsmen, nor *thy* rich neighbours ; lest they also bid thee again, and a recompense be made thee.

13. But when thou makest a feast, call the poor, the maimed, the lame, the blind :

14. And thou shalt be blessed : for they cannot recompense thee : for thou shalt be recompensed at the resurrection of the just.

15. ¶ And when one of them that sat at meat with him heard these things ; he said unto him, Blessed *is* he that shall eat bread in the kingdom of God.

CHAP. XXII.

1. And Jesus answered and spake unto them again by parables ; and said,

16. Then said he unto him,

St. MATTHEW, XXII. St. MARK, XII. St. LUKE, XX., XIV. St. JOHN, XIII.

2. The kingdom of heaven is like unto a certain king, which made a marriage for his son,

3. And sent forth his servants to call them that were bidden to the wedding. And they would not come.

4. Again he sent forth other servants, saying, Tell them which are bidden, Behold I have prepared my dinner: my oxen and *my* fatlings *are* killed: and all things *are* ready. Come unto the marriage.

A certain man made a great supper, and bade many.

17. And sent his servant at supper time, to say to them that were bidden, Come;

5. But they made light of *it;* and went their ways: one to his farm;

another to his merchandize:

for all things are now ready.

18. And they all with one *consent*, began to make excuse; The first said unto him, I have bought a piece of ground; and I must needs go and see it: I pray thee have me excused.

19. And another said, I have bought five yoke of oxen; and I go to prove them; I pray thee have me excused.

20. And another said, I have married a wife; and therefore I cannot come.

6. And the remnant took his servants and entreated *them* spitefully, and slew *them*.

7. But when the king heard *thereof*, he was wroth: and he sent forth his armies, and destroyed those murderers, and burned up their city.

8. Then said he to his servants, The wedding is ready; but they which were bidden were not worthy.

9. Go ye therefore into the highways, and as many as ye shall find, bid to the marriage.

21. So that servant came, and shewed his lord these things. Then the master of the house, being angry, said to his servant;

Go out quickly into the streets and lanes of the city, and bring in hither the poor, and the maimed, and the halt, and the blind.

22. And the servant said, Lord it is done as thou hast commanded; and yet there is room.

23. And the lord said unto the servant, Go out into the highways and hedges, and compel *them* to come in, that my house may be filled.

10. So those servants went out into the highways, and gathered together all, as many as they found, both bad and good: and the wedding was furnished with guests.

11. And when the king came in to see the guests, he saw there a man which had not on a wedding garment;

12. And he saith unto him,

24. For I say unto you that none of those men which were bidden shall taste of my supper.

Continued P. 55.

St. MATTHEW, XXII.   St. MARK, XII.   St. LUKE, XX.   St. JOHN, XIII.

Friend, how camest thou in hither not having a wedding garment? and he was speechless.

13. Then said the king to the servants, Bind him hand and foot, and take him away, and cast *him* into outer darkness : there shall be weeping and gnashing of teeth.

14. For many are called, but few *are* chosen.

M. XX. 16.

15. ¶ Then went the Pharisees and took counsel how they might entangle him in *his* talk.

16. And they sent out unto him their disciples, with the Herodians,

13. ¶ And they send unto him certain of the Pharisees and of the Herodians,
to catch him in *his* words.

Chap. XX., from P. 128.
20. And they watched *him*, and sent forth spies, which should feign themselves just men ; that they might take hold of his words ; that so they might deliver him unto the power and authority of the Governor.

saying, Master, We know that thou art true, and teachest the way of God in truth ; neither carest thou for any *man*: for thou regardest not the person of men.

14. And when they were come, they say unto him ; Master, We know that thou art true ; and carest for no man ; for thou regardest not the person of men ; but teachest the way of God in truth :

21. And they asked him, saying, Master, We know that thou sayest and teachest rightly ; neither acceptest thou the person of *any* ; but teachest the way of God truly :

17. Tell us therefore, What thinkest thou ; Is it lawful to give tribute unto Cæsar ; or not ?

Is it lawful to give tribute to Cæsar, or not ?

15. Shall we give ? or shall we not give ? But he, knowing their hypocrisy, said unto them ; Why tempt ye me ?

22. Is it lawful for us to give tribute unto Cæsar ; or no ?

18. But Jesus perceived their wickedness ; and said ; Why tempt ye me,
ye hypocrites ?

23. But he perceived their craftiness and said unto them ; Why tempt ye me ?

19. Shew me the tribute money.

Bring me a penny, that I may see *it*.

16. And they brought *it*.

24. Shew me a penny.

And they brought unto him a penny.

20. And he said unto them, Whose *is* this image and superscription ?

And he saith unto them, Whose *is* this image and superscription ?

Whose image and superscription hath it ? They answered, and said, Cæsar's.

21. They say unto him, Cæsar's. Then saith he unto them ;
Render therefore unto Cæsar the things which are Cæsar's ; and unto God the things that are God's.

And they said unto him, Cæsar's.

17. And Jesus answering, said unto them, Render to Cæsar the things that are Cæsar's and to God the things that are God's.

25. And he said unto them, Render therefore unto Cæsar the things which be Cæsar's ; and unto God the things which be God's.

26. And they could not take hold of his words before the people :

22. When they had heard *these words*, they marvelled,
and left him, and went their way.

And they marvelled at him.

and they marvelled at his answer, and held their peace.

23. ¶ The same day, came to him the Sadducees, which say, that there is no resurrection ;
and asked him ;

18. ¶ Then come unto him the Sadducees, which say, there is no resurrection ;
and they asked him, saying ;

27. Then came *to him* certain of the Sadducees, which deny that there is any resurrection ; and they asked him,

24. Saying, Master, Moses said, If a man die, having no children, his brother

19. Master, Moses wrote unto us, If a man's brother die, and leave *his* wife *behind him*, and leave no children, that his brother should take his wife, and raise up seed unto his brother.

28. Saying ; Master, Moses wrote unto us ; If any man's brother die, having a wife, and he die without children ; that his brother should take his wife, and raise up seed unto his brother.

shall marry his wife, and raise up seed unto his brother.

25. Now there were with us seven brethren : and the first when he had married a wife, deceased ; and, having no issue, left his wife

20. Now there were seven brethren ;
and the first took a wife ;
and dying, left no seed.

29. There were therefore seven brethren ;
and the first took a wife,
and died without children.

St. MATTHEW, XXII. | St. MARK, XII. | St. LUKE, XX., X. | St. JOHN, XIII.

St. MATTHEW, XXII.

unto his brother :

26. Likewise the second also ; and the third ; unto the seventh.

27. And last of all the woman died also.

28. Therefore, in the resurrection, whose wife shall she be of the seven ? For they all had her.

29. Jesus answered and said unto them, ye do err, not knowing the scriptures, nor the power of God.

30. For in the resurrection they neither marry, nor are given in marriage,

but are as the angels of God in heaven.

31. But as touching the resurrection of the dead, have ye not read that which was spoken unto you by God ; saying,

32. I am the God of Abraham, and the God of Isaac, and the God of Jacob.

God is not the God of the dead,

but of the living.

33. And when the multitude heard this, they were astonished at his doctrine.

34. ¶ But when the Pharisees had heard that he had put the Sadducees to silence, they were gathered together.

35. Then one of them, which was a lawyer asked him a question, tempting him ;

36. Master, which is the great commandment in the law?

37. Jesus said unto him,

St. MARK, XII.

21. And the second took her, and died : neither left he any seed : and the third likewise ;

22. And the seven had her ; and left no seed :

last of all, the woman died also.

23. In the resurrection therefore, when they shall rise, Whose wife shall she be of them ? For the seven had her to wife.

24. And Jesus answering, said unto them, Do ye not therefore err, because ye know not the scriptures, neither the power of God ?

25. For when they shall rise from the dead they neither marry, nor are given in marriage,

but are as the angels which are in heaven.

26. And as touching the dead, that they rise, have ye not read in the book of Moses, how in the bush God spake unto him, saying, I am the God of Abraham, and the God of Isaac, and the God of Jacob?

27. He is not the God of the dead,

but the God of the living :

Ye therefore do greatly err.

28. ¶ And one of the Scribes came, and having heard them reasoning together, and perceiving that he had answered them well,

asked him, Which is the first commandment of all ?

29. And Jesus answered him, The first of all the commandments is, Hear O Israel, The Lord our God is one God :

St. LUKE, XX., X.

30. And the second took her to wife ; and he died childless.

31. And the third took her : and in like manner the seven also : and they left no children ; and died.

32. Last of all, the woman died also.

33. Therefore in the resurrection, Whose wife of them is she ? For seven had her to wife.

34. And Jesus answering, said unto them,

The children of this world marry, and are given in marriage ;

35. But they which shall be accounted worthy to obtain that world and the resurrection from the dead, neither marry nor are given in marriage.

36. Neither can they die any more : for they are equal unto the angels :

and are the children of God : being the children of the resurrection.

37. Now, that the dead are raised even Moses shewed at the bush when he called the Lord the God of Abraham, and the God of Isaac and the God of Jacob.

38. For he is not a God of the dead, but of the living : for all live unto him.

39. ¶ Then certain of the Scribes answering, said, Master, Thou hast well said.

40. And after that they durst not ask him any question at all.
Continued P. 134.
Chap. X., from P. 68.

25. And behold a certain lawyer stood up, and tempted him, saying, Master, what shall I do to inherit eternal life?

26. He said unto him, What is written in the law? How readest thou ?

27. And he answering said,

M. XXII. 35.

M. XXII. 46.

Mk. XII. 28, P. 132.

St. MATTHEW, XXII.	St. MARK, XII.	St. LUKE, XX., X.	St. JOHN, XIII.
Thou shalt love the Lord thy God with all thy heart, and with all thy mind.	30. And thou shalt love the Lord thy God with all thy heart, and with all thy soul, and with all thy mind, and with all thy strength. This *is* the first commandment.	Thou shalt love the Lord thy God with all thy heart, and with all thy soul, and with all thy strength, and with all thy mind :	
38. This is the first and great commandment.	31. And the second *is* like, *namely*, this, Thou shalt love thy neighbour as thyself.		
39. And the second *is* like unto it, Thou shalt love thy neighbour as thyself.		and thy neighbour as thyself.	
40. On these two commandments hang all the law and the prophets.	There is none other commandment greater than these.		
	32. And the Scribe said unto him, Well, Master, thou hast said the truth : for there is one God : and there is none other but he :		
	33. And to love him with all the heart, and with all the understanding, and with all the strength, and to love *his* neighbour as himself, is more than all whole burnt offerings and sacrifices.		
	34. And when Jesus saw that he answered discreetly, he said unto him, Thou art not far from the kingdom of God.	28. And he said unto him, Thou hast answered right : this do, and thou shalt live.	
		29. But *he*, willing to justify himself, said unto Jesus, And who is my neighbour ?	
		30. And Jesus answering said, A certain *man* went down from Jerusalem to Jericho, and fell among thieves, which stripped him of his raiment, and wounded *him*, and departed, leaving *him* half dead.	
		31. And by chance there came down a certain priest that way : and when he saw him, he passed by on the other side.	
		32. And likewise a Levite, when he was at the place, came, and looked *on him*, and passed by on the other side.	
		33. But a certain Samaritan, as he journeyed, came where he was, and when he saw him, he had compassion *on him*,	
		34. And went to *him*, and bound up his wounds, pouring in oil and wine, and set him on his own beast, and brought him to an inn, and took care of him.	
		35. And on the morrow, when he departed he took out two pence, and gave *them* to the host, and said unto him, take care of him : and whatsoever thou spendest more, when I come again I will repay thee.	
		36. Which now of these three, thinkest thou, was neighbour unto him that fell among the thieves ?	
		37. And he said, He that	

St. MATTHEW, XXII.   St. MARK, XII.   St. LUKE, X., XX.   St. JOHN, XIII.

shewed mercy on him. Then said Jesus unto him, Go, and do thou likewise.

Continued P. 125.

Chap. XX., from P. 132.

41. ¶ While the Pharisees were gathered together, Jesus asked them,

35. ¶ And Jesus answered and said while he taught in the temple,

41. And he said unto them,

42. Saying, What think ye of Christ? Whose son is he? They say unto him, *The son* of David.

How say the scribes that Christ

How say they that Christ

is the son of David?

is David's son?

43. He saith unto them, How then doth David in spirit call him Lord? saying,

36. For David himself said by the Holy Ghost,

42. And David himself saith in the book of Psalms,

44. The Lord said unto my Lord,

The Lord said to my Lord,

The Lord said unto my Lord,

Sit thou on my right hand,

Sit thou on my right hand,

Sit thou on my right hand,

till I make thine enemies thy footstool?

till I make thine enemies thy footstool.

43. Till I make thine enemies thy footstool.

45. If David then call him Lord,

37. David therefore himself calleth him Lord; and whence is he *then* his son?

44. David therefore calleth him, Lord; How is he then his son?

How is he his son?

46. And no man was able to answer him a word: neither durst any *man* from that day forth ask him any more *questions.* (1)

and no man after that durst ask him *any question.* (1)

CHAP. XXIII.

1. Then spake Jesus to the multitude and to his disciples,

And the common people heard him gladly.

45. ¶ Then in the audience of all the people he said unto his disciples,

2. Saying, The scribes and the Pharisees sit in Moses' seat:

38. ¶ And he said unto them in his doctrine,

3. All therefore whatsoever they bid you observe, *that* observe and do: But do not ye after their works: for they say, and do not.

Beware of the Scribes,

46. Beware of the scribes;

4. For they bind heavy burdens and grievous to be borne; and lay *them* on men's shoulders: but they *themselves* will not move them with one of their fingers. (2)

See L. XI., 46, P. 136.

5. But all their works they do for to be seen of men: They make broad their phylacteries, and enlarge the borders of their garments,

which love to go in long clothing;

which desire to walk in long robes;

6. And love the uppermost rooms at feasts, and the chief seats in the synagogues,

7. And greetings in the markets, and to be called of men, Rabbi, Rabbi.

and *love* salutations in the market places;

and love greetings in the markets;

8. But be not ye called Rabbi: for one is your master, *even* Christ: and all ye are brethren.

39. And the chief seats in the synagogues, and the uppermost rooms at feasts;

and the highest seats in the synagogues; and the chief rooms at feasts;

9. And call no *man* your father upon the earth: for one is your father, which is in heaven.

10. Neither be ye called masters: for one is your master, *even* Christ.

11. But he that is greatest among you shall be your servant.

(1) Mk. XII. 34; L. XX. 40, P. 132.
(2) L. XI. 45, 46, P. 136.

(1) M. XXII. 46; L. XX. 40, P. 132.

12. And whosoever shall exalt himself shall be abased; and he that shall humble himself shall be exalted. (1)

13. ¶ But woe unto you, scribes and Pharisees, hypocrites! For ye shut up the kingdom of heaven against men. For ye neither go in *yourselves*; neither suffer ye them that are entering to go in.

14. Woe unto you scribes and Pharisees, hypocrites! For ye devour widows' houses and for a pretence make long prayer, therefore ye shall receive the greater damnation. (2)

15. Woe unto you, scribes and Pharisees, hypocrites! For ye compass sea and land to make one proselyte, and when he is made, ye make him twofold more the child of hell than yourselves.

16. Woe unto you, ye blind guides, which say, Whosoever shall swear by the temple it is nothing; but whosoever shall swear by the gold of the temple, he is a debtor!

17. *Ye* fools, and blind: for whether is greater, the gold, or the temple that sanctifieth the gold?

18. And whosoever shall swear by the altar, it is nothing: but whosoever sweareth by the gift that is upon it, he is guilty.

19. *Ye* fools, and blind: for whether *is* greater, the gift, or the altar that sanctifieth the gift;

20. Whoso therefore shall swear by the altar, sweareth by it, and by all things thereon.

21. And whoso shall swear by the temple, sweareth by it, and by him that dwelleth therein.

22. And he that shall swear by heaven, sweareth by the throne of God, and by him that sitteth thereon.

23. Woe unto you, scribes and Pharisees, hypocrites! for ye pay tithe of mint and anise and cummin; and have omitted the weightier *matters* of law, judgment, mercy and faith. These ought ye to have done, and not to leave the other undone.

24. *Ye* blind guides, which strain at a gnat, and swallow a camel!

25. Woe unto you, scribes and Pharisees, hypocrites!

(1) L. XIV. 11, P. 129. XVIII. 14, P. 111.

40. Which devour widows' houses, and for a pretence make long prayers:
These shall receive greater damnation.

Continued P. 133.

47. Which devour widows' houses, and for a shew make long prayers.
The same shall receive greater damnation.

For Chap. XXI., see P. 133.

Chap. XI., from P. 136.

42. But woe unto you, Pharisees! for ye tithe mint and rue and all manner of herbs; and pass over judgment and the love of God. These ought ye to have done, and not to leave the other undone.

43. Woe unto you, Pharisees! For ye love the uppermost seats in the synagogues, and greetings in the markets.

L. XX. 46; P. 134. M. XXIII. 6.

Continued P. 136.

(2) [v. 14. *Not in any ancient MS.* —*Alford.*]

Chap. XI., from P. 38.

37. ¶ And as he spake, a certain Pharisee besought him to dine with him: and he went in and sat down to meat.

38. And when the Pharisee saw *it*, he marvelled that he had not first washed before dinner.

39. And the Lord said unto him, Now do ye Pharisees make clean the outside of the cup and the platter; but your inward part is full of ravening and wickedness.

40. *Ye fools!* Did not he that made that which is without, make that which is within also?

41. But rather give alms of such things as ye have; and behold, all things are clean unto you.

Continued P. 135.

for ye make clean the outside of the cup and of the platter, but within they are full of extortion and excess.

From P. 135.

44. Woe unto you scribes and Pharisees, hypocrites! For ye are as graves which appear not, and the men that walk over *them* are not aware *of them*.

26. *Thou* blind Pharisee, cleanse first that *which is within* the cup and platter, that the outside of them may be clean also.

27. Woe unto you scribes and Pharisees, hypocrites! For ye are like unto whited sepulchres; which indeed appear beautiful outward, but are within full of dead *men's* bones, and of all uncleanness.

28. Even so ye also outwardly appear righteous unto men; but within ye are full of hypocrisy and iniquity.

45. Then answered one of the lawyers, and said unto him, Master, Thus saying, thou reproachest us also.

46. And he said, Woe unto you also, *ye* lawyers! For ye lade men with burdens grievous to be borne, and ye yourselves touch not the burdens with one of your fingers. M. XXIII. 4.

29. Woe unto you, scribes and Pharisees, hypocrites!
Because ye build the tombs of the Prophets, and garnish the sepulchres of the righteous,

30. And say, If we had been in the days of our fathers we would not have been partakers with them in the blood of the prophets.

31. Wherefore ye be witnesses unto yourselves, that ye are the children of them which killed the prophets.

32. Fill ye up then the measure of your fathers.

33. *Ye* serpents! *ye* generation of vipers! how can ye escape the damnation of hell?

34. ¶ Wherefore behold, I send unto you Prophets, and wise men,

47. Woe unto you!
for ye build the sepulchres of the Prophets,

and your fathers killed them.

48. Truly ye bear witness that ye allow the deeds of your fathers: for they indeed killed them; and ye build their sepulchres.

49. Therefore also said the wisdom of God, I will send them Prophets and Apostles, and *some* of them they shall slay and persecute:

137

 St. MATTHEW, XXIII.   St. MARK, XII.   St. LUKE, XI., XIII.   St. JOHN, XIII.

and scribes : and *some* of them ye shall kill and crucify ; and *some* of them shall ye scourge in your synagogues ; and persecute *them* from city to city.

35. That upon you may come all the righteous blood shed upon the earth, from the blood of righteous Abel, unto the blood of Zacharias, son of Barachias, whom ye slew between the temple and the altar.

36. Verily I say unto you, All these things shall come upon this generation.

37. O Jerusalem, Jerusalem, *Thou* that killest the prophets, and stonest them which are sent unto thee, how often would I have gathered thy children together, even as a hen gathereth her chicken under *her* wings ; and ye would not !

38. Behold your house is left unto you desolate.

39. For I say unto you, Ye shall not see me henceforth, till ye shall say, Blessed *is* he that cometh in the name of the Lord.

50. That the blood of all the prophets which was shed from the foundation of the world may be required of this generation ;

51. From the blood of Abel, unto the blood of Zacharias which perished between the altar and the temple.
Verily, I say unto you, It shall be required of this generation.

52. Woe unto you, lawyers ! for ye have taken away the key of knowledge ; ye enter not in yourselves, and them that were entering in ye hindered.

53. And as he said these things unto them, the scribes and the Pharisees began to urge him vehemently, and to provoke him to speak of many things :

54. Laying wait for him, and seeking to catch something out of his mouth, that they might accuse him.

For Chap. XII., see P. 54.

Chap. XIII., from P. 42.
31. ¶ The same day there came certain of the Pharisees, saying unto him, Get thee out and depart hence ; for Herod will kill thee.

32. And he said unto them, Go ye and tell that fox ; behold I cast out devils, and I do cures to-day and to-morrow, and the third *day* I shall be perfected.

33. Nevertheless I must walk to-day, and to-morrow, and the *day* following ; for it cannot be that a prophet perish out of Jerusalem.

34. O Jerusalem, Jerusalem, which killest the prophets, and stonest them that are sent unto thee ; how often would I have gathered thy children together as a hen *doth gather* her brood under *her* wings, and ye would not !

35. Behold your house is left unto you desolate : and verily I say unto you, Ye shall not see me until *the time* come when ye shall say, Blessed *is* he that cometh in the name of the Lord.

For Chap. XIV., see P. 128.

19

From P. 135.

CHAP. XXI. *(from P. 135).*

41. ¶ And Jesus sat over against the treasury
and beheld how the people
cast money into the treasury : and many that were rich cast in much.
42. And there came a certain poor widow; and she threw in two mites : which make a farthing.
43. And he called *unto him* his disciples, and saith unto them,
Verily I say unto you, that this poor widow hath cast more in, than all they which have cast into the treasury :
44. For all *they* did cast in of their abundance ;
but she of her want did cast in all that she had ; *even* all her living.

1. And he looked up and saw the rich men casting their gifts into the treasury.

2. And he saw also a certain poor widow casting in thither two mites.

3. And he said, Of a truth I say unto you, that this poor widow hath cast in more than they all :
4. For all these have of their abundance cast in unto the offerings of God :
but she of her penury hath cast in all the living that she had.

CHAP. XXIV.

CHAP. XIII.

1. And Jesus went out, and departed from the temple :
and his disciples came to *him* for to show him the buildings of the temple.
2. And Jesus said unto them, See ye not all these things? Verily I say unto you, There shall not be left here one stone upon another that shall not be thrown down.
3. ¶ And as he sat upon the mount of Olives

the disciples came unto him privately, saying,

Tell us when shall these things be? and what *shall* be the sign of thy coming, and of the end of the world :
4. And Jesus answered and said unto them, Take heed that no man deceive you.
5. For many shall come in my name saying
I am Christ ; and shall deceive many.

6. And ye shall hear of wars, and rumours of wars : see that ye be not troubled : for all *these things* must come to pass : but the end is not yet.
7. For nation shall rise against nation, and kingdom against kingdom ; and there shall be famines, and pestilences, and earthquakes,

1. And as he went out of the temple, one of his disciples saith unto him, Master, see what manner of stones, and what buildings *are here!*
2. And Jesus answering, said unto him, seest thou these great buildings?
There shall not be left one stone upon another that shall not be thrown down.
3. And as he sat upon the mount of Olives, over against the temple,
Peter and James and John and Andrew asked him privately,

4. Tell us, When shall these things be? and what *shall* be the sign when all these things shall be fulfilled?
5. And Jesus answering them, began to say, Take heed lest any *man* deceive you.
6. For many shall come in my name, saying,
I am *Christ ;* and shall deceive many.

7. And when ye shall hear of wars, and rumours of wars, be ye not troubled :
for *such things* must needs be : but the end *shall* not *be* yet.
8. For nation shall rise against nation, and kingdom against kingdom, and there shall be earthquakes in divers places ;

5. ¶ And as some spake of the temple how it was adorned with goodly stones and gifts, he said,

6. *As for* these things which ye behold, the days will come in the which there shall not be left one stone upon another that shall not be thrown down.

7. And they asked him, saying, Master, But when shall these things be? And what sign *will there be* when these things shall come to pass?

8. And he said, Take heed that ye be not deceived :
For many shall come in my name, saying,
I am *Christ ;*
and the time draweth near. Go ye not therefore after them.
9. But when ye shall hear of wars and commotions, be not terrified : for these things must first come to pass : but the end *is* not by and by.
10. Then said he unto them, Nation shall rise against nation ; and kingdom against kingdom :
11. And great earthquakes shall

St. MATTHEW, XXIV. | St. MARK, XIII. | St. LUKE, XXI. | St. JOHN, XIII.

in divers places :

and there shall be famines and troubles,

be in divers places, and famines, and pestilences,
and fearful sights, and great signs shall there be from heaven.

8. All these *are* the beginning of sorrows.

These *are* the beginnings of sorrows.

9. Then shall they deliver you up to be afflicted,

9. ¶ But take heed to yourselves : for they shall deliver you up to councils, and in the synagogues ye shall be beaten :
and ye shall be brought before rulers and kings for my sake ; for a testimony against them.

12. But before all these, they shall lay their hands on you, and persecute *you ;* delivering you up to the synagogues, and in prisons, being brought before kings and rulers for my name's sake.
13. And it shall turn to you for a testimony.

and shall kill you : (1)
and ye shall be hated of all nations for my name's sake

See v. 13.

See v. 17.

See v. 14.

10. And the Gospel must first be published among all nations.
11. But when they shall lead *you,* and deliver you up ; take no thought before hand what ye shall speak, neither do ye premeditate :
but whatsoever shall be given you in that hour, that speak ye ; for it is not ye that speak, but the Holy Ghost.
12. Now the brother shall betray the brother to death ; and the father the son ; and children shall rise up against *their* parents : and
shall cause them to be put to death.
13. And ye shall be hated of all *men* for my name's sake :

14. Settle *it* therefore in your hearts, not to meditate before what ye shall answer.
15. For I will give you a mouth and wisdom, which all your adversaries shall not be able to gainsay nor resist.
16. And ye shall be betrayed both by parents and brethren, and kinsfolk, and friends.

And *some* of you shall they cause to be put to death.
17. And ye shall be hated of all *men* for my name's sake.
18. But there shall not an hair of your head perish.
19. In your patience possess ye your souls.

10. And then shall many be offended, and shall betray one another ; and shall hate one another.

See v. 9.

v. 13.

v. 17.

11. And many false prophets shall rise, and shall deceive many.
12. And because iniquity shall abound, the love of many shall wax cold.
13. But he that shall endure unto the end, the same shall be saved.
14. And this Gospel of the kingdom shall be preached in all the world for a witness unto all nations :
and then shall the end come.
15. When ye therefore shall see the abomination of desolation, spoken of by Daniel the Prophet, stand in the holy place, (whoso readeth let him understand ;)

but he that shall endure unto the end the same shall be saved.

See v. 10.

14. ¶ But when ye shall see the abomination of desolation, spoken of by Daniel the Prophet, standing where it ought not, (let him that readeth understand,)

20. And when ye shall see Jerusalem compassed with armies,

then know that the desolation thereof is nigh.

St. MATTHEW, XXIV.

St. MARK, XIII.

St. LUKE, XXI. XVII.

St. JOHN, XIII.

16. Then let them which be in Judea flee into the mountains :

then let them that be in Judea flee to the mountains :

21. Then let them which are in Judea flee to the mountain ;
and let them which are in the midst of it depart out ; and let not them that are in the countries enter thereinto.
22. For these be the days of vengeance, that all things which are written may be fulfilled.
Continued below.

17. Let him which is on the housetop not come down to take anything out of his house.
18. Neither let him which is in the field return back to take his clothes.

15. And let him that is on the housetop not go down into the house, neither enter *therein*, to take anything out of his house :
16. And let him that is in the field not turn back again for to take up his garment.

Chap. XVII., from P. 142.
31. In that day he which shall be upon the house-top, and his stuff in the house, let him not come down to take it away :
and he that is in the field, let him likewise not return back.
32. Remember Lot's wife.
33. Whosoever shall seek to save his life, shall lose it ; and whosoever shall lose his life shall preserve it.
Continued P. 142.

19. And woe unto them that are with child, and to them that give suck in those days?

17. But woe to them that are with child, and to them that give suck in those days !

Chap. XXI., resumed.
23. But woe unto them that are with child, and to them that give suck in those days ! For there shall be great distress in the land and wrath upon this people.
24. And they shall fall by the edge of the sword ; and shall be led away captive into all nations : and Jerusalem shall be trodden down of the Gentiles, until the times of the Gentiles be fulfilled.
Continued P. 141.

20. But pray ye that your flight be not in the winter ;
neither on the sabbath day ;
21. For then shall be great tribulation, such as was not since the beginning of the world to this time,
no, nor ever shall be.
22. And except those days should be shortened there should no flesh be saved : but for the elect's sake
those days shall be shortened.

18. And pray ye that your flight be not in the winter.
19. For in those days shall be affliction, such as was not from the beginning of the creation which God created unto this time; neither shall be.
20. And except that the Lord had shortened those days, no flesh should be saved : but for the elect's sake, whom he hath chosen, he hath shortened the days.

Chap. XVII., from P. 119.
20. ¶ And when he was demanded of the Pharisees, when the kingdom of God should come ; he answered them, and said : The kingdom of God cometh not with observation :

23. Then if any man shall say unto you, Lo, here *is* Christ, or there !

21. And then if any man shall say to you, Lo, here *is* Christ, or Lo, *he is* there !

21. Neither shall they say, Lo here ! or, Lo there !

St. MATTHEW, XXIV.   St. MARK, XIII.   St. LUKE, XVII., XXI.   St. JOHN, XIII.

believe *it* not.

believe *him* not.

for behold the kingdom of God is within you.

24. For there shall arise false Christs, and false prophets, and shall shew great signs and wonders ; insomuch that, if *it were* possible, they shall deceive the very elect.

25. Behold, I have told you before.

22. For false Christs and false prophets shall rise ; and shall shew signs and wonders to seduce, if *it were* possible, even the elect.

23. But take ye heed : behold, I have foretold you all things.

22. And he said unto the disciples, The days will come, when ye shall desire to see one of the days of the Son of man, and ye shall not see *it :*
23. And they shall say to you, See here ; or see there : Go not after *them ;* nor follow *them.*

26. Wherefore if they shall say unto you, Behold he is in the desert; go not forth : Behold *he is* in the secret chambers ; believe *it* not.

27. For as the lightning cometh out of the east, and shineth even unto the west ;
so shall also the coming of the Son of man be.

24. For as the lightning that lighteneth out of the *one* part under heaven shineth unto the other *part* under heaven ; so shall also the Son of man be in his day.
25. But first must he suffer many things : and be rejected of this generation.

Continued P. 142.

28. For wheresoever the carcase is, there will the eagles be gathered together.

See L. XVII., 37, P. 142, 143.

29. Immediately after the tribulation of those days shall the sun be darkened, and the moon shall not give her light,
and the stars shall fall from heaven,

24. ¶ But in those days, after that tribulation, the sun shall be darkened, and the moon shall not give her light,
25. And the stars of heaven shall fall,

Chap. XXI., from P. 140.
25. ¶ And there shall be signs in the sun,
and in the moon,
and in the stars ;

and upon the earth distress of nations, with perplexity : the sea and the waves roaring ;
26. Men's hearts failing them for fear, and for looking after those things which are coming on the earth.

and the powers of the heavens shall be shaken.
30. And then shall appear the sign of the Son of man in heaven : and then shall all the tribes of the earth mourn:
And they shall see the Son of man coming in the clouds of heaven, (1) with power and great glory.

and the powers that are in heaven shall be shaken.

26. And then shall they see the Son of man coming in the clouds, with great power and glory.

For the powers of heaven shall be shaken.

27. And then shall they see the Son of man coming in a cloud with power and great glory.

28. And when these things begin to come to pass ; then look up, and lift up your heads ; for your redemption draweth nigh.

31. And he shall send his angels, with a great sound of a trumpet,

27. And then shall he send his

(1) M. IV. 17.

ST. MATTHEW, XXIV. | ST. MARK, XIII. | ST. LUKE, XXI., XVII. | ST. JOHN, XIII.

ST. MATTHEW, XXIV.

and they shall gather together his elect from the four winds, from one end of heaven to the other.

32. Now learn a parable of the fig tree : When his branch is yet tender, and putteth forth leaves, ye know that summer *is* nigh :

33. So likewise ye, when ye shall see all these things, know that it is near : *even* at the doors.

34. Verily, I say unto you this generation shall not pass, Till all these things be fulfilled.

35. Heaven and earth shall pass away, but my word shall not pass away.

36. ¶ But of that day and hour knoweth no *man ;* no, not the angels of heaven ;

but my Father only.

37. But as the days of Noe were, so shall also the coming of the Son of man be.

38. For as in the days that were before the flood they were eating and drinking, marrying, and giving in marriage, until the day that Noe entered into the ark,

39. And knew not until the flood came and took them all away ;

so shall also the coming of the Son of man be.

40. Then shall two be in the field ; the one shall be taken, and the other left.

41. Two *women shall be* grinding at the mill ; the one shall be taken, and the other left.

ST. MARK, XIII.

angels, and shall gather together his elect from the four winds, from the uttermost part of the earth to the uttermost part of heaven.

28. Now learn a parable of the fig tree : When her branch is yet tender, and putteth forth leaves, ye know that summer is near :

29. So ye in like manner, when ye shall see these things come to pass, know that it is nigh ; *even* at the doors.

30. Verily, I say unto you, That this generation shall not pass till all these things be done.

31. Heaven and earth shall pass away, but my words shall not pass away.

32. ¶ But of that day, and *that* hour, knoweth no man : no, not the angels which are in heaven neither the Son ; but the Father.

ST. LUKE, XXI., XVII.

Chap. XXI., continued.

29. And he spake to them a parable :

Behold the fig tree, and all the trees :

30. When they now shoot forth, ye see and know of your own selves that summer is now nigh at hand.

31. So likewise ye, when ye see these things come to pass, know ye that the kingdom of God is nigh at hand.

32. Verily, I say unto you, This generation shall not pass away till all be fulfilled.

33. Heaven and earth shall pass away : but my words shall not pass away.

Continued P. 143.

Chap. XVII., from P. 141.

26. And as it was in the days of Noe, so shall it be also in the days of the Son of man.

27. They did eat, they drank, they married wives, they were given in marriage, until the day that Noe entered into the ark, and the flood came and destroyed them all.

28. Likewise also as it was in the days of Lot ; they did eat, they drank, they bought, they sold, they planted, they builded :

29. But, the same day that Lot went out of Sodom, it rained fire and brimstone from heaven, and destroyed *them* all.

30. Even thus shall it be in the day when the Son of man is revealed.

Continued P. 140.

Chap. XVII., from P. 140.

34. I tell you, in that night, there shall be two *men* in one bed : the one shall be taken, and the other left.

36. Two *men* shall be in the field : the one shall be taken, and the other left.

35. Two *women* shall be grinding together : the one shall be taken, and the other left.

37. And they answered and said

[*Verse 36 not in any of the old MSS.—Alford.*]

unto him, Where, Lord ? And he said unto them, Wheresoever the body *is*, thither will the eagles be gathered together.   M. XXIV. 28.

For Chap. XVIII., see P. 110.

Chap. XXI., from P. 142.
34. ¶ And take heed to yourselves, lest at any time your hearts be overcharged with surfeiting, and drunkenness, and cares of this life ; and *so* that day come upon you unawares.
35. For as a snare shall it come on all them that dwell on the face of the whole earth.

42. ¶ Watch therefore : for ye know not what hour your Lord doth come. (1)

33. Take ye heed, watch and pray : for ye know not when the time is. (1)

36. Watch ye therefore, and pray always, that ye may be accounted worthy to escape all these things that shall come to pass, and to stand before the Son of man.
Continued P. 144.

Chap. XII., from P. 39.
32. Fear not, little flock, for it is your Father's good pleasure to give you the kingdom.
33. Sell that ye have, and give alms ; provide yourselves bags which wax not old, a treasure in the heavens that faileth not ; where no thief approacheth, neither moth corrupteth.   M. VI. 20, 21.
34. For where your treasure is, there will your heart be also.
35. Let your loins be girded about, and *your* lights burning :
36. And ye yourselves like unto men that wait for their Lord   M. XXV. 7, 10. when he will return from the wedding ; that when he cometh and knocketh, they may open unto him immediately.
37. Blessed *are* those servants whom the Lord when he cometh shall find watching : Verily I say unto you, that he shall gird himself, and make them to sit down to meat, and will come forth and serve them.
38. And if he shall come in the second watch, or come in the third watch, and *find* them so, blessed are those servants.

43. But know this, that if the good man of the house had known in what watch the thief would come, he would have watched, and would not have suffered his house to be broken up.

34. *For the Son of man is* as a man taking a far journey, who left his house, and gave authority to his servants, and to every man his work, and commanded the porter to watch.

39. And this know, that if the good man of the house had known what hour the thief would come, he would have watched, and not have suffered his house to be broken through.

(1) M. XXV. 13.

(1) Mk. XIII. 35. P. 144.

ST. MATTHEW, XXIV. ST. MARK, XIII. ST. LUKE, XII. XXI. ST. JOHN, XIII.

44. Therefore be ye also ready : for in such an hour as ye think not, the Son of man cometh.

45. Who then is a faithful and wise servant whom his Lord hath made ruler over his household, to give them meat in due season ?

46. Blessed is that servant whom his Lord when he cometh shall find so doing.
47. Verily, I say unto you, That he shall make him ruler over all his goods,
48. But if that evil servant shall say in his heart, My Lord delayeth his coming ;
49. And shall begin to smite his fellow servants, and to eat and drink with the drunken ;
50. The Lord of that servant shall come in a day when he looketh not for him, and in an hour that he is not aware of ;
51. And shall cut him asunder, and appoint him his portion with the hypocrites : there shall be weeping and gnashing of teeth.

M. VIII. 12.
XXV. 30.
XIII. 42, 50.

35. Watch ye therefore, for ye know not when the master of the house cometh ; at even, or at midnight, or at the cock crowing, or in the morning.
36. Lest coming suddenly he find you sleeping.
37. And what I say unto you, I say unto all watch.

For Chap. XIV., see P. 148.

40. Be ye therefore ready also, for the son of man cometh in an hour ye think not.

41. ¶ Then Peter said unto him, Lord, speakest thou this parable unto us ? or even to all ?
42. And the Lord said, Who then is that faithful and wise steward whom his Lord shall make ruler over his household, to give them their portion of meat in due season ?
43. Blessed is that servant whom his Lord, when he cometh, shall find so doing.
44. Of a truth I say unto you, That he will make him ruler over all that he hath.
45. But and if that servant say in his heart, My Lord delayeth his coming ; and shall begin to beat the men servants and maidens and to eat and drink and to be drunken ;
46. The Lord of that servant will come in a day when he looketh not for him, and at an hour when he is not aware, and will cut him in sunder, and will appoint him his portion with the unbelievers.

47. And that servant which knew his Lord's will, and prepared not himself, neither did according to his will, shall be beaten with many stripes.
48. But he that knew not, and did commit things worthy of stripes, shall be beaten with few stripes. For unto whomsoever much is given, of him shall be much required : and to whom men have committed much, of him they will ask the more.
49. ¶ I am come to send fire on the earth ; and what will I, if it be already kindled ?
50. But I have a baptism to be baptized with, and how am I straightened till it be accomplished !
Continued P. 55.
Chap. XXI., from P. 143.
37. And in the day time he was teaching in the temple : and at night he went out, and abode in the mount that is called the mount of Olives.
38. And all the people came early in the morning to him in the Temple for to hear him.

For Chap. XXII. see P. 148.

Query, whether these verses should be before v 51 of L. XII , P. 55.

Chap. XXV.

1. Then shall the kingdom of heaven be likened unto ten virgins which took their lamps, and went forth to meet the bridegroom.

2. And five of them were wise, and five *were* foolish.

3. They that *were* foolish took their lamps, and took no oil with them :

4. But the wise took oil in their vessels with their lamps.

5. While the bridegroom tarried they all slumbered and slept.

6. And at midnight there was a cry made, Behold, the bridegroom cometh ; go ye out to meet him.

7. Then all these virgins arose, and trimmed their lamps :*   * L. XII. 35, P. 143.

8. And the foolish said unto the wise, give us of your oil ; for our lamps are gone out.

9. But the wise answered, saying, *Not so:* lest there be not enough for us and you : but go ye rather to them that sell, and buy for yourselves.

10. And while they went to buy, the bridegroom came. And they that were ready went in with him to the marriage : and the door was shut.†   † L. XII. 36, P. 143.

11. Afterwards came also the other virgins, saying, Lord, Lord, open to us.

12. But he answered, and said, Verily I say unto you, I know you not.

13. Watch therefore,* for ye know neither the day nor the hour wherein the Son of man cometh.   * M. XXIV. 42.

Chap. XIX., from P. 121.

11. And as they heard these things, he added and spake a parable, because he was nigh to Jerusalem, and because they thought that the kingdom of God should immediately appear.

14. ¶ For the *kingdom of heaven* is as a man travelling into a far country,   *See Mk. XIII.,* 34, P. 143.

12. He said therefore* A certain nobleman went into a far country

to receive for himself a kingdom, and to return.

13. And he called his ten servants, and delivered them ten pounds, and said unto them, Occupy till I come.

who called his own servants, and delivered unto them his goods.

15. And unto one he gave five talents, to another two, and to another one, to every man according to his several ability : and straightway took his journey.

* The similarity of these verses, L. XIX. 12 to 26, to those of St. Matthew XXV. 14 to 29 ; and the necessity of keeping St. Matthew as the standard of order ; decided the placing here of these verses, (12 to 26). Though the context of verses L. XIX. 11, 27, 28, would indicate that the passage might have been correctly inserted in continuance of Luke, XIX. 10, P. 121.

ST. MATTHEW, XXV.   ST. MARK, XIV.   ST. LUKE, XIX.   ST. JOHN, XIII.

14. But his citizens hated him, and sent a message after him, saying, We will not have this *man* to reign over us.

16. Then he that had received the five talents went and traded with the same, and made *them* other five talents.

17. And likewise he that *had received* two ; he also gained other two.

18. But he that had received one, went and digged in the earth, and hid his Lord's money.

19. After a long time the Lord of those servants cometh,

15. And it came to pass, that when he was returned,
having received the kingdom, then he commanded these servants to he called unto him to whom he had given the money, that he might know how much every man had gained by trading.

16. Then came the first, saying, Lord,

and reckoneth with them.

20. And so he that had received five talents came, and brought other five talents, saying, Lord, Thou deliveredst unto me five talents ; behold I have gained beside them five talents more.

21. His Lord said unto him, Well done, *thou* good and faithful servant : Thou hast been faithful over a few things : I will make thee ruler over many things : enter thou into the joy of thy Lord.

22. He also that had received two talents came, and said, Lord, Thou deliveredst unto me two talents : behold, I have gained two other talents besides them.

23. His Lord said unto him, Well done, good and faithful servant : thou hast been faithful over a few things : I will make thee ruler over many things : enter thou into the joy of thy Lord.

24. Then he which had received the one talent came, and said, Lord, I knew thee that thou art an hard man ; reaping where thou hast not sown, and gathering where thou hast not strawed :

25. And I was afraid ; and went and hid thy talent in the earth. Lo, *there* thou hast *that is* thine.

26. His Lord answered and said unto him,

Thou pound hath gained ten pounds.

17. And he said unto him, Well, thou good servant : because thou hast been faithful in a very little, have thou authority over ten cities.

18. And the second [came, saying, Lord,

thy pound hath gained five pounds.

19. And he said likewiss to him, Be thou also over five cities.

20. And another came, saying, Lord, behold, *here is* thy pound, which I have kept laid up in a napkin :

21. For I feared thee, because thou art an austere man. Thou takest up that thou layedst not down ; and reapest that thou didst not sow.

22. And he saith unto him,

Thou wicked and slothful servant ! Thou knewest that I reap where I sowed not ; and gather where I have not strawed :

27. Thou oughtest therefore to

Out of thine own mouth I will judge thee, *thou* wicked servant. Thou knewest that I was an austere man, taking up that I laid not down ; and reaping that I did not sow.

ST. MATTHEW, XXV. | ST. MARK, XIV. | ST. LUKE, XIX. | ST. JOHN, XIII.

have put my money to the exchangers, and *then* at my coming, I should have received mine own with usury.

28. Take therefore the talent from him, and give *it* to him which hath ten talents.

29. For unto every one that hath, shall be given, and he shall have abundance ; but from him that hath not, shall be taken away even that which he hath.

M. XIII. 12.

30. And cast ye the unprofitable servant into outer darkness. There shall be weeping and gnashing of teeth.

M. VIII. 12 ;
XXIV. 51.

31. ¶ When the Son of man shall come in his glory, and all the holy angels with him, then shall he sit upon the throne of his glory :
32. And before him shall be gathered all nations : and he shall separate them one from another, as a shepherd divideth *his* sheep from the goats :
33. And he shall set the sheep on his right hand ; but the goats on the left.
34. Then shall the king say unto them on his right hand, Come, ye blessed of my Father, inherit the kingdom prepared for you from the foundation of the world :
35. For I was an hungred, and ye gave me meat : I was thirsty, and ye gave me drink : I was a stranger, and ye took me in :
36. Naked and ye clothed me : I was sick and ye visited me : I was in prison, and ye came unto me.
37. Then shall the righteous answer him, saying, Lord, when saw we thee an hungred, and fed *thee?* or thirsty, and gave *thee* drink?
38. When saw we thee a stranger, and took *thee* in ? or naked, and clothed *thee?*

XIX. 23. Wherefore then gavest not thou my money into the bank, that at my coming, I might have required mine own with usury ?
24. And he said unto them that stood by, Take from him the pound, and give *it* to him that hath ten pounds.
25. (And they said unto him, Lord, He hath ten pounds.)
26. For I say unto you, That unto every one which hath, shall be given : and from him that hath not, even that he hath shall be taken away from him.

L. VIII. 18, P. 67.

27. But those mine enemies, which would not that I should reign over them, bring hither and slay *them* before me.
28. ¶ And when he had thus spoken, he went before, ascending up to Jerusalem.
Continued P. 121.

ST. MATTHEW, XXVI. | ST. MARK, XIV. | ST. LUKE, XXII. | ST. JOHN, XIII, XII.

39. Or when saw we thee sick, or in prison, and came unto thee!

40. And the king shall answer, and say unto them, Verily I say unto you, inasmuch as ye have done it unto one of the least of these my brethren, ye have done it unto me.

41. Then shall ye say also unto them on the left hand, Depart from me, ye cursed, into everlasting fire, prepared for the devil and his angels:

42. For I was an hungred, and ye gave me no meat: I was thirsty, and ye gave me no drink:

43. I was a stranger, and ye took me not in: naked, and ye clothed me not: sick, and in prison, and ye visited me not.

44. Then shall they also answer him, saying, Lord, when saw we thee an hungred, or athirst, or a stranger, or naked, or sick, or in prison, and did not minister unto thee?

45. Then shall he answer them, saying, Verily, I say unto you, Inasmuch as he did it not to one of the least of these, ye did it not to me.

46. And these shall go away into everlasting punishment, but the righteous into life eternal.

CHAP. XXVI. | CHAP. XIV. | CHAP. XXII. | CHAP. XII.

1. And it came to pass when Jesus had finished all these sayings, he said unto his disciples,

2. Ye know that after two days is the feast of the Passover, | 1. After two days was the feast of the Passover, | 1. Now the feast of unleavened bread drew nigh, which is called the Passover. | 1. Then Jesus six days before the Passover, came to

and the son of man is betrayed to be crucified. | and of the unleavened bread:

3. Then assembled together the chief Priests and the scribes, and the elders of the people unto the palace of the high Priest,

| and the chief Priests and the scribes | 2. And the chief Priests and scribes

who was called Caiaphas,*

4. And consulted that they might take Jesus, by subtlety, and kill him. | sought how they might take him by craft, and put him to death. | sought how they might kill him;

5. But they said, Not on the feast day lest there be an uproar among the people. | 2. But they said, Not on the feast day, lest there be an uproar of the people. | for they feared the people.

Continued P. 151.

* L. III. 2, P. 13.

St. MATTHEW, XXVI.	St. MARK, XIV.	St. LUKE, VII., XXII.	St. JOHN, XII., XIII.
6. ¶ Now when Jesus was in Bethany,	3. ¶ And being in Bethany,	*Chap. VII., from P. 59.*	Bethany, where Lazarus was which had been dead, whom he raised from the dead.
			(5th visit.)
		36. ¶ And one of the Pharisees* desired him that he would eat with him. And he went into the Pharisee's house, and sat down to meat. (1.)	
in the house of Simon the leper,	in the house of Simon the leper, as he sat at meat,		
			2. There they made him a supper ; and Martha served : but Lazarus was one of them that sat at the table with him.
7. There came to him a woman having,	there came a woman having	37. And behold, a woman in the city, which was a sinner, when she knew that *Jesus* sat at meat in the Pharisee's house, brought an alabaster box of ointment,	3. Then took Mary
an alabaster box of very precious ointment,	an alabaster box of ointment of spikenard, very precious :		a pound of ointment of spikenard, very costly,
		38. And stood at his feet behind *him* weeping, and began to wash his feet with tears, and did wipe *them* with the hairs of her head, and kissed his feet, and anointed *them* with the ointment.	and anointed the feet of Jesus, and wiped his feet with her hair :
and poured it on his head as he sat *at meat*.	and she brake the box, and poured *it* on his head.		and the house was filled with the odour of the ointment.
		39. Now when the Pharisee which had bidden him (2) saw *it*, he spake within himself, saying, This man, if he were a Prophet, would have known who, and what manner of woman *this is* that toucheth him ; for she is a sinner.	
		40. And Jesus answering, said unto him, Simon,*	
8. But when his disciples saw *it*, they had indignation, saying, To what purpose *is* this waste?	4. And there were some that had indignation within themselves, and said, Why was this waste of the ointment made?	* See v. 36.	4. Then saith one of his disciples, Judas Iscariot, Simon's *son* which should betray him. (1)
9. For this ointment might have been sold for much, and given to the poor.	5. For it might have been sold for more than three hundred pence, and have been given to the poor. And they murmured against her.		5. Why was not this ointment sold for three hundred pence and given to the poor?
			6. This he said, not that he cared for the poor ; but because he was a thief, and had the bag ; and bare what was put therein.
10. When Jesus understood *it*, he said unto them, Why trouble ye the woman ?	6. And Jesus said, Let her alone : why trouble ye her ?		7. Then said Jesus, let her alone.
			Against the day of my burying hath she kept this (2)
for she hath wrought a good work upon me.	she hath wrought a good work on me.		8. For the poor always ye have with you ;
11. For ye have the poor always with you ;	7. For ye have the poor with you always, and whensoever ye will ye may do them good.		
but me ye have not always.	but me ye have not always.		but me ye have not always
		* v. 40 ; J. XII. 4 ; M. XXVI. 6.	(1) L. VII. 36, *above.*
		(1) L. XI. 37, P. 196.	(2) M. XXVI. 12.
		(2) M. XXVI. 6.	

ST. MATTHEW, XXVI. | ST. MARK, XIV. | ST. LUKE, VII. XXII. | ST. JOHN, XII. XIII.

12. For in that she hath poured this ointment on my body, she did *it* for my burial.

13. Verily I say unto you, Wheresoever this Gospel shall be preached in the whole world, *there* shall also this, that this woman hath done, be told for a memorial of her.

8. She hath done what she could : she is come aforehand to anoint my body to the burying.

9. Verily I say unto you, Wheresoever this Gospel shall be preached throughout the whole world, *this* also that she hath done shall be spoken of for a memorial of her.

I have somewhat to say unto thee. And he saith, Master, say on.

41. There was a certain creditor which had two debtors : the one owed five hundred pence, and the other fifty.

42. And when they had nothing to pay, he frankly forgave them both. Tell me therefore, which of them will love him most?

43. Simon answered and said, I suppose that *he* to whom he forgave most. And he said unto him, Thou hast rightly judged.

44. And he turned to the woman, and said unto Simon, Seest thou this woman? I entered into thine house : thou gavest me no water for my feet; but she hath washed my feet with tears, and wiped *them* with the hairs of her head.

45. Thou gavest me no kiss ; but this woman, since the time I came in hath not ceased to kiss my feet.

46. My head with oil thou didst not anoint ; but this woman hath anointed my feet with ointment.

47. Wherefore I say unto thee, Her sins which are many, are forgiven ; for she loved much ; but to whom little is forgiven, *the same* loveth little.

48. And he said unto her, Thy sins are forgiven.

49. And they that sat at meat with him began to say within themselves, Who is this that forgiveth sins also?

50. And he said to the woman, Thy faith hath saved thee, go in peace.

L. XI. 37, 38. P. 136.

For Chap. VIII., see P. 66.

9. Much people of the Jews therefore knew that he was there : and they came not for Jesus' sake only, but that they might see Lazarus also, whom he had raised from the dead. (1)

10. ¶ But the chief priests consulted that they might put Lazarus also to death : (2)

(1) J. XI. 43, P. 114.
(2) J. XI. 47.

ST. MATTHEW, XXVI.   ST. MARK, XIV.   ST. LUKE, XXII.   ST. JOHN, XII, XIII.

ST. JOHN, XII, XIII.

C. XII. 11. Because that by reason of him many of the Jews went away, and believed on Jesus.

Continued P. 122.

ST. LUKE, XXII.

Chap. XXII., from P. 148.
3. ¶ Then entered Satan into Judas, surnamed Iscariot, being of the number of the twelve.

ST. MATTHEW, XXVI.

14. ¶ Then one of the twelve, called Judas Iscariot, (1)

went unto the chief priests,

ST. MARK, XIV.

10. ¶ And Judas Iscariot, one of the twelve,

went unto the chief priests,

ST. LUKE, XXII.

4. And he went his way, and communed with the chief Priests and Captains,

ST. MATTHEW

15. And said *unto them,* What will ye give me, and I will deliver him unto you?

And they covenanted with him for thirty pieces of silver.
16. And from that time he sought opportunity to betray him.

ST. MARK

to betray him unto them.
11. And when they heard it, they were glad, and promised to give him money.
And he sought how he might conveniently betray him.

ST. LUKE

how he might betray him unto them.

5. And they were glad, and covenanted to give him money.
6. And he promised, and sought opportunities to betray him unto them,
in the absence of the multitude.

ST. MATTHEW

17. ¶ Now the first *day* of the *feast of* unleavened bread, the disciples came to Jesus, saying unto him, Where wilt thou that we prepare for thee to eat the passover?

18. And he said,

ST. MARK

12. ¶ And the first day of unleavened bread, when they killed the passover,
his disciples said unto him, Where wilt thou that we go and prepare that thou mayest eat the passover?
13. And he sendeth forth two of his disciples, and saith unto them,

ST. LUKE

7. ¶ Then came the day of unleavened bread, when the passover must be killed.

8. And he sent Peter and John,
saying,
Go, and prepare us the passover, that we may eat.
9. And they said unto him, Where wilt thou that we prepare?
10. And he said unto them,

ST. MATTHEW

Go into the city,
to such a man,

ST. MARK

Go ye into the city, and there shall meet you a man bearing a pitcher of water: follow him.

ST. LUKE

Behold, when ye are entered into the city, there shall a man meet you, bearing a pitcher of water; follow him into the house where he entereth in.

ST. MATTHEW

and say unto him,
The Master saith, my time is at hand: I will keep the passover at thy house, with my disciples.

ST. MARK

14. And wheresoever he shall go in, say ye to the good man of the house, The Master saith, Where is the guest chamber where I shall eat the passover with my disciples?

ST. LUKE

11. And ye shall say unto the good man of the house, The Master saith unto thee, Where is the guest chamber where I shall eat the passover with my disciples?

ST. MARK

15. And he will shew you a large upper room furnished *and* prepared:
There make ready for us.
16. And his disciples went forth, and came into the city, and found as he had said unto them: and they made ready the passover.

ST. LUKE

12. And he shall shew you a large upper room, furnished:

there make ready.
13. And they went,

and found as he had said unto them: and they made ready the passover.

ST. MATTHEW

19. And the disciples did as Jesus had appointed them;

and they made ready the passover.

ST. JOHN

CHAP. XIII.

From P. 124.

1. Now before the feast of the passover, when Jesus knew that his hour was come that he should depart out of this world unto the Father, having loved his own which were in the world, he loved them unto the end.

ST. MATTHEW

20. Now when the even was

ST. MARK

17. And in the evening he

ST. LUKE

14. And when the hour was

(1) J. XIII. 2, P. 152

St. MATTHEW, XXVI.	St. MARK, XIV.	St. LUKE, XXII.	St. JOHN, XIII.

come, he sat down with the twelve.

21. And as they did eat,

cometh with the twelve.

18. And as they sat and did eat,

come, he sat down and the twelve apostles with him.
Continued P. 153.

2. And supper being ended, the devil having now put into the heart of Judas Iscariot, Simon's *son*, to betray him, (1)

3. Jesus, knowing that the Father had given all things into his hands, and that he was come from God, and went to God;

4. He riseth from supper, and laid aside his garments, and took a towel and girded himself.

5. After that he poureth water into a bason, and began to wash the disciples' feet, and to wipe *them*, with the towel wherewith he was girded.

6. Then cometh he to Simon Peter : and Peter said unto him, Lord dost thou wash my feet !

7. Jesus answered and said unto him, What I do thou knowest not now : but thou shalt know hereafter.

8. Peter saith unto. him, Thou shalt never wash my feet. Jesus answered him, If I wash thee not, thou hast no part with me.

9. Simon Peter saith unto him, Lord, not my feet only, but also *my* hands and *my* head.

10. Jesus saith to him, He that is washed needeth not save to wash *his* feet ; but is clean every whit : and ye are clean, but not all.

11. For he knew who should betray him : therefore said he, ye are not all clean.

12. So after he had washed their feet, and had taken his garments, and was set down again, he said unto them, Know ye what I have done to you ?

13. Ye call me, Master, and Lord ; and ye say well : for so I am.

14. If I then, *your* Lord and Master, have washed your feet : ye also ought to wash one another's feet.

15. For I have given you an example, that ye should do as I have done to you.

16. Verily, verily, I say unto you, The servant is not greater than his Lord : neither he that is sent, greater than he that sent him. (2)

17. If ye know these things, happy are ye if ye do them.

18. ¶ I speak not of you all :

(1) J. XIII. 27 P. 154 ; M. XXVI. 14.
(2) M. X. 24.

I know whom I have chosen: but that the scripture may be fulfilled, he that eateth bread with me hath lifted up his heel against me.

19. Now I tell you before it come, that when it is come to pass, ye may believe that I am *he.*

20. Verily, verily, I say unto you, He that receiveth whomsoever I send, receiveth me, and he that receiveth me, receiveth him that sent me.

21. When Jesus had thus said he was troubled in spirit : and testified, and said, Verily, verily, I say unto you, That one of you shall betray me.

Jesus said, Verily, I say unto you,

22. Then the disciples looked one on another doubting of whom he spake.

he said, Verily, I say unto you, That one of you shall betray me.

One of you which eateth with me shall betray me.

23. Now there was leaning on Jesus' bosom one of his disciples, whom Jesus loved.

22. And they were exceeding sorrowful, and began every one of them to say unto him, Lord, is it I ?

19. And they began to be sorrowful, and to say unto him, one by one,

Chap. XXII.
23. And they began to inquire among themselves, which of them it was that should do this thing.
Continued P. 118.

24. Simon Peter therefore beckoned to him, that he should ask who it should be of whom he spake.

Is it I ? and another *said, is* it I ?

25. He then, lying on Jesus' breast, saith unto him, Lord, Who is it ?

23. And he answered and said, He that dippeth *his* hand with me in the dish, the same shall betray me.

20. And he answered and said unto them, *It is* one of the twelve that dippeth with me in the dish.

From P. 154.
21. ¶ But behold the hand of him that betrayeth me *is* with me on the table.

26. Jesus answered, He it is to whom I shall give a sop, when I have dipped *it.*
And when he had dipped the sop, he gave *it* to Judas Iscariot, *the son* of Simon.

24. The Son of man goeth as it is written of him : but woe unto that man by whom the Son of man is betrayed ! It had been good for that man if he had not been born.

21. The Son of man indeed goeth as it written of him : but woe to that man by whom the Son of man is betrayed ! Good were it for that man if he had never been born.

22. And truly the Son of man goeth as it was determined : but woe unto that man by whom he is betrayed !
Continued above.

25. Then Judas, which betrayed him, answered and said, Master, Is it I ? He said unto him, Thou hast said.

Chap. XXII., from P. 152.
15. And he said unto them, With desire I have desired to eat this passover with you before I suffer :
16. For I say unto you, I will not any more eat thereof, until it be fulfilled in the kingdom of God.

26. ¶ And as they were eating, Jesus took bread, and blessed *it,* and brake *it,* and gave *it* to the disciples, and said, Take ; eat : This is my body.

22. ¶ And as they did eat, Jesus took bread and blessed, and brake *it,* and gave to them, and said, Take ; eat ; This is my body.

19. ¶ And he took bread, and gave thanks, and brake *it,* and gave unto them saying, This is my body which is given for you : This do in remembrance of me.

Transposed.

27. And he took the cup, and gave thanks, and gave *it* to them, saying, Drink ye all of it ;

23. And he took the cup ; and when he had given thanks, he gave *it* to them : and they all drank of it.

17. And he took the cup, and gave thanks, and said, Take this, and divide *it* among yourselves.

St. MATTHEW, XXVI.	St. MARK, XIV.	St. LUKE, XXII.	St. JOHN, XIII.
28. For this is my blood of the new testament, which is shed for many for the remission of sins.	24. And he said unto them, This is my blood of the new testament, which is shed for many.	20. Likewise also the cup after supper, saying, This cup *is* the new testament in my blood, which is shed for you.	*Transposed.*
29. But I say unto you, I will not drink henceforth of this fruit of the vine until that day when I drink it new with you in my Father's kingdom.	25. Verily I say unto you, I will drink no more of the fruit of the vine until that day that I drink it new in the kingdom of God.	18. For I say unto you, I will not drink of the fruit of the vine until the kingdom of God shall come.	*Resumed.*

Continued P. 153.

L. XXII. 3. P. 151.

M. XXVI. 23; Mk. XIV. 20.
L. XXII. 21; J. XIII. 26; P. 153.

27. And after the sop Satan entered into him. Then said Jesus unto him, That thou doest, do quickly.

28. Now no man at the table knew for what intent he spake this unto him.

29. For some *of them* thought, because Judas had the bag, that Jesus had said unto him, Buy *those things* that we have need of against the feast : or, that he should give something to the poor.

30. He then, having received the sop went immediately out. And it was night.

31. ¶ Therefore when he was gone out, Jesus said, Now is the Son of man glorified : and God is glorified in him.

32. If God be glorified in him, God shall also glorify him in himself : and shall straightway glorify him.

33. Little children, Yet a little while I am with you. Ye shall seek me : and as I said unto the Jews, Whither I go ye cannot come : so now I say to you.

34. A new commandment I give unto you, That ye love one another ; as I have loved you, that ye also love one another.

J. XV. 17, P. 158.

35. By this shall all *men* know that ye are my disciples, if ye have love one to another.

36. ¶ Simon Peter said unto him, Lord, whither goest thou ? Jesus answered him, Whither I go, thou canst not follow me now ; but thou shall follow me afterwards.

30. And when they had sung an hymn, they went out into the mount of Olives. (1)	26. ¶ And when they had sung an hymn, they went out into the mount of Olives.		
31. Then saith Jesus unto them, All ye shall be offended because of me this night : for it is written, I will smite the shepherd, and the sheep of the flock shall be scattered abroad.	27. And Jesus saith unto them, All ye shall be offended because of me this night : for it is written, I will smite the shepherd, and the sheep shall be scattered.		
32. But after I am risen again, I will go before you into Galilee. (2)	21. But after that I am risen, I will go before you into Galilee.		

Chap. XXII., from P. 116.

31. ¶ And the Lord said, Simon, Simon, behold Satan [hath desired *to have* you ;] that he may sift *you* as wheat.

32. But I have prayed for

[*hath prevailed to have you all.*"— *Alford.*]

(1) J. XVIII, 1. L. XXII, 39, P. 162.
(2) M. XXVIII, 7, 10.
Mk. XVI, 7, P. 177.

St. MATTHEW, XXVI.	St. MARK, XIV.	St. LUKE, XXII.	St. JOHN, XIV.

St. LUKE, XXII.
thee, that thy faith fail not: and when thou art converted, strengthen thy brethren.

St. MATTHEW, XXVI.
33. Peter answered and said unto him, Though all *men* shall be offended because of thee, *yet* will I never be offended.

St. MARK, XIV.
29. But Peter said unto him, Although all shall be offended, yet *will* not I.

St. LUKE, XXII.
33. And he said unto him, Lord, I am ready to go with thee both into prison and to death.

St. JOHN, XIV.
37. Peter said unto him, Lord, Why cannot I follow thee now? I will lay down my life for thy sake.

St. MATTHEW, XXVI.
34. Jesus said unto him,

St. MARK, XIV.
30. And Jesus saith unto him,

St. LUKE, XXII.
34. And he said,

St. JOHN, XIV.
38. Jesus answered him, Wilt thou lay down thy life for my sake?

St. MATTHEW, XXVI.
Verily I say unto thee, That this night, before the cock crow,
    thou shalt deny me thrice.
35. Peter said unto him, Though I should die with thee, yet will I not deny thee.

Likewise said all the disciples,
   Continued P. 162.

St. MARK, XIV.
Verily I say unto thee, that this day, *even* in this night, before the cock crow twice, thou shalt deny me thrice.
31. But he spake the more vehemently, If I should die with thee, I will not deny thee in any wise.
Likewise also said they all.

St. LUKE, XXII.
I tell thee, Peter, The cock shall not crow this day, before that thou shalt thrice deny that thou knowest me.
Continued P. 162.

St. JOHN, XIV.
Verily, verily, I say unto thee, The cock shall not crow, till thou hast denied me thrice.

CHAP. XIV.
1. Let not your heart be troubled. Ye believe in God; believe also in me.
2. In my Father's house are many mansions. If *it were* not so, I would have told you. I go to prepare a place for you.
3. And if I go, and prepare a place for you, I will come again, and receive you unto myself : that where I am, *there* ye may be also.
4. And whither I go ye know; and the way ye know.
5. Thomas saith unto him, Lord, We know not whither thou goest : and how can we know the way?
6. Jesus saith unto him, I am the way, the truth, and the life. No man cometh unto the Father but by me.
7. If ye had known me, ye should have known my Father also : and from henceforth ye know him, and have seen him.
8. Philip saith unto him, Lord, show us the Father, and it sufficeth us.
9. Jesus saith unto him, Have I been so long time with you, and yet hast thou not known me, Philip? He that hath seen me, hath seen the Father. And how sayest thou *then*, Shew us the Father?
10. Believest thou not that I am in the Father, and the Father in me? The words that I speak unto you I speak not of myself : but the Father that dwelleth in me, he doeth the works.
11. Believe me that I *am* in the Father, and the Father in me : or else believe me for the very work's sake.
12. Verily, verily, I say unto you, He that believeth on me, the works that I do shall he do

also. And greater *works* than these shall he do : because I go unto my Father.

13. And whatsoever ye shall ask in my name, that will I do : that the Father may be glorified in the Son.

14. If ye shall ask anything in my name I will do it.

15. ¶ If ye love me, keep my commandments.

16. And I will pray the Father, and he shall give you another comforter that he may abide with you for ever.

17. *Even* the Spirit of truth, whom the world cannot receive ; because it seeth him not, neither knoweth him. But ye know him : for he dwelleth with you, and shall be in you.

18. I will not leave you comfortless. I will come to you.

19. Yet a little while ; and the world seeth me no more : but ye see me. Because I live, ye shall live also.

20. At that day ye shall know that I *am* in my Father ; and ye in me ; and I in you.

21. He that hath my commandments and keepeth them, he it is that loveth me : and he that loveth me shall be loved of my Father : and I will love him, and will manifest myself to him.

22. Judas saith unto him, not Iscariot, Lord, How is it that thou wilt manifest thyself unto us, and not unto the world ?

23. Jesus answered and said unto him, If a man love me, he will keep my words : and my Father will love him : and we will come unto him, and make our abode with him.

24. He that loveth me not, keepeth not my sayings ; and the word which ye hear is not mine ; but the Father's which sent me.

25. These things have I spoken unto you, being *yet* present with you.

26. But the Comforter, *which is* the Holy Ghost, whom the Father will send in my name, he shall teach you all things, and bring all things to your remembrance whatsoever I have said unto you. (1)

(1) J. XV. 26.
XVI. 7, P., 158.

27. Peace I leave with you ; my peace I give unto you : not as the world giveth give I unto you. Let not your heart be troubled : neither let it be afraid.

28. Ye have heard how I said unto you, I go away, and come *again* unto you. If ye loved me, ye would rejoice ; because I said, I go unto the Father : for my Father is greater than I.

29. And now I have told you before it come to pass, that when it is come to pass, ye might believe.

157

ST. MATTHEW, XXVI.   ST. MARK, XIV.   ST. LUKE, XXII.   ST. JOHN XV.,

30. Hereafter I will not talk much with you, for the Prince of this world cometh, and hath nothing in me.

31. But that the world may know that I love the Father; and as the Father gave me commandment even so I do. Arise, let us go hence.

CHAP. XV.

1. I am the true vine, and my Father is the husbandman.

2. Every branch in me that beareth not fruit he taketh away: and every *branch* that beareth fruit he purgeth it, that it may bring forth more fruit.

3. Now ye are clean through the word which I have spoken unto you.

4. Abide in me, and I in you. As the branch cannot bear fruit of itself, except it abide in the vine; no more can ye except ye abide in me.

5. I am the vine, Ye *are* the branches. He that abideth in me, and I in him, the same bringeth forth much fruit: for without me ye can do nothing.

6. If a man abide not in me, he is cast forth as a branch, and is withered: and men gather them, and cast *them* into the fire, and they are burned.

7. If ye abide in me, and my words abide in you, ye shall ask what ye will, and it shall be done unto you.

8. Herein is my Father glorified, that ye bear much fruit: so shall ye be my disciples.

9. As the Father hath loved me; so have I loved you; continue ye in my love.

10. If ye keep my commandments ye shall abide in my love: even as I have kept my Father's commandments, and abide in his love.

11. These things have I spoken unto you, that my joy might remain in you, and *that* your joy might be full.

12. This is my commandment, that ye love one another; as I have loved you.

13. Greater love hath no man than this, That a man lay down his life for his friends.

14. Ye are my friends if ye do whatsoever I command you.

15. Henceforth I call you not servants: for the servant knoweth not what his Lord doeth. But I have called you friends: for all things that I have heard of my Father I have made known unto you.

16. Ye have not chosen me, but I have chosen you, and ordained you, that ye should go and bring forth fruit, and *that* your fruit should remain, that whatsoever ye shall ask of

the Father in my name, he may give it you.

17. These things I command you, That ye love one another.

18. If the world hate you, ye know that it hated me before it *hated* you.

19. If ye were of the world, the world would love his own : but because ye are not of the world, but I have chosen you out of the world, therefore the world hateth you.

20. Remember the word that I said unto you, The servant is not greater than his Lord. If they have persecuted me, they will also persecute you. If they have kept my saying, they will keep yours also.

21. But all these things will they do unto you for my Name's sake; because they know not him that sent me.

22. If I had not come and spoken unto them, they had not had sin : but now they have no cloke for their sin.

23. He that hateth me, hateth my Father also.

24. If I had not done among them the works which none other man did, they had not had sin ; but now have they both seen and hated both me and my Father.

25. But *this cometh to pass*, that the word might be fulfilled that is written in their law, They hated me without a cause.

26. But when the Comforter is come, whom I will send unto you from the Father, *even* the Spirit of truth which proceedeth from the Father, he shall testify of me.

27. And ye also shall bear witness, because ye have been with me from the beginning.

Chap. XVI.

1. These things have I spoken unto you that ye should not be offended.

2. They shall put you out of the synagogues : yea, the time cometh, that whosoever killeth you will think he doeth God service.

3. And these things they will do unto you, because they have not known the Father, nor me.

4. But these things have I told you, that when the time shall come, ye may remember that I told you of them. And these things I said not unto you at the beginning, because I was with you.

5. But now I go my way to him that sent me : and none of you asketh me, Whither goest thou ?

6. But because I have said these things unto you, sorrow hath filled your heart.

7. Nevertheless I tell you the truth. It is expedient for you that I go away. For if I go not away the Comforter will not come unto you.

159

St. MATTHEW, XXVI.   St. MARK, XIV.   St. LUKE, XXII.   ST. JOHN, XVI.

But if I depart I will send him unto you.

8. And when he is come, he will reprove the world of sin, and of righteousness, and of judgment:

9. Of sin, because they believe not on me:

10. Of righteousness, because I go to my Father, and ye see me no more:

11. Of judgment, because the Prince of this world is judged.

12. I have yet many things to say unto you, but ye cannot bear them now.

13. Howbeit, when he, the Spirit of truth is come, he will guide you into all truth; for he shall not speak of himself: but whatsoever he shall hear, *that* shall he speak: and he will shew you things to come.

14. He shall glorify me; for he shall receive of mine, and shall shew *it* unto you.

16. A little while, and ye shall not see me, and again a little while, and ye shall see me, because I go to the Father.

17. Then said *some* of his disciples among themselves, What is this that he saith unto us, a little while and ye shall not see me: and again a little while and ye shall see me, and because I go to the Father?

18. They said therefore, What is this that he saith, a little while? We cannot tell what he saith.

19. Now Jesus knew that they were desirous to ask him, and said unto them, Do ye enquire among yourselves of that I said, a little while and ye shall not see him: and again a little while and ye shall see me?

20. Verily, verily I say unto you, That ye shall weep and lament, but the world shall rejoice: and ye shall be sorrowful, but your sorrow shall be turned into joy.

21. A woman when she is in travail hath sorrow, because her hour is come: but as soon as she is delivered of the child, she remembereth no more the anguish, for joy that a man is born into the world.

22. And ye now therefore have sorrow. But I will see you again, and your heart shall rejoice: and your joy no man taketh from you.

23. And in that day ye shall ask me nothing. Verily, verily I say unto you, Whatsoever ye shall ask the Father in my name, he will give *it* you.

24. Hitherto have ye asked nothing in my name. Ask and ye shall receive: that your joy may be full.

25. These things have I spoken unto you in proverbs. But the time cometh when I shall no more speak unto you in proverbs; but I shall shew you plainly of the Father.

26. At that day ye shall ask in my name : and I say not unto you that I will pray the Father for you :

27. For the Father himself loveth you, because ye have loved me ; and have believed that I came out from God.

28.. I came forth from the Father ; and am come into the world. Again I leave the world, and go to the Father.

29. His disciples said unto him, Lo, now speakest thou plainly; and speakest no proverb.

30. Now we are sure that thou knowest all things and needest not that any man should ask thee : By this we believe that thou camest forth from God.

31. Jesus answered them, Do ye now believe ?

32. Behold, the hour cometh ; yea, is now come, that ye shall be scattered, every man to his own ; and shall leave me alone. And yet I am not alone, because the Father is with me.

33. These things I have spoken unto you that in me ye might have peace. In the world ye shall have tribulation, But be of good cheer ; I have overcome the world.

Chap. XVII.

1. These words spake Jesus ; and lifted up his eyes to heaven and said, Father, The hour is come : glorify thy Son ; that thy Son also may glorify thee :

2. As thou hast given him power over all flesh, that he should give eternal life to as many as thou hast given him.

3. And this is life eternal : that they might know thee the only true God, and Jesus Christ, whom thou hast sent.

4. I have glorified thee on the earth : I have finished the work which thou gavest me to do.

5. And now, O Father, glorify thou me with thine own self, with the glory which I had with thee before the world was.

6. I have manifested thy name unto the men which thou gavest me out of the world. Thine they were ; and thou gavest them me ; and they have kept thy word.

7. Now they have known that all things whatsoever thou hast given me are of thee.

8. For I have given to them the words which thou gavest me. And they have received *them* ; and have known surely that I came out from thee : and they have believed that thou didst send me.

9. I pray for them. I pray not for the world ; but for them which thou hast given me : for they are thine.

10. And all mine are thine, and thine are mine : and I am glorified in them.

11. And now I am no more in the world. But these are in the world : and I come to thee. Holy Father, Keep through thine own name those whom thou hast given me : that they may be one, as we *are.*

12. While I was with them in the world I kept them in thy name. Those that thou gavest me I have kept ; and none of them is lost, but the son of perdition, that the scripture might be fulfilled.

13. And now come I to thee. And these things I speak in the world, that they might have my joy fulfilled in themselves.

14. I have given them thy word, and the world hath hated them ; because they are not of the world ; even as I am not of the world.

15. I pray not that thou shouldest take them out of the world, but that thou shouldest keep them from the evil.

16. They are not of the world ; even as I am not of the world.

17. Sanctify them through thy truth : thy word is truth.

18. As thou hast sent me into the world, even so have I also sent them into the world.

19. And for their sakes I sanctify myself, that they also might be sanctified, through the truth.

20. Neither pray I for these alone ; but for them also which shall believe on me through their word :

21. That they all may be one : as thou, Father, *art* in me, and I in thee : that they also may be one in us : that the world may believe that thou hast sent me.

22. And the glory which thou gavest me, I have given them, that they may be one, even as we are one.

23. I in them ; and thou in me ; that they may be made perfect in one : and that the world may know that thou hast sent me, and hast loved them as thou hast loved me.

24. Father, I will that they also whom thou hast given me be with me where I am, that they may behold my glory which thou hast given me : for thou lovedst me before the foundation of the world.

25. O righteous Father, the world hath not known thee. But I have known thee ; and these have known that thou hast sent me.

26. And I have declared unto them thy name, and will declare *it,* that the love wherewith thou hast loved me, may be in them, and I in them.

St. MATTHEW, XXVI.   St. MARK, XIV.   St. LUKE, XXII.   St. JOHN, XVIII.

Continued from P. 155.

35. And he said unto them, When I sent you without purse and scrip and shoes; lacked ye anything? And they said; Nothing.

M. X. 10 ;
P. X. 4, 17, P. 87.

36. Then said he unto them, But now, he that hath a purse, let him take *it ;* and likewise *his* scrip : and he that hath no sword, let him sell his garment and buy one.

37. For I say unto you, That this that is written must yet be accomplished in me : And he was reckoned among the transgressors : For the things concerning me have an end.

L. XXII 49, 50. P. 164.

38. And they said, Lord, behold, here *are* two swords. And he said unto them ; It is enough.

CHAP. XVIII.

From P. 155.
36. ¶ Then cometh Jesus with them unto a place called Gethsemane :
and saith unto the disciples, Sit ye here, while I go and pray yonder.

32. And they came to a place which was named Gethsemane :

and he saith to his disciples, Sit ye here while I shall pray.

39. ¶ And he came out, and went as he wont, to the mount of Olives : (1) and his disciples also followed him.

1. When Jesus had spoken these words, he went forth with his disciples over the brook Cedron, where was a garden, into the which he entered, and his disciples.

37. And he took with him Peter, and the two sons of Zebedee, and began to be sorrowful, and very heavy.
38. Then saith he unto them, My soul is exceeding sorrowful, even unto death : tarry ye here, and watch with me.
39. And he went a little farther,
and fell on his face, and prayed, saying, O my Father, if it be possible, let this cup pass from me :

33. And he taketh with him Peter and James and John, and began to be sore amazed, and to be very heavy :
34. And saith unto them, My soul is exceedingly sorrowful, unto death : tarry ye here, and watch.
35. And he went forward a little,
and fell on the ground, and prayed that if it were possible the hour might pass from him.
36. And he said, Abba, Father, all things *are* possible unto thee. Take away this cup from me. Nevertheless not what I will, but what thou wilt.

40. And when he was at the place, he said unto them, Pray that ye enter not into temptation.
41. And he was withdrawn from them about a stone's cast, and kneeled down and prayed ;
42. Saying, Father, if thou be willing remove this cup from me : nevertheless not my will, but thine, be done

See J. XII. 27, P. 123.

nevertheless, not as I will, but as thou *wilt.*

43. And there appeared an angel unto him from heaven, strengthening him.
44. And being in agony he prayed more earnestly : and his sweat was as it were great drops of blood falling down to the ground.
45. And when he rose up from prayer and was come to his disciples, he found them sleeping for sorrow.
46. And said unto them,

40. And he cometh unto the disciples, and findeth them asleep ; and saith unto Peter,

37. And he cometh and findeth them sleeping ; and saith unto Peter, Simon, sleepest thou?

What, could ye not watch with me one hour?
41. Watch and pray, that ye enter not into temptation :

Couldst not thou watch one hour?
38. Watch ye and pray, lest ye enter into temptation.

Why sleep ye?

rise and pray lest ye enter into temptation.

(1) M. XXI. 30.

ST. MATTHEW, XXVI. | ST. MARK, XIV. | ST. LUKE, XXII. | ST. JOHN, XVIII.

the spirit indeed *is* willing but the flesh *is* weak.

42. He went away again the second time, and prayed, saying, O my Father, If this cup may not pass away from me, except I drink it, thy will be done.

43. And he came and found them asleep again : for their eyes were heavy.

44. And he left them, and went away again, and prayed the third time, saying the same words.

45. Then cometh he to his disciples, and said unto them, Sleep on now, and take *your* rest : Behold the hour is at hand, and the Son of man is betrayed into the hands of sinners.

46. Rise : let us be going : behold, he is at hand that doth betray me.

47. ¶ And while he yet spake, lo, Judas, one of the twelve came ; and with him a great multitude, with swords and staves, from the chief Priests and Elders of the people.

48. Now he that betrayed him gave them a sign, saying, Whomsoever I shall kiss, that same is he : hold him fast.

49. And forthwith he came to Jesus and said, Hail, master ! and kissed him

50. And Jesus said unto him, Friend, wherefore art thou come?

Then came they and laid hands on Jesus, and took him,

the spirit truly *is* ready but the flesh *is* weak.

39. And again he went away, and prayed,

and spake the same words.

40. And when he returned, he found them asleep again : (for their eyes were heavy)

neither wist they what to answer him.

41. And he cometh a third time, and said unto them, Sleep on now, and take *your* rest. It is enough : the hour is come : behold, the Son of man is betrayed into the hands of sinners.

42. Rise up : let us go : lo, he that betrayeth me is at hand.

43. And immediately, while he yet spake, cometh Judas, one of the twelve, and with him a great multitude, with swords and staves, from the chief Priests and the scribes and the Elders.

44. And he that betrayed him, and given them a token, saying, Whomsoever I shall kiss, that same is he, take him and lead *him* away safely.

45. And as soon as he was come, he goeth straightway to him, and saith, Master, Master, and kissed him.

46. ¶ And they laid their hands on him, and took him,

47. ¶ And while he yet spake, behold a multitude, and he that was called Judas, one of the twelve,

went before them, and drew near unto Jesus to kiss him.

48. But Jesus said unto him, Judas, betrayest thou the Son of man with a kiss ?

2. And Judas also, which betrayed him, knew the place : for Jesus also ofttimes resorted thither with his disciples.

3. Judas then, having received a band *of men*, and officers of the chief priests and Pharisees, cometh thither with lanterns, and torches and weapons.

4. Jesus therefore, knowing all things that should come upon him, went forth and said unto them, Whom seek ye?

5. They answered him, Jesus of Nazareth. Jesus saith unto them, I am *he*. And Judas also which betrayed him, stood with them.

6. As soon then as he had said unto them, I am *he*, they went backward, and fell to the ground.

7. Then asked he them again, Whom seek ye? and they said, Jesus of Nazareth.

8. Jesus answered, I have told you that I am *he*: If therefore ye seek me, let these go their way.

9. That the saying might be fulfilled, which he spake : Of them which thou gavest me have I lost none,

ST. MATTHEW, XXVI.	ST. MARK, XIV.	ST. LUKE, XXII.	ST. JOHN, XVIII.
		49. When they which were about him saw what would follow, they said unto him, Lord, shall we smite with the sword? (1)	
51. And behold, one of them which were with Jesus, stretched out *his* hand, and drew his sword ; and struck a servant of the high priest's ; and smote off his ear.	47. And one of them that stood by drew a sword, and smote a servant of the high priest, and cut off his ear.	50. ¶ And one of them smote the servant of the high Priest, and cut off his right ear.	10. Then, Simon Peter, having a sword, drew it, and smote the high Priest's servant, and cut off his right ear. The servant's name was Malchus.
52. Then said Jesus unto him, Put up again thy sword into his place, for all they that take the sword shall perish with the sword.			11. Then said Jesus unto Peter, Put up thy sword into the sheath. The cup which my Father hath given me, shall I not drink it ?
53. Thinkest thou that I cannot now pray to my Father, and he shall presently give me more than twelve legions of angels ? 54. And how then shall the scriptures be fulfilled, that thus it must be ? 55. In that same hour said Jesus to the multitudes,	48. And Jesus answered and said unto them,	51. And Jesus answered and said, Suffer ye thus far. And he touched his ear, and healed him.	
Are ye come out as against a thief, with swords and staves for to take me? I sat daily with you, teaching in the temple ; and ye laid no hold on me. 56. But all this was done that the scriptures of the prophets might be fulfilled. Then all the disciples forsook him, and fled.	Are ye come out as against a thief, with swords, and *with* staves to take me? 49. I was daily with you in the temple, teaching, and ye took me not ; But the scriptures must be fulfilled. 50. And they all forsook him and fled, 51. And there followed him a certain young man, having a linen cloth cast about *his* naked *body :* and the young men laid hold on him : 52. And he left the linen cloth ; and fled from them naked.	52. Then Jesus said unto the chief Priests and Captains of the temple, and the Elders which were come to him, Be ye come out as against a thief, with swords and staves ? 53. When I was daily with you in the temple, ye stretched forth no hands against me. But this is your hour and the power of darkness.	
			12. Then the band and the Captain and officers of the Jews took Jesus and bound him,
57. ¶ And they that had laid hold on Jesus, led *him* away to Caiaphas, the high priest, (1) where the scribes and the elders were assembled.	53. And they led Jesus away to the high priest. And with him were assembled all the chief priests, and the elders, and the scribes.	54. Then took they him, and led *him,* and brought him into the high Priest's house :	13. And led him away to Annas first : for he was father in law to Caiaphas, which was the high Priest that same year. (1) 14. Now Caiaphas was he which gave counsel to the Jews that it was expedient that one man should die for the people.
58. But Peter followed him afar off	54. And Peter followed him afar off,	and Peter followed afar off.	15. ¶ And Simon Peter followed Jesus, and *so did* another disciple. That disciple was known unto the high Priest ; and went in with Jesus, into the palace of the high Priest.
unto the high priest's palace,	even into the palace of the		

(1) L, III 2, P, 13.   (1) L, XXII, 38, P, 162,   (1) L, III, 2, P, 13,

ST. MATTHEW, XXVI. | ST. MARK, XIV. | ST. LUKE, XXII. | ST. JOHN, XVIII.

16. But Peter stood at the door without. Then went out that other disciple which was known unto the high Priest, and spake unto her that kept the door.

55. And when they had kindled a fire in the midst of the hall,
and were set down together, Peter sat down among them.
Continued P. 166.

and brought in Peter.
Continued P. 166.

and went in, and sat with the servants to see the end.
59. Now the chief Priests and Elders and all the council sought false witness against Jesus to put him to death.
60. But found none: yea, though many false witnesses came yet found they none.
At the last came two false witnesses,
61. And said, This *fellow* said,

I am able to destroy the temple of God, and to build it in three days.

high Priest, and he sat with the servants, and warmed himself at the fire.
55. And the chief Priests and all the council sought for witness against Jesus, to put him to death,
and found none.
56. For many bare false witness against him, but their witness agreed not together.
57. And there arose certain, and bare false witness against him, saying,
58. We heard him say,
I will destroy this temple that is made with hands; and within three days I will build another made without hands.
59. But neither so did their witness agree together.

From P. 166.
66. ¶ And as soon as it was day, the Elders of the people and the chief Priests and the scribes came together; and led him into their council, saying,

62. And the high Priest arose; and said unto him, Answerest thou
nothing? What *is it which* these witness against thee?
63. But Jesus held his peace. And the high Priest answered, and said unto him,
I adjure thee by the living God that thou tell us, whether thou be the Christ the Son of God.
64. Jesus saith unto him,
Thou hast said:
nevertheless I say unto you, Hereafter shall ye see the Son of man sitting on the right hand of power, and coming in the clouds of heaven,

60. And the high Priest stood up in the midst, and asked Jesus, saying, Answerest thou nothing? What *is it which* these witness against thee?
61. But he held his peace, and answered nothing. Again the high Priest asked him, and said unto him,
Art thou the Christ, the Son of the Blessed?
62. And Jesus said,
I am.

And ye shall see the Son of man sitting on the right hand of power, and coming in the clouds of heaven.

67. Art thou the Christ? tell us. And he said unto them, If I tell you, ye will not believe.
68. And if I shall ask *you*, ye will not answer me; [nor let *me go*.] (1)
69. Hereafter shall the Son of man sit on the right hand of the power of God.

70. Then said they all, Art thou then the Son of God? And he said unto them, Ye say that I am.

From P. 166.
19. ¶ The high Priest then asked Jesus of his disciples, and of his doctrine.
20. Jesus answered him, I spake openly to the world: I ever taught in the synagogue, and in the temple, whither the Jews always resort; and in secret have I said nothing.
21. Why askest thou me? Ask them which heard me, what I have said unto them. Behold, they know what I said.
22. And when he had thus spoken, one of the officers which stood by, struck Jesus with the palm of his hand, saying, Answerest thou the high Priest so?

Mk. XIV. 62.

65. Then the high Priest rent his clothes, saying, He hath spoken blasphemy;
What further need have we of witnesses?
Behold, now ye have heard his blasphemy:
66. What think ye?
They answered and said,
He is guilty of death.
67. Then did they spit in his face and buffetted him; and others smote *him* with the palms of their hands.

63. Then the high Priest rent his clothes, and saith,

What need we any further witnesses?
64. Ye have heard the blasphemy:
What think ye?
And they all condemned him to be guilty of death.
65. And some began to spit on him, and to cover his face, and to buffet him;

71. And they said, What need we any further witness? For we ourselves have heard of his own mouth.

For Chap. XXIII., see P. 167.
From P. 166.
63. ¶ And the men that held Jesus, mocked him and smote *him*.

(1) ["Nor let me go" *omitted in several oldest MSS.—Alford.*]

23. Jesus answered him, If I have spoken evil, bear witness of the evil: but if well, why smitest thou me?
Continued P. 166.

(Transposed.)

ST. MATTHEW, XXVI.	ST. MARK. XIV.	ST. LUKE, XXII.	ST. JOHN, XVIII.
		64. And when they had blindfolded him, they struck him on the face, and asked him, saying, Prophecy, who is it that smote thee?	
68. Saying, Prophesy unto us thou Christ: Who is he that smote thee?	and to say unto him, Prophesy: And the servants did strike him with the palms of their hands.	65. And many other things, blasphemously spake they against him. *Continued P. 165.*	
		Chap. XXII., from P. 165.	*From P. 165.*
69. ¶ Now Peter sat without in the palace : and a damsel came unto him, saying,	66. ¶ And as Peter was beneath in the palace there cometh one of the maids of the high Priest.	56. But a certain maid beheld him	17. Then saith the damsel that kept the door unto Peter,
Thou also wast with Jesus of Galilee.	67. And when she saw Peter warming himself, she looked upon him and said, And thou also wast with Jesus of Nazareth.	as he sat by the fire, and earnestly looked upon him, and said, This man was also with him.	Art not thou also *one* of this man's disciples?
70. But he denied before *them* all, saying, I know not what thou sayest.	68. But he denied, saying, I know not, neither understand I what thou sayest.	57. And he denied him saying, Woman, I know him not.	He saith, I am not.
			18. And the servants and officers stood there, who had made a fire of coals ; for it was cold : and they warmed themselves : and Peter stood with them, and warmed himself. *Continued P. 165.* 24. Now Annas had sent him bound unto Caiaphas the high priest. 25. And Simon Peter stood and warmed himself.
		J. XVIII. 10. P. 164.	
71. And when he was gone out into the porch,	and he went out into the porch ; and the cock crew.		They said therefore unto him,
another *maid* saw him, and said unto them that were there, This *fellow* was also with Jesus of Nazareth.	69. And a maid saw him again ; and began to say to them that stood by, This is *one* of them.	58. And after a little while, another saw him, and said, Thou art also of them. And Peter said, Man, I am not.	Art not thou also *one* of his disciples? He denied *it*, and said, I am not.
72. And again he denied, with an oath, I do not know the man. 73. And after awhile came unto *him* they that stood by, and said to Peter, Surely, thou also art *one* of them ; for thy speech betrayeth thee.	70. And he denied it again. And a little after, they that stood by said again to Peter, Surely thou art *one* of them : for thou art a Galilean, and thy speech agreeth thereto.	59. And about the space of one hour after another confidently affirmed, saying, Of a truth this *fellow* also was with him ; for he is a Galilean.	26. One of the servants of the high priest, being *his* kinsman whose ear Peter cut off, saith, Did not I see thee in the garden with him?
74. Then began he to curse and to swear, *saying*, I know not the man. And immediately the cock crew.	71. But he began to curse and to swear, *saying*, I know not this man of whom ye speak. 72. And the second time the cock crew.	60. And Peter said, Man, I know not what thou sayest. And immediately, while he yet spake, the cock crew. 61. And the Lord turned, and looked upon Peter ; And Peter remembered the	27. Peter then denied again. And immediately the cock crew.
75. And Peter remembered the word of Jesus, which said unto him, Before the cock crow, thou shalt deny me thrice. And he went out, and wept bitterly.	And Peter called to mind the word that Jesus said unto him, Before the cock crow twice thou shalt deny me thrice. And when he thought thereon he wept.	word of the Lord, how he had said unto him, Before the cock crow, thou shalt deny me thrice. 62. And Peter went out and wept bitterly. *Continued P. 165.*	

St. MATTHEW, XXVII.	St. MARK, XV.	St. LUKE, XXIII.	St. JOHN, XVIII.

Chap. XXVII.

1. When the morning was come, all the chief Priests and Elders of the people took counsel against Jesus,

to put him to death.

2. And when they had bound him, they led *him* away, and delivered him to Pontius Pilate the Governor.

3. ¶ Then Judas, which had betrayed him, when he saw that he was condemned, repented himself; and brought again the thirty pieces of silver to the chief Priests and Elders,

4. Saying, I have sinned in that I have betrayed the innocent blood. And they said, What *is that* to us? See thou *to that*.

5. And he cast down the thirty pieces of silver in the temple, and departed. And went and hanged himself.

6. And the chief Priests took the silver pieces, and said, It is not lawful to put them into the treasury, because it is the price of blood.

7. And they took counsel, and bought with them the potter's field, to bury strangers in.

8. Wherefore that field was called, the field of blood, unto this day.

9. Then was fulfilled that which was spoken by Jeremy the Prophet, saying, And they took the thirty pieces of silver, the price of him that was valued; whom they of the children of Israel did value;

10. And gave them for the potter's field, as the Lord appointed me.

11. And Jesus stood before the Governor.

Chap. XV.

1. And straightway in the morning the chief Priests held a consultation with the Elders and scribes, and the whole council.

And bound Jesus, and carried *him* away,
and delivered *him* to Pilate.

See Acts I. 18.

Zach. XI. 12, 13.

Chap. XXIII.

1. And the whole multitude of them arose,

and led him unto Pilate.

2. And they began to accuse him, saying,

We found this *fellow* perverting the nation, and forbidding to give tribute to Cæsar; saying, That he himself is Christ, a king.

28. ¶ Then led they Jesus from Caiaphas unto the hall of judgment. And it was early. And they themselves went not into the judgment hall, lest they should be defiled: but that they might eat the passover.

29. Pilate then went out unto them, and said, What accusation bring ye against this man?

30. They answered and said unto him, If he were not a malefactor, we would not have delivered him up unto thee.

31. Then said Pilate unto them, Take ye him and judge him according to your law. The Jews therefore said unto him, It is not lawful for us to put any man to death.

32. That the saying of Jesus might be fulfilled, which he spake, signifying what death he should die.

St. MATTHEW, XXVII.	St. MARK, XV.	St. LUKE, XXIII.	St. JOHN, XVIII.
And the Governor	2. And Pilate	3. And Pilate	33. Then Pilate entered into the judgment hall again, and called Jesus,
asked him saying, Art thou the king of the Jews?	asked him, Art thou the king of the Jews?	asked him, saying, Art thou the king of the Jews?	and said unto him, Art thou the king of the Jews? 34. Jesus answered him, Sayest thou this thing of thyself, or did others tell it thee of me? 35. Pilate answered, Am I a Jew? Thine own nation and the chief Priests have delivered thee unto me. What hast thou done? 36. Jesus answered, My kingdom is not of this world. If my kingdom were of this world, then would my servants fight, that I should not be delivered to the Jews. But now is my kingdom not from hence. 37. Pilate therefore said unto him, Art thou a king then?
And Jesus said unto him, Thou sayest.	And he answering, said unto him, Thou sayest it.	And he answered him, and said Thou sayest it.	Jesus answered, Thou sayest that I am a king. To this end was I born: and for this cause came I into the world; that I should bear witness unto the truth. Every one that is of the truth heareth my voice. 38. Pilate saith unto him, What is truth?
12. And when he was accused of the chief Priests and Elders, he answered nothing. 13. Then said Pilate unto him, Hearest thou not how many things they witness against thee? 14. And he answered him to never a word; insomuch that the Governor marvelled greatly.	3. And the chief Priests accused him of many things: but he answered nothing. 4. And Pilate asked him again, saying, Answerest thou nothing? Behold how many things they witness against thee. 5. But Jesus yet answered nothing: so that Pilate marvelled.		
		4. Then said Pilate to the chief Priests and to the people, I find no fault in this man. 5. And they were the more fierce, saying, He stirreth up the people; teaching throughout all Jewry; beginning from Galilee to this place. 6. When Pilate heard of Galilee, he asked, whether the man were a Galilean? 7. And, as soon as he knew that he belonged to Herod's jurisdiction, he sent him to Herod: who himself was at Jerusalem at that time. 8. ¶ And when Herod saw Jesus, he was exceeding glad. For he was desirous to see him of a long season: because he had heard many things of him: and he hoped to have seen some miracle done by him. 9. Then he questioned with him in many words. But he answered him nothing.	And when he had said this, he went out again unto the Jews, and saith unto them, I find in him no fault at all.

10. And the chief Priests and scribes stood and vehemently accused him.

11. And Herod, with his men of war set him at nought, and mocked *him*,* and arrayed him in a gorgeous robe† : and sent him again to Pilate.

See v. 15.

†*J. XIX.* 2. *P.* 170.

12. ¶ And the same day Pilate and Herod were made friends together : for before they were at enmity between themselves.

13. ¶ And Pilate, when he had called together the chief Priests and the rulers of the people,

14. Said unto them, Ye have brought this man unto me, as one that perverteth the people : and behold, I, having examined *him* before you, have found no fault in this man touching those things whereof ye accuse him :

15. No, nor yet Herod.* For I sent you to him : and, lo, nothing worthy of death is done unto him.

See v. 11, above.

16. I will therefore chastise him, and release *him*.

15. Now at *that*] feast the Governor was wont to release unto the people a prisoner ; whom they would.

16. And they had then a notable prisoner, called Barabbas.

6. Now at *that* feast he released unto them one prisoner, whomsoever they desired.

7. And there was *one*, named Barabbas, *which lay* bound with them that had made insurrection with him : who had committed murder in the insurrection.

8. And the multitude, crying aloud, began to desire *him to do* as he had ever done unto them.

17. (For of necessity he must release one unto them at the feast.)

39. But ye have a custom that I should release unto you one at the Passover ;

17. Therefore when they were gathered together, Pilate said unto them,
Whom will ye that I release unto you? Barabbas, or Jesus which is called Christ?

18. For he knew that for envy they had delivered him.

9. But Pilate answered them, saying,
Will ye that I release unto you the king of the Jews?

10. For he knew that the chief Priests had delivered him for envy.

Will ye therefore that I release unto you the king of the Jews?

19. ¶ When he was set down on the judgment seat, his wife sent unto him, saying, Have thou nothing to do with that just man : for I have suffered many things this day in a dream because of him.

20. But the chief Priests and Elders persuaded the multitude that they should ask Barabbas, and destroy Jesus.

11. But the chief Priests moved the people, that he should rather release Barabbas unto them.

18. And they cried out all at once, saying, Away with this *man ;* and release unto us Barabbas.

19. (Who for certain sedition made in the city, and for murder, was cast into prison.)

40. Then cried they all again, saying, not this man, but Barabbas.

Now Barabbas was a robber. (1)

(1) *Mk. XV.* 7. *P.* 169.

ST. MATTHEW, XXVII.

ST. MARK, XV.

ST. LUKE, XXIII.

ST. JOHN, XIX.

21. The Governor answered, and said unto them, Whether of the twain will ye that I release unto you? They said, Barabbas.

22. Pilate saith unto them,

What shall I do then with Jesus which is called Christ?

They all say unto him, Let him be crucified.

23. And the Governor said, Why? what evil hath he done?

But they cried out the more, saying,
Let him be crucified.

24. ¶ When Pilate saw that he could prevail nothing, but *that* rather a tumult was made, he took water, and washed *his* hands before the multitude, saying, I am innocent of the blood of this just person : see *ye to it.*

25. Then answered all the people, and said, His blood *be* on us, and on our children.

26. ¶ Then released he Barabbas unto them.

And when he had scourged Jesus,
he delivered *him* to be crucified.

27. Then the soldiers of the Governor took Jesus into the common hall, and gathered unto him the whole band *of soldiers.*

28. And they stripped him, and put on him a scarlet robe.

29. ¶ And when they had platted a crown of thorns, they put *it* upon his head ;
and a reed in his right hand ;
and they bowed the knee before him,
and mocked him
saying, Hail, King of the Jews !

30. And they spit upon him, and took the reed, and smote him on the head.

31. And after that they had mocked him, they took the robe off from him? and put his own raiment on him ;
and led him away to crucify *him.*

12. And Pilate answered and said again unto them,

What will ye then that I shall do unto *him* whom ye call the King of the Jews?

13. And they cried out again, Crucify him.

14. Then Pilate said unto them,
Why? What evil hath he done?

And they cried out the more exceedingly, Crucify him.

15. ¶ And so Pilate, willing to content the people,

released Barabbas unto them,

and delivered Jesus,

when he had scourged *him*, to be crucified.

16. And the soldiers led him away into the hall, called Pretorium : and they call together the whole band.

17. And they clothed him with purple : and platted a crown of thorns ;
and put it about his *head.*

18. And began to salute him,

hail, King of the Jews !

19. And they smote him on the head with a reed : and did spit upon him ; and bowing *their* knees worshipped him :

20. And when they had mocked him, they took off the purple from him ; and put his own clothes on him ;
and led him out to crucify him.

20. Pilate therefore, willing to release Jesus, spake again to them.

21. But they cried saying, Crucify *him*, Crucify him.

22. And he said unto them the third time, Why? What evil hath he done?
I have found no cause of death in him ; I will therefore chastise him, and let *him* go.

23. And they were instant, with loud voices, requiring that he might be crucified. And the voices of them and of the chief Priests prevailed.

24. And Pilate gave sentence that it should be as they required.

25. And he released unto them him, that for sedition and murder was cast into prison, whom they had desired. But he delivered Jesus to their will.

J. XIX. 4.

CHAP. XIX.

1. Then Pilate therefore took Jesus, and scourged *him.*

L. XXIII. 11, P. 169.

2. And the soldiers platted a crown of thorns, and put *it* on his head ; and they put on him a purple robe :

3. And said, Hail, King of the Jews ! And they smote him with their hands,

4. Pilate therefore went forth again and saith unto them, Behold, I bring him forth to you, that ye may know that I find no fault in him.

St. MATTHEW, XXVII.　　　St. MARK, XV.　　　St. LUKE, XXIII.　　　St. JOHN, XIX.

M. XXVII. 21.
Mk. XV. 20.

5. Then came Jesus forth, wearing the crown of thorns, and the purple robe, and *Pilate* saith unto them, Behold the man.

L. XXIII. 21. *P.* 170.

6. When the chief Priests therefore and officers saw him, they cried out saying, Crucify *him*, crucify *him*. Pilate saith unto them, Take ye him, and crucify *him;* for I find no fault in him.

See v. 12.

7. The Jews answered him, we have a law, and by our law he ought to die, because he made himself the son of God.

8. ¶ When Pilate therefore heard that saying, he was the more afraid :

9. And went again into the judgment hall, and saith unto Jesus, Whence art thou? But Jesus gave him no answer.

M. XXVII. 14.

10. Then saith Pilate unto him, Speakest thou not unto me? Knowest thou not that I have power to crucify thee, and power to release thee?

11. Jesus answered, Thou couldest have no power *at all* against me, except it were given thee from above; therefore he that delivered me unto thee hath the greater sin.

J. XVIII. 38. *P.* 168.

12. And from thenceforth* Pilate sought to release him. But the Jews cried out, saying, If thou let this man go, thou art not Cæsar's friend. Whosoever maketh himself a king speaketh against Cæsar.

v. 7.

13. ¶ When Pilate therefore heard that saying, he brought Jesus forth, and sat down in the judgment seat, in a place that is called the pavement, but in the Hebrew, Gabbatha.

14. And it was the preparation of the Passover; and about the sixth hour.* And he saith unto the Jews, Behold your king!

* *Mk. XV.* 25. *P.* 172.

15. But they cried out, Away with *him:* away with *him:* crucify him.
Pilate saith unto them, Shall I crucify your king? The chief Priests answered, We have no king but Cæsar.

M. XXVII. 26.
Mk. XV. 15.
L. XXIII. 25.

16. Then delivered he him therefore unto them to be crucified. And they took Jesus, and led *him* away.

32. And as they came out, they found a man of Cyrene, Simon by name, him they compelled to bear his cross.

21. And they compel one Simon a Cyrenian, who passed by, coming out of the country, the father of Alexander and Rufus, to bear his cross.

26. And as they led him away, they laid hold upon one Simon, a Cyrenian, coming out of the country; and on him they laid the cross, that he might bear *it* after Jesus.

27. ¶ And there followed

St. MATTHEW, XXVII.	St. MARK, XV.	St. LUKE, XXIII.	St. JOHN, XIX.

St. LUKE, XXIII.

him a great company of people, and of women, which also bewailed and lamented him.

28. But Jesus turning unto them, said, Daughters of Jerusalem, weep not for me: but weep for yourselves and for your children.

29. For behold the days are coming, in the which they shall say, Blessed are the barren, and the wombs that never bare, and the paps which never gave suck.

30. Then shall they begin to say to the mountains, fall on us: and to the hills, cover us:

31. For if they do these things in a green tree, what shall be done in the dry?

32. And there were also two other, malefactors, led with him to be put to death.

St. JOHN, XIX.

17. And he, hearing his cross, went forth into a place called the place of a skull, which is called in the Hebrew, Golgotha:

St. MATTHEW, XXVII.

33. And when they were come unto a place called Golgotha, that is to say, a place of a skull.

34. ¶ They gave him vinegar to drink mingled with gall: and when he had tasted thereof, he would not drink.

35. And they crucified him:

St. MARK, XV.

22. And they bring him unto the place Golgotha, which is, being interpreted, the place of a skull.

23. And they gave him to drink wine mingled with myrrh: but he received it not.

24. And when they had crucified him,

St. LUKE, XXIII.

33. And when they were come to the place which is called Calvary,

there they crucified him, and the malefactors; one on the right hand, and the other on the left.

34. ¶ Then said Jesus, Father, forgive them: for they know not what they do.
And they parted his raiment, and cast lots.*

St. JOHN, XIX.

18. Where they crucified him, and two other with him; on either side one, and Jesus in the midst.

} J. XIX. 23, 24. P. 173.

St. MATTHEW, XXVII.

and parted his garments, casting lots:

[that it might be fulfilled which was spoken by the prophet, They parted my garments among them, and upon my vesture did they cast lots.]

36. And sitting down they watched him there:

See. v. 41, 42, 43.

St. MARK, XV.

they parted his garments, casting lots upon them, what every man should take.

Not in any of the most ancient MSS.—Alford.

25. And it was the third hour.(1) And they crucified him

Mk. XV. 31. P. 173.

M. XXVII. 34.

26. And the superscription of his accusation was written over:

[This not in some of the early MSS.—Alford.]

St. LUKE, XXIII.

35. And the people stood beholding. And the rulers also with him derided him, saying, He saved others; let him save himself, if he be Christ the chosen of God.

36. And the soldiers also mocked him, coming to him and offering him vinegar,

37. And saying, If thou be the king of the Jews, save thyself.

38. And a superscription also was written over him, [in letters of Greek, and Latin, and Hebrew;]

St. MATTHEW, XXVII.

37. And set up over his head his accusation written,

THIS IS JESUS THE KING* OF THE JEWS.

St. MARK, XV.

THE KING* OF THE JEWS.

St. LUKE, XXIII.

THIS IS THE KING* OF THE JEWS.

St. JOHN, XIX.

19. ¶ And Pilate wrote a title, and put it on the cross; and the writing was,

JESUS OF NAZARETH THE KING* OF THE JEWS.

20. This title then read many of the Jews: for the place where Jesus was crucified was nigh to the city: and it was

* M. XXI. 5, XXVII. 11, 29; Mk. XV. 2. 9. P. 169.; L. XXIII. 3, P. 168.
J. I. 49, VI. 15; XXVIII. 33, 37, 39, P. 168; XIX. 3, 14, P. 173.

(1) J. XIX. 14. P. 171.

written in Hebrew, a*
and Latin.

21. Then said the chi
of the Jews to Pilate,
the King of the Jews'
he said, I am the Ki
Jews.

22. Pilate answered
have written I have w

23. ¶ Then the soldi
they had crucified Je
his garments, and m
parts, to every soldier
and also *his* coat: now
was without seam, wo
the top throughout.

24. They said therefo
themselves, Let us no
but cast lots for it,
shall be. That the
might be fulfilled, whi
They parted my raime
them, and for my ve
they cast lots. Thes
therefore the soldiers (

M. XXVII. 35.

---

38. Then there were two thieves crucified with him; one on the right hand, and another on the left.

27. And with him they crucify two thieves; the one on his right hand and the other on his left.   *See L. XXIII. 33 ; J. XIX. 18.*

28. [And the scripture was fulfilled which saith, And he was numbered with the transgressors.]   [*Not in any of the most ancient MSS.—Alford.*]

39. ¶ And they that passed by reviled him, wagging their heads,

40. And saying, Thou that destroyest the temple, and buildest *it* in three days, save thyself. If thou be the Son of God, come down from the cross.

41. Likewise also the chief Priests mocking *him*, with the scribes and Elders, said,

42. He saved others; himself he cannot save.
If he be the King of Israel, Let him now come down from the cross, and we will believe him.

43. He trusted in God; let him deliver him now, if he will have him: For he said, I am the son of God.

44. The thieves also, which were crucified with him, cast the same in his teeth.

29. And they that passed by railed on him, wagging their heads,
and saying, Ah, thou that destroyest the Temple, and buildest *it* in three days,

30. Save thyself, and come down from the cross.

31. Likewise also the chief Priests, mocking, said, among themselves, with the scribes, He saved others; himself he cannot save.

32. Let Christ the King of Israel descend now from the cross, that we may see and believe.   *See L. XXIII. 35. 37. P. 172.*

And they that were crucified with him reviled him.

39. And one of the malefactors which were hanged railed on him, saying, If thou be Christ, save thyself and us.

40. But the other, answering, rebuked him, saying, Dost not thou fear God, seeing that thou art in the same condemnation?

41. And we indeed justly: for we receive the due reward of our deeds; but this man hath done nothing amiss.

42. And he said unto Jesus, Lord, remember me when thou comest into thy kingdom.

43. And Jesus said unto him, Verily, I say unto thee, Today* shalt thou be with me in Paradise.   ‡ M. XII. 40.

St. MATTHEW, XXVII.	St. MARK, XV.	St. LUKE, XXIII.	St. JOHN, XIX.

St. JOHN, XIX.

25. ¶ Now there stood, by the cross of Jesus, his mother, and his mother's sister, Mary the wife of Cleophas,* and Mary Magdalene.

26. When Jesus therefore saw his mother and the disciples standing by, whom he loved, the said unto his mother, Woman, behold thy Son !

27. Then saith he to the disciple, Behold thy mother ! And from that hour that disciple took her unto his own *home.*

* M. XXVII. 56 ; Mk. XV. 40 ;

St. MATTHEW, XXVII.

45. Now, from the sixth hour,

there was darkness over all the [land,] unto the ninth hour.

[" *earth.*"—*Alford.*]

St. MARK, XV.

33. And when the sixth* hour was come, there was darkness over the whole [land] until the ninth hour.

[" *earth.*"—*Alford.*]

St. LUKE, XXIII.

44. And it was about the sixth hour,†
and there was darkness over all the earth until the ninth hour.

45. And the sun was darkened, and the veil of the temple was rent in the midst.

St. JOHN, XIX.

† *See J. XIX.* 14.

---

46. And about the ninth hour Jesus cried with a loud voice, saying, Eli, Eli, lama sabacthani?
that is to say, my God, my God, why hast thou forsaken me ?

34. And at the ninth hour, Jesus cried with a loud voice, saying, Eloi, Eloi, lama sabacthani ?
which is, being interpreted, my God, my God, why hast thou forsaken me ?

47. Some of them that stood there when they heard *that*, said, This *man* calleth for [Elias.]

[" *Elijah.*"—*Alford.*]

35. And some of them that stood by when they heard *it*, said, Behold he calleth [Elias.]

[" *Elijah.*"—*Alford.*]

28. ¶ After this, Jesus, knowing that all things were now accomplished, that the scripture might be fulfilled, saith, I thirst.

29. Now there was set a vessel full of vinegar : and they filled a sponge with vinegar and put it upon hyssop, and put *it* to his mouth.

30. When Jesus therefore had received the vinegar, he said, It is finished :

---

48. And straightway one of them ran and took a sponge, and filled *it* with vinegar, and put *it* on a reed, and gave him to drink.

49. The rest said, Let be, let us see whether Elias will come to save him.

50. ¶ Jesus, when he had cried again with a loud voice,

36. And one ran and filled a sponge full of vinegar, and put *it* on a reed, and gave him to drink,
saying, Let alone : let us see whether Elias will come to take him down.

37. And Jesus cried with a loud voice,

46. ¶ And when Jesus had cried with a loud voice,
he said, Father, into thy hands I commend my spirit : [and having said thus,
He gave up the ghost.

---

yielded up the ghost.

and gave up the ghost.

and he bowed his head and gave up the ghost.

---

51. And behold the veil of the temple was rent in twain from the top to the bottom : and the earth did quake ; and the rocks rent :

52. And the graves were opened : and many bodies of the saints, which slept, arose,

53. And came out of the graves, after his resurrection ; and went into the holy city ; and appeared unto many.

54. Now when the Centurion, and they that were with him, watching Jesus, saw the earthquake, and those things that were done, they feared greatly, saying,

31. And the veil of the temple was rent in twain from the top to the bottom.

See v. 45.

39. ¶ And when the Centurion, which stood over against him, saw that he so cried out, and gave up the ghost, he said,

47. Now when the Centurion saw what was done, he glorified

* *Mk. XV.* 25, *P*, 172.

St. MATTHEW, XXVII.	St. MARK, XV.	St. LUKE, XXIII.	St. JOHN, XIX.
Truly this was the Son of God.	Truly this man was the Son of God.	God, saying, Certainly this was a righteous man.	" This man was innocent."—A.

Truly this was the Son of God.

Truly this man was the Son of God.

God, saying, Certainly this was a righteous man.

48. And all the people that came together to that sight, beholding the things that were done, smote their breasts, and returned.

55. And many women were there beholding afar off, which followed Jesus from Galilee, ministering unto him.

56. Among which was Mary Magdalene, and Mary the mother of James and Joses, and the mother of Zebedee's children.*

  * { J. XIX. 25, P. 174.
      { M. XIII. 55.

57. When the even was come,

40. There were also women looking on afar off:
among whom was Mary Magdalene, and Mary the mother of James the less, and of Joses, and Salome:

41. (Who also, when he was in Galilee followed him and ministered unto him,) and many other women which came up with him unto Jerusalem.

42. And now, when the even was come, because it was the preparation; that is, the day before* the sabbath:

  * M. XXVII. 62.

49. And all his acquaintance and the women that followed him from Galilee stood afar off, beholding these things.

31. The Jews therefore, because it was the preparation, that the bodies should not remain upon the cross on the sabbath day, (for that sabbath day was an high day) besought Pilate that their legs might be broken, and that they might be taken away.

32. Then came the soldiers, and brake the legs of the first, and of the other which was crucified with him.

33. But when they came to Jesus, and saw that he was dead already, they brake not his legs.

34. But one of the soldiers, with a spear, pierced his side ; and forthwith came thereout blood and water.

35. And he that saw it, bare record : and his record is true : and he knoweth that he saith true, that ye might believe.

36. For these things were done, that the scripture should be fulfilled ; a bone of him shall not be broken.

37. And again another scripture saith ; They shall look on him whom they pierced.

there came a rich man of Arimathea, named Joseph,

43. Joseph of Arimathea, an honorable counsellor, which

50. And behold there was a man named Joseph ; a counsellor : and he was a good man, and a just :

38. ¶ And after this, Joseph of Arimathea,

who also himself was Jesus' disciple :

also waited for the kingdom of God,

51. (The same had not consented to the counsel and deed of them.) He was of Arimathea, a city of the Jews : who also himself waited for the kingdom of God.

being a disciple of Jesus, but secretly for fear of the Jews,

58. He went to Pilate, and begged the body of Jesus.

Then Pilate commanded the body to be delivered.

came and, went in boldly unto Pilate, and craved the body of Jesus.

44. And Pilate marvelled if he were already dead ; and calling unto him the Centurion

52. This man went unto Pilate, and begged the body of Jesus.

53. And he took it down,

besought Pilate that he might take away the body of Jesus : and Pilate gave him leave.

St. MATTHEW, XXVII.	St. MARK, XV.	St. LUKE, XXIII.	St. JOHN, XIX.
	he asked him, Whether he had been any while dead: 45. And, when he knew it of the Centurion, he gave the body to Joseph.		
59. And when Joseph had taken the body,	46. And he bought fine linen, and took him down,		He came, therefore, and took the body of Jesus. 39. And there came also Nicodemus, which at the first came to Jesus by night, and brought a mixture of myrrh and aloes, about an hundred pound weight. (1)
he wrapped it in a clean linen cloth,	and wrapped him in the linen,	and wrapped it in linen.	40. Then took they the body of Jesus, and wound it in linen clothes; with the spices: as the manner of the Jews is to bury. 41. Now in the place where he was buried there was a garden: and in the garden a new sepulchre,
60. And laid it in his own new tomb, which he had hewn out in the rock:	and laid him in a sepulchre which was hewn out of a rock,	and laid it in a sepulchre that was hewn in stone, wherein never man before was laid. 54. And that day was the preparation, and the sabbath drew on.	wherein never man was yet laid. 42. There laid they Jesus therefore, because of the Jews' preparation day;
and he rolled a great stone to the door of the sepulchre; and departed. 61. And there was Mary Magdalene, and the other Mary sitting over against the sepulchre.	and rolled a stone unto the door of the sepulchre. 47. And Mary Magdalene and Mary the mother of Jesus beheld where he was laid.	55. And the women* also which came with him from Galilee followed after, and beheld the sepulchre: and how his body was laid. 56. And they† returned and prepared spices and ointments, and rested the sabbath day, according to the commandment.	for the sepulchre was nigh at hand. _____ * M. XXVII. 55, 56. † J. XIX. 39.
[62. ¶ Now the next day that followed the day of the preparation the chief Priests and Pharisees came together unto Pilate, 63. Saying, Sir, We remember that that deceiver said while he was yet alive, After three days I will rise again. 64. Command therefore that the sepulchre be made sure, until the third day; lest his disciples come by night, and steal him away; and say unto the people, He is risen from the dead. So the last error shall be worse than the first. 65. Pilate said unto them, Ye have a watch: Go your way: make it as sure as ye can. 66. So they went, and made the sepulchre sure: sealing the stone: and setting a watch.]			

ST. MATTHEW, XXVIII.	ST. MARK, XVI.	ST. LUKE, XXIV.	ST. JOHN, XX.

1. In the end of the sabbath,

1. And when the sabbath was past, Mary Magdalene and Mary the *mother* of James and Salome had brought sweet spices, that they might come and anoint him.

1. Now upon the first *day* of the week,

1. The first *day* of the week, cometh Mary Magdalene

as it began to dawn toward the first *day* of the week, came Mary Magdalene and the other Mary to see the sepulchre *

* { M. XXVII. 61.
{ Mk. XV. 47.

2. And, very early in the morning, the first *day* of the week, they* came unto the sepulchre,
* Mk. XV. 47; XVI. 1.

at the rising of the sun.

3. And they said among themselves, Who shall roll us away the stone from the door of the sepulchre? (2)

very early in the morning,

they* came unto the sepulchre,
* L. XXIII. 55. P. 176.
bringing the spices which they had prepared:
and certain *others* with them.

early, when it was yet dark,

unto the sepulchre;

2. And behold, there was a great earthquake. For the angel of the Lord descended from heaven; and came and rolled back the stone from the door: and sat upon it:
3. His countenance was like lightning, and his raiment white as snow:
4. And for fear of him the keepers* did shake; and became as dead *men*.
* M. XXVII. 65.

4. And when they looked they saw that the stone was rolled away: for it was very great.
5. And, entering into the sepulchre,

2. And they found the stone rolled away from the sepulchre.

3. And they entered in;

and found not the body of the Lord Jesus.
4. And it came to pass as they were much perplexed thereabout,

and seeth the stone taken away from the sepulchre. (2)

5. And the angel answered,

they saw a young man, sitting on the right side, clothed in a long white garment.
And they were affrighted.

behold, two men stood by them in shining garments.

5. And as they were afraid, and bowed down *their* faces, to the earth,

and said unto the women:
Fear not ye: for I know that ye seek Jesus which was crucified.
6. He is not here: for he is risen; as he said, Come, see the place where the Lord lay.

6. And he saith unto them, Be not affrighted: ye seek Jesus of Nazareth, which was crucified:
He is risen: he is not here: behold the place where they laid him:

they said unto them;
Why seek ye the living among the dead?
6. He is not here: but is risen. Remember how he spake unto you, when he was yet in Galilee, (1)
7. Saying, The Son of man must be delivered into the hands of sinful men, and be crucified; and the third day rise again. (2)
8. And they remembered his words.

7. And go quickly, and tell his disciples that he is risen from the dead; and behold He goeth before you into Galilee. (1) There shall ye see him. Lo, I have told you.

7. But go your way, tell his disciples, and Peter,

that he goeth before you into Galilee: there shall ye see him: as he said unto you (1)

(1) M. XXVII. 32; XXVIII. 10, 16, 17, 18.

(1) M. XXVI. 32; Mk. XIV. 28.

(1) M. XX. 17, 18, 19.
(2) L. XVIII. 33. P. 118.

St. MATTHEW, XXVIII.	St. MARK, XVI.	St. LUKE, XXIV.	St. JOHN, XX.
8. And they departed quickly from the sepulchre; with fear and great joy: and did run to bring his disciples word.	8. And they went out quickly and fled from the sepulchre; for they trembled and were amazed: neither said they anything to any man; for they were afraid.	9. And returned from the sepulchre, and told all those things unto the eleven, and to all the rest.	
*M. XXVIII. 1, 9, 10. Mk. XVI. 1. L. XXIV. 1, 15. J. XX. 14. P. 179.	9. ¶ Now when *Jesus* was risen, early the first *day* of the week, he appeared first to Mary Magdalene,* out whom he had cast seven devils. 10. *And* she went and told them that had been with her; as they mourned and wept.	10. It was Mary Magdalene, and Joanna, and Mary *the mother* of James, and other *women that were* with them, which told these things unto the apostles.	2. Then SHE† runneth and cometh to Simon Peter and to the other disciple whom Jesus loved, and saith unto them, They have taken away the Lord out of the sepulchre, and WE† know not where they have laid him.† † *M. XXVIII.* 1, 7, 9, 10.
9. ¶ And as they went to tell his disciples, behold Jesus met them, saying, All hail! And they came, and held him by the feet, and worshipped him.	*See J.* 20, 17.		
10. Then said Jesus unto them, Be not afraid: go tell my brethren, that they go into Galilee: and there shall they see me.	*See M. XXVIII.* 7.		
11. ¶ Now when they were going, behold, some of the watch came into the city, and showed unto the chief Priests all the things that were done.	*See M. XXVII.* 65		
12. And when they were assembled with the Elders, and had taken counsel, they gave large money unto the soldiers, 13. Saying, say ye, His disciples came by night and stole him *away* while we slept. 14. And if this come to the Governor's ears, we will persuade him, and secure you. 15. So they took the money and did as they were taught. And this saying is commonly reported among the Jews until this day.	"*Several of the ancient heretics received on* the Gospel of St. Mark: others, among the Catholics, rejected the last twelve verses of this Gospel,— i.e., from v. 9 to 20 of this chap. "*London Encyc.*, 1829, Mark." [The following twelve verses of St. Mark are wanting in the two oldest MSS., the Vatican and Sinaitic.—Alford.] Lond: Encyc: 1829, "Mark."		
16. ¶ Then the eleven disciples went away into Galilee, into a mountain where Jesus had appointed them. 17. And when they saw him they worshipped him. But some doubted. 18. And Jesus came and spake unto them, saying, All power is given unto me in heaven and earth.	*See M, XXVI,* 32; *XXVIII.* 10. *See Mk. XVI.* 11, 13.	*L. XXIV.*, 33. P. 181.	*J. XX.*, 25, 27.
Continued P. 182.	11. And they, when they had heard that he was alive and had been seen of her, believed not.	11. And their words seemed to them as idle tales, and they believed them not. 12. Then arose Peter, and ran unto the sepulchre:	3. Peter therefore went forth and that other disciple, and came to the sepulchre. 4. So they ran both together; and the other disciple did outrun Peter, and came first to the sepulchre.

5. And he stooping down, *and looking in*, saw the linen clothes lying; yet went he not in.

6. Then cometh Simon Peter, following him, and went into the sepulchre; and seeth the linen clothes lie,

and stooping down he beheld the linen clothes laid by themselves,
and departed, wondering in himself at that which was come to pass.

M. XXVII. 5.
M. XXI. 5.
L. XXIV. 4

7. And the napkin that was about his head, not lying with the linen clothes, but wrapped together in a place by itself.

8. Then went in also that other disciple which came first to the sepulchre. And he saw; and believed.

M. XXVII. 63.
XXVIII. 7.

9. For as yet they knew not the scripture that he must rise again from the dead.

10. Then the disciples went away again unto their own home.

11. ¶ But Mary stood without at the sepulchre, weeping. And as she wept, she stooped down, *and looked* into the sepulchre:

M. XXVIII. 5.
Mk. XVI. 5.
L. XXIV. 4.

12. And seeth two angels in white, sitting the one at the head, and the other at the feet, where the body of Jesus had lain.

13. And they say unto her, Woman, Why weepest thou? She saith unto them, Because they have taken away my Lord, and I know not where they have laid him.

M. XXVIII. 6, 9.
Mk. XVI. 7.

14. And when she had thus said, she turned herself back, and saw Jesus standing; and knew not that it was Jesus.

15. Jesus saith unto her, Woman, Why weepest thou? Whom seekest thou? She, supposing him to be the gardener, saith unto him, Sir, if thou have borne him hence, tell me where thou hast laid him, and I will take him away.

16. Jesus saith unto her, Mary! She turned herself, and saith unto him, Rabboni! which is to say, Master.

17. Jesus said unto her, Touch me not:† for I am not yet ascended to my Father: but go to my brethren and say unto them, I ascend unto my Father and your Father; and *to* my God and your God.

† *M. XXVIII. 9.*

M. XXVIII. 7, 10.

18. Mary Magdalene came and told the disciples, that she had seen the Lord; and *that* he had spoken these things unto her.

M. XXVIII. 8.
L. XXIV. 9, 10.

12. ¶ After that, he appeared, in another form, unto two of them; as they walked and went into the country.
See v. 7.

13. ¶ And, behold, two of them went that same day to a village called Emmaus, which was from Jerusalem *about* three score furlongs.
14. And they talked together

of all these things which had happened.

15. And it came to pass that while they communed *together* and reasoned, Jesus himself drew near, and went with them.

16. But their eyes were holden that they should not know him.

17. And he said unto them, What manner of communications *are* these, that ye have one to another, as ye walk, and are sad?

*J. XLV. 25. P. 173.

18. And the one of them whose name was Cleopas* answering, said unto him, Art thou only a stranger in Jerusalem, and hast not known the things which are come to pass there in these days?

19. And he said unto them, What things? And they said unto him, Concerning Jesus of Nazareth: which was a prophet mighty in deed and word, before God and all the people:

20. And how the chief Priests and our rulers delivered him to be condemned to death, and have crucified him.

21. But we trusted that it had been he which should have redeemed Israel. And beside all this, to-day is the third day since these things were done.

22. Yea, and certain women also of our company made us astonished, which were early at the sepulchre:

23. And when they found not his body, they came, saying that

*L. XXIV. 4 to 7. P. 177.

they had also seen a vision of angels; which said, That he was alive.

24. And certain of them which were with us went to the sepulchre, and found *it* even so as the women had said. But him they

† M. XXVIII. 10.

saw not.†

25. Then he said unto them, O fools, and slow of heart to believe all that the prophets have spoken!

26. Ought not Christ to have suffered these things, and to enter into his glory?

27. And beginning at Moses and all the prophets, he expounded unto them, in all the scriptures, the things concerning himself.

28. And they drew nigh unto the village whither they went. And he made as though he would have gone further.

29. But they constrained him, saying, Abide with us: for it is toward evening, and the day is far

181

ST. MATT., XXVIII.   ST. MARK, XVI.   ST. LUKE, XXIV.   ST. JOHN, XX.

spent. And he went in to tarry with them.

30. And it came to pass as he sat at meat with them, he took bread, and blessed *it*, and brake, and gave to them.

31. And their eyes were opened; and they knew him: and he vanished out of their sight.

32. And they said one to another, Did not our heart burn within us while he talked with us, by the way, and while he opened to us the scriptures?

See M. XXVIII. 16.

33. And they rose up, the same hour, and returned to Jerusalem: and found the eleven gathered together, and them that were with them;

See L. XXIV. 12.

34. Saying, the Lord is risen indeed, and hath appeared to Simon,

13. And they went and told *it* unto the residue; neither believed they them.

35. And they told what things *were done* in the way; and how he was known of them in breaking of bread.

* *See Mk. XVI. 7.*

14. Afterwards* he appeared unto the eleven, as they sat at meat;

36. ¶ And as they spake, Jesus himself stood in the midst of them; and saith unto them, Peace *be* unto you.

37. But they were terrified and affrighted, and supposed that they had seen a spirit.

19. ¶ Then the same day at evening, being the first *day* of the week, when the doors were shut where the disciples were assembled; for fear of the Jews; came Jesus, and stood in the midst; and saith unto them, Peace *be* unto you.

* *J. XX. 29.*
† *M. XXVIII. 16.*

and upbraided them with their unbelief* and hardness of heart; because they believed not them which had seen† him after he was risen.

38. And he said unto them, Why are ye troubled? And why do thoughts arise in your hearts? (1)

39. Behold my hands and my feet, that it is I myself! Handle me, and see: For a spirit hath not flesh and bones, as ye see me have.

40. And when he had thus spoken, he shewed them *his* hands and *his* feet.

41. And while they yet believed not for joy, and wondered; he said unto them, Have ye here any meat?†

20. And when he had so said, he shewed unto them *his* hands and his side. Then were the disciples glad, when they saw the Lord.

† *J. XXI. 13.*

42. And they gave him a piece of a broiled fish and of an honeycomb.

43. And he took *it*, and did eat before them.

* *J. XXI. 12, 15.*

44. And he said unto them, These *are* the words which I spake unto you while I was yet with you, that all things must be fulfilled which were written in the law of Moses, and *in* the prophets, and *in* the Psalms, concerning me.

45. Then opened he their understanding, that they might understand the scriptures.

46. And said unto them, Thus it is written; and thus it behoved Christ to suffer; and to rise from the dead the third day.

21. Then said Jesus to them

(1) *M. XXVIII. 17; Mk. XVI. 14; J. XX. 20.*

St. MATTHEW, XXVIII.	St. MARK, XVI.	St. LUKE, XXIV.	St. JOHN, XX.

St. MATTHEW, XXVIII.

19. ¶ Go ye therefore and teach all nations :

baptizing them in the name of the Father, and of the Son, and of the Holy Ghost. (1)

20. Teaching them to observe all things whatsoever I have commanded you.

M. X. 1
Mk. III. 15. *P. 52.*
L. IX. 1.

And lo, I am with you alway ; *even* unto the end of the world (2). Amen.

END OF THE GOSPEL ACCORDING TO ST. MATTHEW.

St. MARK, XVI.

15. And he said unto them, Go ye into all the world, and preach the Gospel to every creature. (1)

16. He that believeth and is baptized shall be saved :

but he that believeth not shall be damned.

17. And these signs shall follow them that believe. In my name shall they cast out devils : they shall speak with new tongues :

18. They shall take up serpents ; and if they drink any deadly thing, it shall not hurt them : they shall lay hands on the sick, and they shall recover.

19. ¶ So then after the Lord had spoken

unto them, he was received up into heaven, and sat on the right hand of God.

20. And they went forth and preached everywhere ; the Lord working with *them* ; and confirming the word with signs following. Amen.

END OF THE GOSPEL ACCORDING TO ST. MARK.

St. LUKE, XXIV.

47. And that repentance (1) and remission of sins should be preached in his name among all nations ; beginning at Jerusalem.

48. And ye are witnesses of these things.

49. ¶ And behold I send the promise of my Father upon you.

But tarry ye in the city of Jerusalem, until ye be endued with power from on high.

50. And he led them out as far as to Bethany. (2) And he lifted up his hands and blessed them.

51. And it came to pass, while he blessed them, he was parted from them ;

and carried up into heaven.

52. And they worshipped him : and returned to Jerusalem with great joy :

53. And were continually in the temple, praising and blessing God. Amen.

END OF THE GOSPEL ACCORDING TO ST. LUKE.

St. JOHN, XX.

again, Peace *be* unto you. As my Father hath sent me, even so send I you.

22. And when he had said this, he breathed on *them ;* and saith unto them, Receive ye the Holy Ghost :

23. Whose soever sins ye remit, they are remitted unto them ; *and* whose soever *sins* ye retain, they are retained. (1)

---

(1) *M. III.* 11—*IV.* 17.
  J. IV. 2. *P.* 25.
  Mk. I. 15. *P.* 18.
   XVI. 15, 16.
  L. XXIV. 47.
(2) *M. XXIV.* 3, 29, 30, 34.
   XV. 13.

(1) *M. IV.* 17 ; *Mk. I.* 15.

(1) *M. IV.* 17.
(2) *M. XXVIII.* 16.
  Mk. XVI. 14. *P.* 181.

(1) *M. XVI.* 19 ; *XVIII.* 18.
  L. XXIV. 47.

24. ¶ But Thomas, one of the twelve, called Didymus, was not with them when Jesus came. (2)

Mk. XVI. 14. P. 131.

25. The other disciples therefore said unto him, We have seen the Lord. But he said unto them, Except I shall see in his hands the print of the nails, and put my finger into the print of the nails; and thrust my hand into his side, I will not believe. (3)

M. XXVIII. 17.
Mk. XVI. 14.

26. ¶ And after eight days, again his disciples were within; and Thomas with them. *Then* came Jesus, the doors being shut, and stood in the midst, and said, Peace *be* unto you.

27. Then saith he to Thomas, Reach hither thy finger; and behold my hands. And reach hither thy hand, and thrust *it* into my side: and be not faithless, but believing.

28. And Thomas answered, and said unto him, My Lord! and my God!

M. XXVIII. 17.
Mk. XVI. 14.
L XXIV. 38. P. 131.
J. XX. 24.

29. Jesus saith unto him, Thomas, Because thou hast seen me, thou hast believed. Blessed *are* they that have not seen, and *yet* have believed.

30. ¶ And many other signs truly did Jesus in the presence of his disciples, which are not written in this book:

31. But these are written, that ye might believe that Jesus is the Christ, the Son of God: and that believing ye might have life, through his name.

CHAP. XXI.

M. XXVIII. 16, 20.
Mk. XVI. 19.
L. XXIV. 50, 51. P. 182.

1. After these things Jesus shewed himself again to the disciples at the sea of Tiberias* and on this wise shewed he *himself.*

2. There were together Simon Peter, and Thomas called Didymus, and Nathaniel of Cana in Galilee, and *the sons* of Zebedee, and two other of his disciples.

3. Simon Peter saith unto them, I go a fishing. They say unto him, We also go with thee. They went forth; and entered into a ship immediately: and that night they caught nothing.

L. XXIV. 41. P. 131.

4. But when the morning was now come, Jesus stood on the shore: But the disciples knew not that it was Jesus.

5. Then Jesus saith unto them, Children, have ye any meat? They answered him, No.

L. V. 4, 6. P. 20.

6. And he said unto them, Cast the net on the right side of the ship, and ye shall find. They cast therefore, and now they were not able to draw it for the multitude of fishes.

7. Therefore that disciple whom Jesus loved, saith unto Peter, It is the Lord. Now when Simon Peter heard that it was the Lord, he girt *his* fisher's coat *unto him*, (for he was naked) and did cast himself into the sea.

8. And the other disciples came in a little ship (for they were not far from land, but as it were two hundred cubits,) dragging the net with fishes.*

* L. V. 7. P. 20.

9. As soon then as they were come to land, they saw a fire of coals there, and fish laid thereon, and bread.

10. Jesus saith unto them, Bring of the fish which ye have now caught.

11. Simon Peter went up, and drew the net to land, full of great fishes; an hundred and fifty and three: and for all there were so many, yet was not the net broken.†

† L. V. 7. P. 20.

12. Jesus saith unto them, Come *and* dine. And none of the disciples durst ask him, Who art thou: Knowing that it was the Lord.

13. Jesus then cometh, and taketh bread, and giveth them; and fish likewise.

J. XX. 14, 19, 26; XXI. 1.
M. XXVIII. 9, 18.
Mk. XVI. 9, 12, 14.
L. XXIV. 15, 36.

14. This is now the third time that Jesus shewed himself to his disciples after that he was risen from the dead.

15. ¶ So when they had dined, Jesus saith to Simon Peter, Simon, *son* of Jonas, Lovest thou me more than these? He saith unto him, Yea, Lord, thou knowest that I love thee. He saith unto him, Feed my lambs.

16. He saith to him again, the second time, Simon, *son* of Jonas,

184

St. JOHN, XXI.

Lovest thou me? He saith unto him, Yea, Lord, Thou knowest that I love thee. He saith unto him, Feed my sheep.

17. He saith unto him the third time, Simon, *son* of Jonas, Lovest thou me? Peter was grieved because he said unto him the third time, lovest thou me: and he said unto him, Lord, Thou knowest all things; Thou knowest that I love thee. Jesus saith unto him, Feed my sheep.

18. Verily, verily, I say unto thee, When thou wast young, thou girdedst thyself, and walkedst whither thou wouldest: but when thou shalt be old; thou shalt stretch forth thy hands, and another shall gird thee; and carry *thee* whither thou wouldest not.

19. This spake he, signifying by what death he should glorify God. And when he had spoken this, he saith unto him; Follow me.

J. XIII. 23. P. 153. { 20. Then Peter, turning about, seeth the disciple whom Jesus loved following; which also leaned on his breast at supper, and said unto him, Lord, which is he that betrayeth thee?

21. Peter seeing him saith to Jesus, Lord, And what *shall* this man do?

M. XVI. 28. ⎫
Mk. IX. 1. P. 86. ⎬ 22. Jesus saith unto him, If I will that he tarry here till I
L. IX. 27. ⎭ come, what *is that* to thee? Follow thou me.

M. XVI. 28. { 23. Then went this saying abroad among the brethren, that that disciple should not die. Yet Jesus said not unto him, Thou shalt not die; but, if I will that he tarry till I come, what *is that* to thee.

24. This is the disciple which testifieth of these things; and wrote these things. And we know that his testimony is true.

25. And there are also many other things which Jesus did; the which if they should be written every one, I suppose that even the world itself could not contain the books that should be written. Amen.

END OF THE GOSPEL ACCORDING TO ST. JOHN.

GENEALOGY OF JESUS.

ACCORDING TO ST. MATTHEW.	ACCORDING TO ST. LUKE.
CHAP. I. *Backwards.*	CHAP. III., 23. *P. 16.*
1. Jesus	1. Jesus
2. Joseph	2. Joseph
3. Jacob	3. Heli
4. Matthan	4. Matthat
5. Eleazar	5. Levi
6. Eliud	6. Melchi
7. Achim	7. Janna
8. Sadoc	8. Joseph
9. Azor	9. Mattathias
10. Eliakim	10. Amos
11. Abiud	11. Naum
	12. Esli
	13. Nagge
	14. Maath
	15. Mattathias
	16. Semei
	17. Joseph
	18. Juda
	19. Joanna
	20. Rhesa
12. Zorobabel	21. Zorobabel ⎫ *(Placed parallel only from*
13. Salathiel	22. Salathiel ⎭ *coincidence of names.)*
	23. Neri
* 14. Jechonias (or Jehoahaz)	24. Melchi
	25. Addi
"And from the carrying away into	26. Cosam
* Babylon unto Christ are 14 gene-	27. Elmodam
rations." M. I., 17.	28. Er
1—15. Josias (or Josiah)	29. Jose
2—16. Amon	30. Eliezer
3—17. Manasses (or Menasseh)	31. Jorim
4—18. Ezekias (or Hezekiah)	32. Matthat
5—19. Achaz	33. Levi
6—20. Joatham (or Jotham)	34. Simeon
7—21. Ozias (or Uzzia)	35. Juda
	36. Joseph
	37. Jonan
	38. Eliakim
8—22. Joram (or Jehoram)	39. Melea
9—23. Josaphat (or Jehosophat)	40. Menan
10—24. Asa	41. Mattatha
11—25. Abia (or Abijam)	42. NATHAN
12—26. Roboam	43. David
13—27. SOLOMON	
14—28. David.	

"And from David until the carrying
away into Babylon are 14 generations." M. I., 17.

ACCORDING TO ST. MATTHEW.		ACCORDING TO ST. LUKE.	
1—29.	Jesse	44.	Jesse
2—30.	Obed	45.	Obed
3—31.	Booz	46.	Booz
4—32.	Salmon	47.	Salmon
5—33.	Naason	48.	Naason
6—34.	Aminadab	49.	Aminadab
7—35.	Aram	50.	Aram
8—36.	Esrom	51.	Esrom
9—37.	Phares	52.	Phares
10—38.	Judas	53.	Juda
11—39.	Jacob	54.	Jacob
12—40.	Isaac	55.	Isaac
13—41.	Abraham	56.	Abraham

41 *Total generations to Abraham.*

"So all the generations from Abraham to David are 14 generations." M. I. 17.

56 *Total generations to Abraham.*

* *The carrying away to Babylon did not take place under Jechonias, but a reign later, under Jehoiachim. Kings XXI. 24, XXVI. 30, 34.*

* *According to II. Kings, VIII., XI., XII., XIV., there is here an omission of 3 descents, viz., Ahaziah*

Johoash, or Joash

Amaziah

which would make 17 generations, instead of 14, from David unto the carrying away to Babylon.

57.	Thara
58.	Nachor
59.	Saruch
60.	Ragan
61.	Phalec
62.	Heber
63.	Sala
64.	Cainan
65.	Arphaxed
66.	Sem
67.	Noe
68.	Lamech
69.	Mathusala
70.	Enoch
71.	Jared
72.	Maleleel
73.	Cainan
74.	Enos
75.	Seth
76.	Adam	"which was *the Son* of God,"

SYNOPSIS of all the *identified* MIRACLES recorded in the FOUR GOSPELS.

Before the Crucifixion, 36—After the Crucifixion, 1—After the Resurrection, 1.

Total, 38.

There is only ONE miracle which is recorded in ALL the FOUR GOSPELS, viz., the miracle of the 5 loaves and 2 fishes. *(M. xiv. 19, 21 —Mk. vi. 31, 44.—L. vi. 9, 17.—J. vi. 9, 13.)*—Of the THREE raised from the dead, ONE is recorded in St. Matthew, St. Mark, and St. Luke; TWO in St. Luke; and ONE in St. John only.

(See subjoined table.)

ST. MATTHEW.	ST. MARK.	ST. LUKE.	ST. JOHN.
Five loaves 2 fishes XIV. 19, 21	same .. VI. 38, 44	same ... ... VI. 9, 17	same ... ... VI. 9, 13
Jesus on sea 25	same 49, 50	——	same 19, 20
Leper cleansed ... VIII. 2	same ... .. I. 42	same ... ... V. 13	——
Peter's wife's mother ... 15	same 31	same ... ... IV. 39	——
Stills a storm ... 16	same ... .. IV. 39	same ... ... VIII. 24	——
Legion cast out (2) ... 33	same (1) ... .. V. 13	same 32	——
Palsy cured ... IX. 6	same ... .. II. 11	same ... ... V. 25	——
Ruler's daughter raised ... 18	same ... .. V. 22, 42	same ...VIII. 41, 55	——
Issue healed 22	same 25	same 44	——
Withered hand ... XII. 13	same ... .. III. 5	same ... ... VI. 10	——
Lunatic cured XVII. 15, 18	Dumb spirit .. IX. 17, 26	u spirit ... IX. 38, 42	——
2 Blind see... ... XX. 30	Bartimeus, &c. .. X. 46, 52	a blind man XVIII. 35, 42	——
Preternat. Darkness XXVII. 45	same ... .. XV. 33	same ... ... XXIII.'44	——

ADDITIONAL in ST. MATTHEW.	ADDITIONAL in ST. MARK.	ADDITIONAL in ST. LUKE.	ADDITIONAL in ST. JOHN.
2 blind cured ... IX. 27	Blind man cured .. VIII. 25	Multitude of fishes V. 6	Water into wine ... II. 9
Dumb man 32		Man of Nain raised VII. 15	Nobleman's son ... IV. 54
Peter on sea XIV. 28, 32		Woman cured ... XIII. 12	Impotent walks ... V. 9
Tribute money XVII. 27		10 Lepers .. ... XVII. 12	Ship arrives ... VI. 21
		Servant's ear ... XXII. 51	Man blind ... IX. 1
			Lazarus raised ... XI. 44
			2nd draught of fishes XXI. 6, 11
			(a)

ONLY in ST. MATTHEW.	ONLY in ST. MATTHEW AND ST. LUKE.	ONLY in ST. MARK AND ST. LUKE.	
Sick brought XIV. 35—VI. 55	Centurion's servant VIII. 13—VII. 10	Unclean spirit I. 23—IV. 33	
Daughter cured XV. 22—VII. 25, 26	One possessed XII. 22—XI. 14		
Many lame, blind 30 32			
7 loaves 32, 38—VIII. 5, 9			
Fig tree XXI. 19—XI. 20			

AFTER the RESURRECTION—One

ONLY in ST. JOHN.
2nd draught of fishes XXI. 6, 11
(a)

NOTES ON THE FOREGOING PARALLEL.

The close identity which is evident between those parallel portions of St. Matthew's, St. Mark's, and St. Luke's Gospels, which *commence with the third chapter and terminate at the end of the first verse of the twenty-eighth chapter of St. Matthew's text*, seems to demonstrate that, within those limits, the staple both of St. Mark's and St. Luke's Gospel was drawn either from St. Matthew's, or from some original common to all three of them; although in the residue of their Gospel St. Mark and St. Luke entirely quit St. Matthew's Text.

St. Mark *(a)* has omitted various passages of St. Matthew's present Gospel; and in particular his two first chapters, (comprising the genealogy, the miraculous conception, the birth of Jesus, and the visit of the Magi), as well as the entire sermon: (contained in St. Matthew's fifth, sixth, and seventh chapters), and all St. Mark's reappearances of Christ after his resurrection differ entirely from those recorded by St. Matthew (Mk. XVI. 9, 12, 14, 19). He has also made some few additions *(c)* to St. Matthew's Text.

St. Luke, *(b)* who declares that he wrote for the use of Theophilus " those things believed among them as delivered by eye witnesses and ministers," has commenced by substituting for the two first chapters of St. Matthew two new ones; has distributed Matthew's sermon in detached verses through the sixth, eighth, eleventh, twelfth, thirteenth, fourteenth, and sixteenth chapters of his own gospel; has explained certain of Matthew's original passages; and has made repeated additions to them *(d)*, some of which appear to have been deduced from the text of St. Mark *(f)*. St. Luke is the only evangelist who notices the abnormal conception of the Baptist's mother; or, who relates any incidents of Jesus' life, between his circumcision when an infant, and his baptism by John in manhood. Both St. Luke and St. Mark ignore those reappearances of Christ recorded by St. Matthew, and supply others (L. XXIV. 15 to 31, 36, 50, 51).

A similar comparison of St. John's Gospel with St. Matthew's produces striking results. St. John entirely omits the miraculous conception, and the birth of Jesus, His genealogy, His baptism by John, His temptation. The sermon, His peregrination and teachings in the provinces, all His prophecies set forth in St. Matthew's twenty-fourth chapter, His institution of the eucharist, and the eternal Hell. Instead of the forty days spent in the wilderness, he represents Jesus at the marriage feast in Cana; and in place of His progress through the provinces, St. John relates four extra visits to Jerusalem. He describes totally dissimilar reappearances after the resurrection (J. XX. 14 to 17, 19, 26; XXI. 7); and promulgates new and mystical revelations concerning the godhead of Christ—*(See Compendium of Texts)*.

The frequent, and sometimes the peculiar, use of Peter's name, as well in St. Matthew's as in the two other Synoptic Gospels *(g)* is remarkable, and may be suggestive.

NOTES REFERRED TO IN P. 190.

(a) *Tertullian and others assert that MARK was amanuensis of St. Peter, who dictated this Gospel to him.*
Lond. Encycl: 1829. "Mark."

(b) *LUKE, "the companion of Paul." "Irenæus says that St. Luke digested in writing what St. Paul preached to the Gentiles: and Gregory Nazainzen states that St. Luke wrote with the assistance of St. Paul."*
Idem. "Luke."

(c) ADDITIONAL in ST. MARK'S GOSPEL.—Mk. I. 1 to 3, 15, 29—III. 9, 13, 20, 21—IV. 24, 26 to 29, 36—V. 3 to 6, 42—VI. 13, 19, 23, 37, 52—VII. 3, 4, 33 to 36—VIII. 22 to 26—IX. 15, 16, 21 to 24, 26, 27, 49, 50—X. 24, 30, 49, 50—XI. 11, 35—XII. 32, 33—XIII. 10—XIV. 51, 52—XV. 7, 8, 25—XVI. 5, 9, 10, 14, 17, 18, 19.

(d) ADDITIONAL in ST. LUKE'S GOSPEL.—Chaps. I. and II.—III. 5, 6, 10 to 15, 23 to 38—IV. 17 to 20—V. 2 to 10, 39—VI. 12, 13, 17 to 19, 24 to 26, 33 to 36, 38—VII. 3, 10 to 17, 21, 29, 30, 36 to 50—VIII. 1 to 3, 21—IX. 37, 42, 51, to 62—X. 1 to 12, 17 to 20, 29 to 42—XI. 5 to 8, 27, 28, 40, 41, 45, 46, 52 to 54—XII. 13 to 21, 32 to 38, 47, 48, 54 to 57 —XIII. 1 to 17, 22, 23, 25, 29 to 35—XIV. 1 to 15, 28 to 33—XV. 1, 2, 3, 6 to 32—XVI. 1 to 31—XVII. 7 to 20, 22, 28, 29, 34—XVIII. 1 to 14.—XIX. 1 to 18, 40 to 44—XX. 29 to 42—XXI. 11, 18 to 24, 32, 34, 35, 37, 38—XXII. 15, 16, 29, 35 to 38, 43, 44, 48, 49, 51, 70—XXIII. 2, 4 to 16, 19 to 24, 27 to 32, 36, 39 to 43, 45, 48, 56—XXIV. 6, 7, 10, 12, 13 to **50, 51,** 52, 53.

(e) EXTRA TEXTS IN ST. MARK REPEATED BY ST. LUKE.				(f) EXTRA TEXTS IN ST. MARK REPEATED WITH ADDITIONS BY ST. LUKE.			
Mk. I. 22 to 29.	...	...	L. IV. 32 to 44.	Mk. I. 25.	...	...	L. IV. 35.
V. 9, 10.	...	...	VIII. 30, 31.	II. 4.	...	...	V. 18, 19.
III. 8, 10.	...	...	VI. 17. 18.	V. 18 to 21.	...	...	VIII. 38 to 44.
IX. 38 to 40.	...	...	IX. 49, 50.	29 to 33.	...	...	44 to 47.
XII. 41 to 44.	...	...	XXI. 1 to 4.	41 to 43.	...	...	54 to 56.
				VI. 15, 16.	...	...	IX. 8, 9.
				31.	...	...	10.

(g) ST. MATTHEW.	ST. MARK.	ST. LUKE.	ST. JOHN.
IV. 18.	I. 16, 29, 30.	V. 3 to 10.	I. 40 to 44.
VIII. **14**	III. 16—V. 37.	IV. 38.	VI. 68.
X. 2.		VI. 14.	
		VIII. 45, 51.	
XIV. **28,**			
XV. **15.**			
XVI. **16** to **19, 22, 23.**	VIII. 29, 32, 33.	IX. 20.	
XVII. 1, 4, **24, 25, 26.**	IX. 2, 5.	28, 32, 33.	
XVIII. 21.			
		XII. 41.	
XIX. 27.	X. 28.	XVIII. 25.	
	XI. **21.**		
	XIII. 3.		
XXVI. 33, 35.	XIV. 29.	XXII. 8, 31, 34.	XIII. 6, 8, 9, 24, 86, 87.
37, 40.	33, 37.		XVIII. 10, 11, 15.
58.	54.	54, 55, 58.	16.
69, 73, **75.**	66, 70, **72.**	60, 61, **62.**	17, 18, 25, 26, 27.
	XVI. **7.**		
		XXIV. **12.**	
		34.	
		XX. **2, 3, 4, 6.**	
		XXI. **2, 3, 7, 11, 15,** 16, 7, 20, **21.**	

COMPENDIUM OF THE CHIEF TEXTS, TEACHINGS

St. MATTHEW.			St. MARK.		
CH.	PRACTICAL.	MYSTICAL.	CH.	PRACTICAL.	MYSTICAL.
IV. 10	Thou shalt worship the Lord thy God : him only shalt thou serve.				
23.		Preaching the Gospel of the kingdom.	I. 14		Preaching the Gospel of the kingdom of God.
17.		Jesus began to preach —Repent, kingdom of Heaven at hand.	15.		The kingdom of heaven is at hand : repent : believe the Gospel.

ATTRIBUTED TO JESUS IN THE FOUR GOSPELS.

	St. LUKE.			St. JOHN.	
CH.	PRACTICAL.	MYSTICAL.	CH.	PRACTICAL.	MYSTICAL.
IV. 8.	Same.				
			I. 1.		In the beginning was the Word. Was with God—was God.
			2.		Was in the beginning with God.
			3.		All things were made by him.
			7.		John Baptist's witness.
			9.		The true light.
			10.		He was in the world.
			12.		Power to receivers to become Sons of God.
			13.		Which were born of God. The Word
			14.		was made flesh and dwelt among us.
			17.		The law by Moses. Grace and Truth by Christ.
18.		The Lord hath anointed me to preach the Gospel to the poor, &c.	18.	No man hath seen God.	The only begotten Son, He declared Him.
43.		I must preach the kingdom of God to other cities.	III.		
			3.		Born again.
			5.		Of water, and the Spirit.
			13.		He came down from heaven. The Son of man which is in heaven.
			35.		The Father hath given all things into his hands.
			17.		To save, not to condemn the world.
			IV.		
			10.		Living water.
			22.		Salvation is of the Jews.
			23.		True worshippers shall worship the Father in spirit,
			24.		God is a Spirit.
			25. } 26. }		The Messiah—the Christ. I am he.
			V.		
			17.		My Father worketh—I work.
			19.		The Son can do nothing of himself.
			V.		
			21.		The Son quickeneth whom he will.
			22.		Judgment committed to the Son.
			23.		Honour the Son as the Father.
			24.		He believing is passed from death to life.
			27.		The Son executes judgment.
			29.		Resurrection to life; or to damnation.

26

St. MATTHEW.   St. MARK.

CH.	PRACTICAL.	MYSTICAL.	CH.	PRACTICAL.	MYSTICAL.
V.					
3.	Blessed the poor in spirit	...		...	...
4.	They that mourn				
5.	The meek				
6.	Have thirst for righteousness				
7.	The merciful				
8.	The poor in spirit shall see God				
9.	The peacemakers				
10.	Persecuted for righteousness				
11.	Reviled for my sake	...	...		...
15.	Candle under a bushel	...	...	IV. 21.	similar
17.		Come to fulfil the law			
19. {	Whoever shall break one of these commandments, &c.				
21. } 22. }	Angry with brother				
25.	Agree quickly	...	...		...
28.	Adultery of heart				
29.	Right eye offend	} Whole body cast into	IX.	Eye offend thee	
30.	Right hand offend	} hell	43. 47.	Foot offend thee	
32.	Divorce not, except, &c.				
34.	Swear not at all				
39.	Smite on one cheek	...	...		...
42.	Give to him that asks				
44.	Love your enemies				
45.	That ye be children of your				
48.	Father in heaven				
VI.	Be perfect, even as, &c.	...	...	...	...
1. 4.	Give alms secretly				
5. 8.	Pray to the Father in secret				
6.	Enter into thy closet				
7.	Use not vain repetitions				
9.	After this manner pray, Our Father which art in heaven, &c.	...	...	XI. 25.	Forgive, that your Father may forgive
18.	Fasting				
20.	Treasures in heaven				
23.	If the eye be evil	...	...		...
24.	Cannot serve two masters				
25.	No thought for your life, &c.				
33.	Seek the kingdom of God	...	...	...	...
VII.					
1.	Judge not	...	...	...	...
3.	Mote in brother's eye	...	...	...	...
5.	And thine own eye				
6.	Give not holy things to dogs				
7.	Ask and it shall be given	...	...	...	...
11.	Your Father shall give good things to them that ask him	...	...	...	...
12.	What men should do to you, do to them	...	...	...	...
13.	Enter at the strait gate				

Sт. LUKE.   Sт. JOHN.

CH.	PRACTICAL.	MYSTICAL.	CH.	PRACTICAL.	MYSTICAL.
			V. 30.		I execute the will of the Father which sent me.
			36.		The works that I do, bear witness of me.
			39.		Search the scriptures, they testify of me.
VI. 20.	same				
21.	Hunger now ye that weep now				
22.	similar				
VIII. 16.	similar				
XII. 58.	same				
VI. 29.	similar				
30.	similar				
27.	same				
35.	similar				
36.	Be merciful as, &c.				
XI.					
2.	When ye pray say, Our Father which art in heaven, &c				
42.	similar				
XVI. 13.	same				
XII. 22.	same				
31.	same				
VI. 38.	Give good measure				
37.	Judge not				
41.	same				
XI. 9.	Ask, &c.				
13.	Your Father shall give the Holy Spirit to them that ask				
VI. 31.	same				
XIII. 24.	same				

St. MATTHEW.   St. MARK.

CH.	PRACTICAL.	MYSTICAL.	CH.	PRACTICAL.	MYSTICAL.
VII. 15.	Beware of false prophets				
21.	Not every one that saith } Lord, Lord }	...	...	...	...
23.	Depart from me ye that work iniquity	...	...	...	...
24.	Whoso heareth and doeth, &c., a wise man	...	...	...	...
VIII. 12.	Outer darkness				
22.	Follow me : let the dead bury their dead, &c.				
IX.					
13.	I will have mercy not sacrifice				
	I did not come to call the righteous but sinners to repentance	...	II. 17.	same	...
16.	New cloth into old garment	...	21.	similar	...
X.					
32.	Whoso confesses me before men, him will I confess before my Father	...	...	...	...
23.		Ye shall not have gone over the cities of Israel till the Son of man be come			
33.	But whoso shall deny me, } &c., before my Father }	...	...	...	...
34.	I came not to send peace but a sword				
36.	A man's foes shall be they } of his own household }	...	...	...	...
XI. 27.		All things are delivered to me of my Father			
		Neither knoweth any man the Father save the Son and he to whom the Son will reveal him	...	...	...
9.	... ...	More than a prophet	...	...	...
13.	The prophets and the law until John	...	...	...	...
21.	They would have repented	...	...	...	...
XII. 8.	The Son of man Lord of Sabbath	...	II. 28.	same	...
6.	In this place is one greater } than the temple }				
31.	... ...	Sin against the Holy Ghost	III. 29	...	similar	...
36.	Every idle word accounted for				

ST. LUKE.   ST. JOHN.

CH.		PRACTICAL.	MYSTICAL.	CH.	PRACTICAL.	MYSTICAL.
VI.	46.	Why call me Lord, &c.				
XIII.	25.	Once the door shut I know you not				
	27.	similar				
	30.	The last shall be first				
VI.	47.	Whoso heareth my sayings and doeth them, is like, &c.				
IX.	62.	No man having put hand to looking back is fit for the	the plough and kingdom of God.			
V.	32.	same				
	36.	similar				
XII.	8.	Him will I confess before the angels of God				
	9.	{ deny me before the { angels of God				
	51.	I came not to send peace rather division				
	53.	{ The Father divided against { the Son, &c.				
X.	22.	... ...	similar			
VII.	26.	... ...	much more than a prophet			
XVI.	16.	... ...	similar			
X.	13.	They had repented long ago				
VI.	5.	same		VII. 23.	Angry? Made a man whole on the Sabbath.	
XIII.	6.	Parable. Fig tree				
XII.	10.	... ...	similar			

St. MATTHEW.			St. MARK.		
CH.	PRACTICAL.	MYSTICAL.	CH.	PRACTICAL.	MYSTICAL.
48.	Who is my mother ? who my brethren				
49.	Behold my mother, &c.		III. 33.	similar ...	...
50.	Whoso do the will of my Father, is my brother, sister, mother	... ...	35.		
XIII. 13.	Parable : the sower	... ...	IV. 4.	similar ...	...
12.	Who hath ,to him shall be given. From him who hath				
XXV. 29.	not shall be taken away.	... ...	25.	same	...
XIII. 24.	Parable : the tares				
31.	Parable : mustard seed	... ...	26.	Parable, seed and harvest	...
33.	Parable : leaven	... ...	31.	similar ...	...
					...
42. } 50. }	*	Furnace of fire weeping and gnashing of teeth		... ...	...
XXIV. 51.	Portion with hypocrites			... ...	...
XV. 11.	Not that which goeth into the mouth defileth		VII. 15.	same	
19.	Evil thoughts, murders, &c.		22.	similar	
XVI. 16.		The Christ the Son of the living God	VIII. 29.	The Christ ...	...
18.	Thou art Peter, on this rock I will build my church whatsoever thou bind, &c.	... ...		... ...	...
23.	Get thee behind me	Satan	33.	same	

* VIII. 12 ; XIII. 42, 50 ; XXII.
13 ; XXIV. 51 ; XXV. 3*.

St. LUKE.   St. JOHN.

CH.	PRACTICAL.	MYSTICAL.	CH.	PRACTICAL.	MYSTICAL.
VIII. 21.	My mother and my brethren are those which hear the word of God and do it.				
5.	similar				
18.	same				
XIII. 19.	similar				
21.	same				
28.	Weeping and gnashing of teeth				
XII. 46.	portion with unbelievers				
			VI. 27.	...	Labor not for meat that perisheth but enduring to everlasting life, which Son of man shall give.
			VI.		
			35.	...	I am the bread of life.
			38.	...	I came down to do the Father's will.
			40.	...	That seeing the Son and believing on him may have eternal life, and I will raise him up at last day.
			46.	...	He which is of God hath seen the Father.
			51.	...	I am the living bread which came down from heaven. My flesh I will give for the life of the world.
			53.	...	Except ye eat the flesh of the Son of man, and drink his blood, ye have no life in you.
			54.	...	Whoso eateth, &c., and drinketh, &c., hath eternal life : and I will raise him up at the last day.
			57.	...	As the living Father hath sent me, and I live by the Father, &c.
			58.	...	This is that bread which came down from heaven.
			62.	...	What if ye shall see the Son of man ascend up where he was before ?
			63.	...	The words I speak unto you are spirit and are life.
IX. 20.	The Christ of God	... ...	69.	...	Thou art Christ the Son of the living God.
	...	... ...		see J. XX. 23.	

	ST. MATTHEW.			ST. MARK.	
CH.	PRACTICAL.	MYSTICAL.	CH.	PRACTICAL.	MYSTICAL.
24.	If any will come after me let him deny himself and take up his cross	... ...	34.	similar ...	... ...
27.		Son of man shall come in the glory of his Father.	38.	similar ...	... ...
28.	shall reward every one according to his works ...	some standing here shall not taste death till they see the Son of man coming in his kingdom.	IX. 1.	... ...	Some standing, &c., till they have seen the kingdom of God come with power.
XVII. 5.		A voice out of the cloud, this is my beloved Son	IX. 7.	... ...	same ..
XVIII. 1.	Who is greatest ?	... ...	34.	same ...	... ...
2.	He called a child	... ...	36.	same ...	... ...
3.	Except as children not enter, &c.				
5.	Whoso receiveth such in my name receiveth me	... ...	37.	same ...	... ...
6.	But whoso shall offend one such, &c.	... ...	42.	similar ...	... ...
10.	Their angels do always behold the face of my Father				
XIX. 14.	Of such is the kingdom of heaven	... ...	X. 14.	similar ...	... ...
			IX. 48.	... ...	Worm dieth not and the fire is not quenched
			49.	... ...	Every one shall be salted with fire
			50.	... ...	Have salt in yourselves
XVIII. 8.				and have peace one with another	
		Cast into everlasting fire	43.	... ...	To go into hell, into the fire that never shall be quenched.
9.	enter into life	... ...		Enter the kingdom of God	
8—9.	If thy right hand If thine eye offend*	... ...	47.	... ...	... ..
12.	Parable : sheep lost				
14.	Not the will of your Father that one of these little ones perish				
15.	If thy brother trespass				
22.	Forgive until seventy times seven }	... ...		... ...	... ..
20.	Where two or three are gathered				

* V. 29, 30.

	St. LUKE.				St. JOHN.	
CH.	PRACTICAL.	MYSTICAL.	CH.	PRACTICAL	MYSTICAL.	

CH.	PRACTICAL.	MYSTICAL.	CH.	PRACTICAL	MYSTICAL.
23.	similar				
26.	similar				
27.	Some, &c., till they see the kingdom of God				
IX.					
35.	... ...	same			
46.	same				
47.	same				
48.	same				
XVII. 2.	similar				
XVIII. 16.	same				
XV. 4.	similar				
7—10.	Joy in heaven over one sinner that repenteth				
8.	Parable : woman losing one piece of silver				
11—32.	Prodigal son				
XVI. 1.	Wise steward				
16.	Law and prophets until John				
19.	Parable : rich man and beggar Lazarus				
XVIII. 4.	Seven times in a day				

27

CH.	PRACTICAL.	MYSTICAL.	CH.	PRACTICAL.	MYSTICAL.
	ST. MATTHEW.			ST. MARK.	
23,	Parable: King accounting with his servant	... ...	... ...		...

Sᴛ. LUKE.   Sᴛ. JOHN.

CH	PRACTICAL	MYSTICAL.	CH.	PRACTICAL.	MYSTICAL.
7.	Parable : servant ploughing		VII.		
			16.	My doctrine is not mine	but his that sent me.
			17.		If any man do his will he shall know of his doctrine
			VII.		
			19.	Did not Moses give you the law, and none keep it ?	
			29.	... ...	I know him and am from him
			33.	... ...	a little while I go to him
			37.	Come to me & drink	
			39.	... ...	Jesus not yet glorified
			VIII. 11.	Go, sin no more	
			12.	.. ...	I am the light of the world
			16. 18. 29.	... ...	I am not alone—the Father which sent me—I and the Father
			23.	... ...	Ye from beneath. I from above
			24.	If ye believe not ye shall die in your sins.	
			28. 26. 40.	... ...	When ye shall have lifted up the Son. I speak what I have heard— seen—of him—have heard of God.
			34.	Whoso committeth sin is the servant of sin	
			36.	... ...	If the Son shall make you free
			38.	... ...	I speak that which I have seen of my Father
			42.	... ...	I proceeded from God : neither came I ; He sent me.
			47.	. ..	He that is of God heareth.
			51.	... ...	If a man keep my sayings, he shall never see death.
			54.	... ...	It is my Father that honoureth me, and your God.
			55.	... ...	I know him.
			56.	... ...	Abraham rejoiced to see my day.
			58.	... ...	Before Abraham was I am.
			IX.		
			5.	... ...	As long as I am in the world, I am the light of the world.
			35—37.	... ...	The Son of God talketh with thee.
			39.	... ...	For judgment I am come.
			X. 11.	Parable of the sheepfold : I am the good Shepherd	
			16.	There shall be one fold and one Shepherd	
			17.		Father loves me because I lay down my life, that, &c.
			X. 18.	No man taketh it I lay it down	This command I received of my Father.
			27.	My sheep hear my voice	
			28.	... ...	I give them eternal life.
			30.	... ...	I and my Father are one.
			35. 36.	... ...	If ye call them gods to whom the word of God came, say ye thou blasphemest because I said, I a⸱ the Son of God

CH.	PRACTICAL.	MYSTICAL.	CH.	PRACTICAL.	MYSTICAL.
XIX. 9.	Whoso put away his wife, and whoso marry her: committeth adultery.	...	X. 11—12.	similar ...	
14.	Suffer little children, &c of such is the kingdom of God	... ...	14.	similar ...	
16.	What shall I do that I may have eternal life?	... ..	17.	same ...	
17.	Keep the commandments	... ...	19.	Thou knowest the commandments	
	Why call me good? none but God	... ...	18.	same ...	
18.	Do no murder, &c. Thou shalt not commit adultery, &c.	... ...	19.	——— do not commit adultery, &c.	
18.	Thou shalt not bear false witness.	... ...		do not bear false witness	
19.	Honor thy father and thy mother	... ...		same ...	
21.	Sell, &c., and follow me	... ...	21.	same ...	
24.	Camel through eye of a needle	... ...	25.	same ...	
*30.	Many first shall be last many last shall be first	... ...	31.	same ...	
XX. 1.	Parable: kingdom of heaven a householder				
23.	To sit on my right hand, &c. not mine to give	... ...	40.	same ...	
28.	To give his life a ransom for many	... ...		———	
XXI. 9.		Hosanna! Son of David	XI. 10.		Hosanna! blessed, &c.
43.	The kingdom of God shall be taken from you and given to a nation, &c.				
XXI. 13.	My house the house of prayer	.. ...	XI. 17.	similar ...	
25.	The baptism of John, whence?	... ...	30.	same ...	
28.	Parable: two sons.				
33.	Parable: planter of a vineyard	... ...	XII. 1.	similar ...	
42.	Stone the builders rejected	... ...	10.	same ...	
XXII. 1—14.	Parable: marriage supper	... ...		...	

*M. XX. 16.

St. LUKE. St. JOHN.

CH.	PRACTICAL.	MYSTICAL.	CH.	PRACTICAL.	MYSTICAL.
			38.	...	... The Father is in me and I in him.
XVI.			XI. 25.	...	... I am the resurrection and the life.
18.	similar				
XVIII.					
1—9.	Parables : Unjust judge—				
10—14.	Pharisee & publican				
17.	similar				
18.	same				
20.	same				
19.	same				
20.	Do not commit adultery, do not kill ; do not steal.				
20.	same				
...	same				
22.	same				
25.	same				
XIX.					
10.	Come to save that lost				
38.	...	... Blessed be the King	XII. 13.	...	... Hosanna ! blessed King of Israel.
			24.	Except a corn die, &c.	
			25.	...	... He that loveth life shall lose it. He that hateth life shall keep life eternal.
			31.	...	... Now shall the Prince of this world be cut off.
			32.	...	... If I be lifted up, I will draw all, &c.
			XII. 36.	..	... Believe in the light, that ye be children.
			44.	...	... He that believeth on me believeth
			45.	...	... on him—seeth me seeth him.
			48.	...	... He that rejecteth me the word shall judge.
			49. 50.	...	... I have not spoken of myself, but,
XX. 46.	similar	... .	II. 16.	similar	As the Father said, so I speak.
X. 42.	That good part.				
XX.					
4.	same				
9.	similar				
17.	same				
XIV. 8.	Parable : sit not in highest rooms				

| | ST. MATTHEW. | | | ST. MARK. | |
CH.	PRACTICAL.	MYSTICAL.	CH.	PRACTICAL.	MYSTICAL.
21.	Render unto Cæsar, &c. and unto God, &c.	... ...	XII. 17.	same	... ...
31.	...	In the resurrection they neither marry, &c., but are as the angels ..			
			25.	...	similar ...
36.	Which the great commandment?	...	28.	Which the first commandment	... ...
37.	Love the Lord thy God, &c.	...	30.	same	... ...
39.	Love thy neighbour as self	...	31.	same	... ..
40.	On these two commandments hang all the law and the prophets	...	29. 32. 33. 34.	There is one God, none other. To love him, &c., and to love his neighbour as himself, not far from kingdom of God.	... ..
			31.	There is no commandment greater	
42.	...	Christ, whose son is he? The son of David.	35.	...	varied ...
XXIII.9	One is your Father which is in heaven				
11.	The greatest among you shall be your servant				
12.	Whoso exalteth himself, &c.				
XXIV. 27, 28.	Prophesy, destruction of the temple	...	XIII. 2 to 23.	similar	... ...
29. 30. 31.	Immediately after tribulation of those days, &c., judgment day		24—26.	similar	... ..
34.	This generation shall not pass till all these things be fulfilled	.. ...	30.	same	...
44.	Be ready; for, &c.	...	35.	watch	...
XXV. 1.	Parable: ten virgins				
14.	Parable: man travelling to far country, ten talents	...	XIII. 34.	similar	...
*30.	...	Outer darkness — weeping, wailing, gnashing of teeth			
33.	Sheep right hand, goats left hand				
41.	...	Everlasting fire, devil and his angels			
†46.	These shall go away into everlasting punishment, but the righteous into life eternal				
XXVI. 26.	...	This is my body	XIV. 22.	...	same ...
28.	...	This is my blood	24.	...	same ..

* XXII. 13.
† XVIII. 8.

	St. LUKE.			St. JOHN.	
CH.	PRACTICAL	MYSTICAL.	CH.	PRACTICAL.	MYSTICAL.
XX, 25.	same				
35.	similar				
X. 25.	What to do to inherit eternal life.				
27.	same And thy neighbour, &c.				
28.	This do and thou shalt live				
XX. 41.	varied				
XIII.33.	A prophet cannot perish out of Jerusalem				
XXI. 6, 24.	similar				
25, 27.	similar				
32.	same				
36.	Watch and pray always				
XII. 40.	same				
47.	Beaten with many stripes				
48.	Beaten with few stripes				
XIX. 13.	Ten pounds				
		Mine enemies which would not I should reign over them, bring —slay them before me.			
XXII. 19.	.. ...	same			
20.	.. ...	same			

St. MATTHEW   St. MARK.

CH.	PRACTICAL.	MYSTICAL.	CH.	PRACTICAL.	MYSTICAL.
29.					
32.	... ...	In my Father's kingdom	25.	...	New in the kingdom of God ...
	After I am risen again I will go before you into Galilee	..	28.	...	...
64.	... ...	Ye shall see the Son of man sitting on the right hand of power and coming in the clouds, &c.	62.	...	Son of man on the right hand of power and coming, &c.
XXVII 46.	.. ..	Eli, lama sabachthani	XV. 34.	...	Eloi, Eloi, lama sabachthani

St. LUKE. | St. JOHN.

CH.	PRACTICAL.	MYSTICAL.	CH.	PRACTICAL.	MYSTICAL.
19.	This do in remembrance of me				
			XIII. 34.	A new commandment I give, Love one another	
			35.	By this shall all men know	
18.	..	... Until the kingdom of God shall come			
			XIV. 1.	Ye believe in God	Believe also in me
			2.	...	In my Father's house are many mansions
			6.	...	I am the way, the truth
			7.	...	Henceforth ye know him and have seen him
			9.	...	He that hath seen me hath seen the Father
			10.	...	I am in the Father and the Father in me He doeth the works
			11.	...	Else believe me for the very works' sake
			12.	...	Because I go unto my Father
			16.	...	He shall give you another Comforter
			17.	...	Even the spirit of truth
			18.	...	I will come to you
			24.) 21.)	He that loveth me not, keepeth not my sayings	He that loveth me shall be loved of my Father
			20.	...	The Comforter shall teach you* and bring to remembrance my sayings
			XV. 28.) 1.)	...	For my Father is greater than I. I am the vine, my Father the husbandman
			XV. 5.	...	Ye are the branches
			10.	If ye keep my commandments ye shall abide in my love	
			XVI. 15.	...	All things the Father hath are mine
			16.	A little while and ye	shall not see me
			28.	...	I came from the Father, I go to the Father
			XVII. 3.	...	Thee, the only true God, and Jesus Christ whom thou hast sent
			5.	..	Glory which I had before the world was
			8.	I have given the	thou gavest me. I came out from thee
			13.	...	and now I come to thee
			21.	...	as thou, Father, art mine and I in thee
			24.	...	Thou lovedst me before the foundation of the world
69	Hereafter shall	the son of man sit on the right hand of the power of God	XVIII.	...	...
XXIII. 43.	To-day shalt thou be with me in Paradise		36.	...	My kingdom is not of this world

* XXV. 26, XVI. 7.

St. MATTHEW.

St. MARK.

CH.	PRACTICAL.	MYSTICAL.	CH.	PRACTICAL.	MYSTICAL.
XXVIII 19.	Go ye teach all nations	baptizing them in the name of the Father and of the Son and of the Holy Ghost	XVI. 15.	Go ye into all the world and preach the Gospel to every creature	
			16.	...	... He that believeth and is baptized shall be saved but he that believeth not shall be damned
20.	I am with you alway, even unto the end of the world.				
			17.		And these things shall follow them that believe—in my name shall they cast out devils. They shall speak with unknown tongues
			18.		They shall take up serpents. They shall drink any deadly thing, &c. They shall lay hands on the sick, &c.

RESURRECTION.

<table>
<tr><th colspan="3">Sт. LUKE.</th><th colspan="3">Sт. JOHN.</th></tr>
<tr><th>CH.</th><th>PRACTICAL.</th><th>MYSTICAL.</th><th>CH.</th><th>PRACTICAL.</th><th>MYSTICAL.</th></tr>
<tr><td></td><td></td><td></td><td>XX.
23.</td><td>Whosesoever sins ye remit they are remitted :
Whosesoever sins ye retain they are retained.</td><td></td></tr>
<tr><td>XXIV.
47.</td><td>And that repentance and remission of sins should be preached in his name among all nations</td><td></td><td>21.</td><td>Peace be unto you,</td><td>as my Father hath sent me even so send I you.</td></tr>
<tr><td>49.</td><td>..</td><td>... And behold, I send the promise of my Father upon you</td><td>22.

XXI.
15,16,17.</td><td>

Feed my lambs.
Feed my sheep</td><td>And when he had said this he breathed on them, and saith unto them, Receive ye the Holy Ghost.</td></tr>
</table>

Just Published

(FOR THE SERVICE OF THE CLERGY OF ALL DENOMINATIONS,
AND OF OTHER HONEST INQUIRERS),

AN ANALYSIS OF THE PARALLEL GOSPELS.

QUARTO, IN CLOTH, 6/6.

London:
LONGMANS, GREEN & CO., PATERNOSTER ROW.

AND ALL BOOKSELLERS.

1876.

ImTheStory.com

Personalized Classic Books in many genre's

Unique gift for kids, partners, friends, colleagues

Customize:

- Character Names
- Upload your own front/back cover images (optional)
- Inscribe a personal message/dedication on the
  inside page (optional)

Customize many titles Including
- Alice in Wonderland
- Romeo and Juliet
- The Wizard of Oz
- A Christmas Carol
- Dracula
- Dr. Jekyll & Mr. Hyde
- And more...

CPSIA information can be obtained
at www.ICGtesting.com
Printed in the USA
BVOW06s2324240517
485138BV00009B/65/P

9 781313 535045